GREATER LONDON
The Politics of Metropolitan Reform

D1362185

AN ADVANCED STUDY IN POLITICAL SCIENCE

GREATER LONDON

The Politics of Metropolitan Reform

FRANK SMALLWOOD
Dartmouth College

The Bobbs-Merrill Company, Inc.
A SUBSIDIARY OF HOWARD W. SAMS & CO., INC.
Publishers / Indianapolis / New York / Kansas City

Robert C. Wood, Consulting Editor
THE MASSACHUSETTS INSTITUTE OF TECHNOLOGY

To Ann

Acknowledgments

A great many people provided the welcome assistance that went into the making of this book.

At the outset, a deep debt of gratitude is due the members of the Department of Government at Dartmouth College and the Administration and the Trustees of the College for providing me with a Dartmouth Faculty Fellowship, which made the entire study project possible.

A number of colleagues offered most helpful advice on my initial research design, most especially Professors Samir Anabtawi, George Belknap, Robert Dentler, H. Wentworth Eldredge, Bradbury Seasholes, Vincent Starzinger, Richard Sterling, and Robert C. Wood.

Upon my arrival in England, I was fortunate in making contact with the Greater London Study Group at the London School of Economics. All members of this group provided a great deal of invaluable guidance. In this regard, I am most heavily indebted to Professor William Robson and to L. J. Sharpe. The warm friendships that were forged during my London visit represent one of the most pleasant and satisfying side-benefits of the entire study project.

Five individuals—Wallace Sayre, Paul Ylvisaker, Henry Ehrmann and, once again, Robert C. Wood and L. J. Sharpe—took the time and trouble to offer detailed comments on the original draft of my manuscript, and I am most grateful to each of them.

Two additional sources of help went into the making of the study project and, in the final analysis, the book would not have been possible without either of them. The first was provided by my wife, Ann, who, on the surface, served as constructive critic, dexterous cartographer, and master of the international logistics that are part and parcel of keeping a family of four young children on the move for more than a year. Beneath the surface, she provided the personal support, strength, and encouragement that made the entire project feasible. It is difficult to find the words that could adequately express the deep thanks I owe to her.

The second source of help was embodied by the numerous Londoners who took the pains to submit to lengthy interviews on all aspects of the reorganization program. A listing of these persons is contained in an appendix to the study. In every case, I was treated with sympathetic interest that extended well above and beyond the normal bounds of courtesy.

Needless to say, none of the above individuals bears responsibility for any of the observations or conclusions that appear on the following pages. The book represents my own evaluation of the Greater London reform program as I interpreted this program. In partial repayment to all concerned, I have attempted to discharge this responsibility as fairly and as objectively as possible, in the hope that the study may provide some new insight into this fascinating phenomenon of metropolitan government.

FRANK SMALLWOOD

Hanover, New Hampshire
October 1964

Contents

x   *Contents*

Maps and Tables

Part I

SCOPE
AND
CHRONOLOGY

In England and America one has . . . the feeling that
it is the growing, and not the decaying forces of society
which create the most disquieting problems.
—Graham Wallas, *Human Nature in Politics*

1. The Scope of the Study

Nearly a quarter of a century ago, when America first became aware of the challenges inherent in its burgeoning forces of metropolitan growth, Victor Jones observed that "the politics of metropolitan integration are the most important aspect of the problem."[1]

Some twenty years later, another observer of the metropolitan scene, Stanley Scott, was forced to conclude, "The literature of political science, and of the other social sciences, is very thin when it comes to providing answers for the many questions raised by . . . metropolitan government re-organization proposals."[2]

The basic lag between research and reality represents the initial impetus that led to the study that follows. Paradoxically, the study is designed to shed light on some of the factors that may influence the success, or failure, of metropolitan governmental reform efforts in the United States, by analyzing the political response to one current reorganization plan abroad—the creation of a new Greater London government by Act of Parliament, which received Royal Assent on July 31, 1963.

While obviously there are basic environmental differences between the metropolitan politics of London and those of the American city, this very fact provided the underlying rationale for the study effort. It

[1] Victor Jones, "The Politics of Integration in Metropolitan Areas," *Annals: American Academy of Political and Social Science,* CCVII (June 1940), 161.

[2] Stanley Scott, "Research on Governmental Reorganization in Metropolitan Areas," *Two Notes on Metropolitan Research* (The Maxwell Graduate School of Citizenship and Public Affairs, June 1961), p. 11.

was felt that, if any common denominators could be found under such varying conditions, they might tell us something significant about the more general workings of our metropolitan political systems.

The study indicates that such common denominators do exist. First and foremost among them is the fundamental fact that the London reorganization plan sparked off a bitter political conflict. While somewhat different from the controversies that have occurred over metropolitan governmental programs in such American cities as Cleveland, Miami, and St. Louis, this conflict was a highly volatile, and a highly relevant, political fight nonetheless.

This is not to argue that the struggle over the Greater London plan represents any perfect carbon copy of American agonies with metropolitan politics. Chapter 8 highlights certain basic environmental factors in London that stand in marked contrast to American experience in this regard. In addition, some crucial procedural differences were evident. As is stressed repeatedly in the study, the final process of approval—"the locus of the power to decide"[3]—in London was quite dissimilar from that which we utilize in the United States. Whereas we look to the electorate to wrestle with the issue of metropolitan reform through a public referendum, in England it is a higher authority— the Government and the Parliament—that makes the final decisions on this issue. Chapter 11 indicates how this basic procedural difference led to some fascinating shifts in political strategies and, in so doing, it indicates the very telling impact that procedural innovations can have upon the inner workings of the political process.

Yet, despite these differences, there are a great many parallels between what happened in London and what has transpired in America on this issue of metropolitan government reorganization.

Whereas the differences between London's response and the American cities' response to metropolitan reform are primarily static in their emphasis on structure and procedure, the similarities are dynamic in their concern with the raw human emotions that strike close to the heart of politics in the fullest sense of this term. The hopes and fears, the stakes and strategies, the shifts in deployment of resources that char-

[3] Scott, "Research on Reorganization," p. 17.

acterized the political infighting over the Greater London plan were, in many respects, remarkably akin to those which have been observed in American cities.

Thus, for example, if one substitutes the word "Labour" for "Democratic," and the word "Conservative" for "Republican," it is possible to gain a high degree of insight into the London story simply by noting Edward C. Banfield's description of "The Politics of Metropolitan Area Organization" in the United States:

> In general, the large cities are heavily Democratic and the suburban rings heavily Republican. . . . These facts suggest that for many years to come it will be difficult or impossible to integrate local governments where the two-party system operates. . . . In effect, advocates of consolidation schemes are asking the Democrats to give up control of the central cities, or, at least, to place it in jeopardy.[4]

Similarly, one does not need to substitute any words at all to make the following observation by Luther Gulick directly relevant to the London scene:

> Each defined human institution, especially when created by law and endowed with even the smallest modicum of power, tends to develop into an independent "institutional personality." This involves not only asserting itself, but also extending itself and seeking to perpetuate itself. This is apparently a law of group structure, as it is of individual existence. And among governmental institutions, the suicide complex is notably absent. . . . The existence of a fixed and immortal boundary tends to create and sustain a fixed and immortal governmental institution.[5]

It was factors of underlying similarity such as these that prompted the enlargement of the present study beyond an organizational appraisal of the administrative details of the Greater London plan. During the course of the study, it became increasingly more obvious that the

[4] Edward C. Banfield, "The Politics of Metropolitan Area Organization," *Midwest Journal of Political Science*, I (May 1957), 82, 86.

[5] Luther Gulick, *The Metropolitan Problem and American Ideas* (New York: Alfred A. Knopf, 1962), p. 36.

problem of metropolitan governmental reform represents the type of catalytic agent that serves as a promising base for research into more general phenomena of political response that can extend well beyond specific questions of metropolitan organization itself.

This is so, first, because this issue is highly political in its overarching implications. It is political owing to both the nature of the participants and the nature of the subject matter involved. The major participants are governments, and, by basic definition, they are intimately concerned with the central questions of politics and power. The subject matter, too, is highly caustic—the distribution of governmental authority, the allocation of finances, the disruption of "fixed and immortal" boundaries, and innumerable similar problems contain a decidedly strong political orientation. Although, in the abstract world of theory, the issue of local governmental reform may appear to be antiseptic, or even sterile, in the vibrant world of political reality, such an issue is highly contentious by its very nature.

In addition, this issue contains a readily identifiable central focus that tends to give coherence to the entire research analysis. This focus is to be found in the reform plan itself. Such a plan represents a concrete target that demands some type of definite reply. The plan may be implemented, or modified, or defeated, or even sidetracked, but it must be acknowledged in one way or another. Once the process of reform begins to unfold, some type of subsequent response must inevitably follow.

Finally, this same basic issue of metropolitan reform is currently receiving world-wide attention, but it is receiving attention in a variety of different environmental contexts. On all parts of the globe, from Tokyo to Toronto, urban governments are wrestling with the problems of twentieth-century growth and are attempting to arrive at some meaningful political solutions to this problem. This presents a unique opportunity to the political observer, because it means that a basically similar experiment is being performed under a wide variety of laboratory conditions. Under these circumstances, it would be tragic not to grasp the full potentialities of this opportunity by utilizing this development as a basis for political, as well as organizational, analysis.

Indeed, in conducting such an analysis, we can hope to learn something from, and contribute something to, the larger questions of political integration that face our modern age. In many respects, today's metropolis represents a fascinating base for the study of "micropolitics." If we can believe an increasingly heavy body of literature, the metropolis is characterized by a growing economic, and even cultural, intradependence. Yet, the problems of political fragmentation are far from resolved. In the words of L. P. Green, ". . . local government systems were designed in their essentials before the advent of the modern city, and there is no place in them for the urban leviathans of modern times."[6]

To the extent that this is the case, the problems of metropolitan political integration represent something of a miniaturization of similar problems at a national, and even perhaps at an international, level. It would be absurd, of course, to push this analogy too far; but it most certainly should not be totally ignored. Matthew Holden's 1962 American Political Science Association paper on "The Governance of the Metropolis as a Problem in Diplomacy" and Douglas Price's 1963 paper on "Comparative Analysis in State and Local Politics: Potential and Problems" both indicate the promise that is inherent in such an approach.

As a result of the above considerations, the present study branches out beyond a purely organizational appraisal of the Greater London plan into an analysis of the kinds of participants and the kinds of tactics and strategies that went into the making of the political response to this plan. The broad model utilized for this purpose is borrowed from the general format developed by Wallace Sayre and Herbert Kaufman in their analysis of New York City's political system.[7] The contest that took place over the Greater London plan is viewed as actually being a contest, and the study attempts to identify the basic where, who, what, and how—the arena, the contestants, the stakes, and the strategies—that characterized this contest.

[6] L. P. Green, *Provincial Metropolis* (London: Allen & Unwin Ltd., 1959), p. 20.

[7] Wallace S. Sayre and Herbert Kaufman, *Governing New York City* (New York: Russell Sage Foundation, 1960).

In turn, Gabriel Almond's "input-output" categories are used to provide meaningful subdivisions under the Sayre-Kaufman model. Almond has suggested that all political systems are characterized by certain basic, and universal, functions. Some of these functions have a predominantly "input" orientation to the extent that they feed into the system, and some are related to the "ouputs" that are produced by the system. Almond lists seven such functional categories (illustrative examples are provided in parentheses):[8]

A. INPUT FUNCTIONS
1. Political Socialization and Recruitment (e.g., social foundations and attitudes)
2. Interest Articulation (e.g., anomic demonstrations, formal interest associations)
3. Interest Aggregation (e.g., political coalitions, party systems)
4. Political Communication (e.g., informal discussions, mass media)
B. OUTPUT FUNCTIONS
5. Rule-Making (e.g., legislative functions)
6. Rule-Application (e.g., executive functions)
7. Rule-Adjudication (e.g., judicial functions)

On the input side, the study gives particular consideration to aspects of "political socialization and recruitment" in Chapters 3, 4, and 7; to "interest articulation" in Chapter 6; to "interest aggregation" in Chapter 5; and to "political communication" in Chapters 8 and 13. The entire issue of reform is, of course, directly concerned with the output side of Almond's analysis, since it deals with an attempt to modify the output agencies of local government, most especially the "rule-application" agencies.

One of the most reassuring aspects of the analysis is the fact that the entire story unfolded with a reasonable degree of predictability. While the arguments and the strategies employed by both the proponents and the opponents of reform were not always immediately obvious, they did make considerable sense when viewed within the totality of the

    [8] Gabriel A. Almond and James S. Coleman (eds.), *The Politics of the Developing Areas* (Princeton: Princeton University Press, 1960), p. 17.

prevailing situation. Robert Dahl's *homo politicus,* as observed in New Haven, was quite readily identifiable as *homo politicus Londinium.*

In addition to its concern with metropolitan politics, the study has a purely descriptive objective in the historic sense of this term. Once again during the course of research, it became obvious that the central issue of metropolitan governmental reform is the type of problem that cuts a wide swath across many aspects of contemporary society. One cannot understand the concerns expressed over the Greater London plan by the London Teachers' Association, for example, without being aware of the general workings of the English educational system—the Eleven Plus examination; the difference between a comprehensive, a secondary modern, and a grammar school; and a host of similar considerations. Likewise, one cannot appreciate the protests of the Local Medical Committee for the County of London without knowing something about the key administrative changes that took place under the National Health Act of 1946.

Hence, in telling the story of the response to the Greater London plan, it is necessary to describe a great many current developments in English life as they relate to this plan. It is hoped that the reader will gain some benefit from such an exposure, above and beyond anything he may learn about metropolitan politics as such.

This, then, is the story of a community conflict in the classic sense of the term. It is a story that hopefully will have relevance both to an American and to an English audience.

2. London's Governmental Reform: A Chronological Summary

On July 29, 1957, Her Majesty's Government advised Parliament of its intention to create a new Royal Commission on Local Government in Greater London, thus setting into motion a reform effort that was destined to develop into a full-fledged political struggle. Before analyzing this struggle in any depth, it is necessary to gain a background understanding of the basic time sequence under which this reform effort actually unfolded.

This chapter is designed to summarize, in chronological fashion, the major events that occurred between the time of the Government's original announcement to Parliament in July 1957 and the time the new London Government Bill received Royal Assent on July 31, 1963. The summary does not attempt to probe into the deeper and more complex political influences—the motivational concerns, the tactical alignments, the operational strategies—that shaped the positions of the various groups actually participating in the struggle over reform. Instead, it is designed to serve as an outline guide, setting the stage for the more detailed analysis of just such political considerations that is set forth in subsequent chapters of the study.

The Organization of the Royal Commission   1957

The Government, more particularly the Ministry of Housing and Local Government, faced three immediate decisions once it had advised Parliament of its intention to establish the Royal Commission:

10

a. the formulation of the Commission's charge;
b. the selection of the Commission's membership; and
c. the delineation of the geographical frame of reference that was to serve as the base for the Commission's study program.

THE COMMISSION'S CHARGE

Although the wording of the Commission's substantive charge was a topic that invoked little if any significant debate, the Commission's interpretation of this charge was destined to exercise a profound influence over the entire political battle that lay ahead. By Her Majesty's Warrant dated December 10, 1957, the Commission was directed:

> To examine the present system and working of local government in the Greater London area; to recommend whether any, and if so what, changes in local government structure and the distribution of local authority functions in the area, or in any part of it, would better secure effective and convenient local government; and to regard, for these purposes, local government as not including the administration of police, or of water. . . .[1]

The key words in the above charge were the twin criteria of "effective" and "convenient" local government.

The Commission experienced little difficulty in interpreting the first of these terms. "Effective" local government was viewed as referring to the "output" aspects of the governmental process, more particularly to the efficiency with which the local authorities provided various specialized functional services. It was precisely this consideration of functional "output" that had dominated London's local governmental development throughout the preceding century. Since the time of the creation of the original London Police district in 1829, a host of special boards, special commissions, and other special authorities had been added to London's governmental system in an unending stream, in an effort to discharge particular functional services within the growing metropolis.

[1] Rpt., Cmnd. 1164 (i.e., "The Report of the Royal Commission on Local Government in Greater London" [London: Her Majesty's Stationery Office, October 1960]), p. 1.

It was the Royal Commission's interpretation of the second criterion —"convenient" local government—that represented something of a departure from past practice. As defined by the Commission, "convenient" local government was government that was "near at hand; easy of access." Specifically, the Commission viewed "convenient" local government as being "close to the people," and it later elaborated on this viewpoint in a remarkable philosophical portrayal of the local governmental process, which was spelled out in Chapter VI of its report:

> Local government, as we see it, is not just a machine or a piece of organisation. . . . Local government seems to us to be much more like a living thing, an organism, in which each part or function is not self-contained, or connected externally with other parts. Each part is integrally concerned with each other part. . . .
>
> In contrast to some other systems of government, representative government properly so called seeks to give outward form to the inward unity of a living community. Local government is with us an instance of democracy at work, and no amount of potential administrative efficiency could make up for the loss of active participation in the work by capable, public spirited people elected by, responsible to, and in touch with those who elect them.[2]

Here, indeed, were the elements of a significant approach to the problems of London's local government. This government was to be evaluated not only in terms of its "output" capacity to deliver specific services, but also in terms of "input" considerations involving political recruitment, political responsiveness, and democratic control. London's government was to be judged by not one, but two criteria. In the words of the Royal Commission, it was to be evaluated in terms of the twin tests of "administrative efficiency, and the health of representative government, as well as the organic relationship of both."

It was this dual emphasis on the "output" and the "input" aspects of the governmental process that represented a departure from previous practice, not only in London but in the United States as well. In America, as Robert C. Wood has noted, the great majority of our local governmental institutions, especially in our large metropolitan

2 *Ibid.*, p. 59.

areas, has been shaped almost entirely in terms of functional considerations alone:

> Technical specialist after technical specialist moved from one city to another, engaging in painstaking examinations of the current conditions of his own narrow proficiency, and solemnly proclaimed that no public health department could work properly unless it had a clientele of at least 50,000 people. . . . Little real attention was paid to the construction of meaningful political communities, or to the question of obtaining political responsibility.[3]

Now, in London, a new Royal Commission was indicating a concern over just such questions of political responsibility and the construction of meaningful political communities. By so doing, it was shaping the entire course of the struggle over reform that lay ahead.

THE COMMISSION'S MEMBERSHIP

The Government's second major consideration—the Commission's membership—did represent a significant issue of potential controversy. There is no doubt that, in naming the Commission, the Government placed key emphasis on the criterion of impartiality. Above all else, the Government attempted to name commissioners who were removed from the London governmental scene, and, as the listing in Table I (page 14) indicates, none of the commissioners did, in fact, have any direct experience with a London local authority.

Despite, or in part because of, this quest for impartiality, three different criticisms were leveled against the composition of the Commission.

In the first instance, some critics held not only that the Commission's membership was unfamiliar with the subject of London's government in particular, but also that the commissioners were not adequately versed in the wider subject of local government in general. This criticism was grounded in the fact that some of the commissioners had never served on any local governmental authority at any level and,

---

[3] Robert C. Wood, "A Division of Powers in Metropolitan Areas," in A. A. Maass (ed.), *Area and Power* (Glencoe: The Free Press, 1959), pp. 58-60.

hence, they were supposedly lacking in a "feel" for the "inner work-ings" of the local governmental process as such.

The response to this charge was that what the Commission may have lost in familiarity, it more than gained in objectivity. In the words of one of the Commission's supporters, "the independence of the members was one of the assets of the Commission."[4]

TABLE I

Members of the Royal Commission
on Local Government in Greater London
1957

Sir Edwin S. Herbert, K.B.E., Chairman
Sir Edwin, a solicitor, served as chairman or deputy chairman of several companies, including William Deacons Bank Ltd. and Associated Redif-fusion Ltd. He served as chairman of a number of official committees, including the Committee of Inquiry into the Electricity Supply Industry in 1954. Sir Edwin was designated a Life Peer in December 1963 and sub-sequently assumed the title Baron Tangley.

Sir John C. Wrigley, K.B.E., C.B.
Sir John, a retired civil servant, formerly served as the Joint Deputy Secretary in the Ministry of Health.

Sir Charles R. Morris
Sir Charles, the Vice-Chancellor of Leeds University, previously served as the Headmaster of King Edward School, Birmingham. Formerly, he was a fellow of Balliol College and an Oxford City Councillor.

Mr. Paul S. Cadbury, C.B.E.
Mr. Cadbury, Vice-Chairman of Cadbury Brothers, Ltd., had served in Birmingham local government and as a member of the Central Housing Advisory Committee.

Mr. William H. Lawson, C.B.E.
Mr. Lawson, a chartered accountant, was past president of the Institute of Chartered Accountants. A member of the Southern Electricity Board, he had served on various Government committees.

4 William A. Robson, "The Reform of London Government," *Public Admin-istration,* XXXIX (Spring 1961), 60.

Miss Alice C. Johnston, C.B.E.

Miss Johnston, a member of the National Assistance Board, was a former tutor at the Bonar Law College. During the war, she served in the Women's Voluntary Service and in the Civil Service.

Professor W. J. M. Mackenzie

Professor Mackenzie, a Professor of Government at the Victoria University at Manchester, served in the Civil Service during the war, had been an advisor to many Government commissions and committees, and had written numerous articles on local government.

A second criticism held that the Commission was weighted with technical specialists rather than with more socially oriented generalists:

> Members' experience and expertise equipped them to deal admirably with the more technical problems of local government, such as planning and administrative patterns necessary to secure optimum efficiency where this can be measured in technical terms. But local government provides, above all, services for citizens who measure its value at the point of direct contact. Regrettably the only member of the Commission who possessed such essential knowledge was the Social Services Administrator of the Women's Voluntary Services. In view of the heavy weighting of the Commission on the technical side, it is unfortunate . . . that she was not buttressed by a social scientist.[5]

To the best of my knowledge, no rebuttal was made to this charge. In fairness to the commissioners, however, it is difficult to read their report without concluding that they adopted a considerably more generalist view toward the government of Greater London than that displayed by any other body in the long history of London's circuitous governmental development.

Finally, there was the criticism that the Commission harbored a Conservative Party political bias—a charge that never really came out in the open, but one that lurked in the background during subsequent debates. Thus, on one occasion, a critic of the Commission asserted

[5] Marjorie McIntosh, "The Report of the Royal Commission on Local Government in Greater London," *British Journal of Sociology,* XII, No. 3 (September 1961), 238.

that "there was nobody on the Commission with a Labour point of view"[6]—an assertion that is debatable on a number of grounds. At least two of the seven Commission members were definite supporters of the Labour Party, and there is no evidence to indicate that any of the remaining five harbored any strong anti-Labour Party prejudice. Actually, only one member of the Commission, Miss Johnston, had an identifiable Conservative link—through her previous service as a tutor of the Bonar Law College, which was a Conservative establishment at the time. Certainly, however, it is difficult to view Miss Johnston, or any of the other commissioners, as a "political appointee" who was selected to represent Conservative Party interests. Under British Constitutional practice, Royal Commissions are expected to be non-partisan, and there is no indication that the Herbert Commission was any exception in this regard.

Actually, this criticism never reached serious proportions with respect to the work of the Royal Commission itself. The question of political motivation was raised once again, however, and this time with considerably more justification, after the Commission had finally completed its study and the Government was faced with the choice of whether to act upon or to ignore the Commission's recommendations.

THE COMMISSION'S GEOGRAPHICAL JURISDICTION

The third decision the Government faced prior to the inauguration of the new study related to the delineation of the Commission's review area. As finally specified in its Warrant, the Commission's review was confined to:

> The Greater London area as comprising the Metropolitan Police District together with the City of London, the Boroughs of Dartford, Romford and Watford, the Urban Districts of Caterham and Warlingham, Chorley Wood, Hornchurch, Rickmansworth, and Walton and Weybridge, and the Parish of Watford Rural in the Watford Rural District.[7]

[6] Parliamentary Debates (Hansard), House of Lords, Vol. CCXXXVIII, No. 49 (14 March 1962), col. 191; hereafter cited as Hansard.

[7] Rpt., Cmnd. 1164, p. 1.

This review area, based primarily on the Metropolitan Police District as originally conceived in 1829, encompassed some 845 square miles, extending for about a sixteen-mile radius from central London. Thus, the Commission's study was to coincide closely with the geographic area located inside London's Green Belt, including the whole of London and Middlesex counties; significant metropolitan portions of Essex, Surrey, and Kent counties; and a small corner of Hertfordshire County.

This final consideration of geographical jurisdiction created the most significant controversy of all. The major stream of criticism was that this geographical area was too small. Critics of this persuasion pointed to the 1944 Abercrombie Plan for Greater London's postwar development (which had extended for a thirty- rather than a fifteen-mile radius from central London) and argued that the real problems of metropolitan growth were taking place beyond the confines of the Green Belt and, hence, beyond the fringes of the Commission's purview. This argument was subsequently picked up by neutral observers from the press, by professional associations with a more direct interest in regional planning, and, above all, by those local governmental authorities that were later to oppose the Royal Commission's final recommendations.

While it would be foolhardy to pretend that this stream of criticism was without any validity, one point should be clarified at the outset, before this argument is analyzed in greater detail at a later stage of this study. This is the fact that this third line of criticism emerged in full form only after the Royal Commission had completed its study, and only after the potential political impact of its recommendations became apparent. Despite all the homage paid to the Abercrombie concepts at this later juncture, only one local authority (the Metropolitan Borough of Camberwell) and one independent group (the London School of Economics) argued at the outset that the Commission's geographical frame of reference was too small.

Instead, initial objections from the local authorities went in just the opposite direction. In 1957, before the new study got under way, the

Commission's "proposed terms of reference were sent to all local authorities in the Greater London area, and while quite a few thought that the area was too large, only one took the general point that the area ought to be larger—that was the Camberwell Metropolitan Borough Council who thought the area should include the Metropolitan Green Belt."[8]

These, then, were the major decisions the government made regarding the Commission's charge, membership, and geographical jurisdiction to set the stage for the new review of London's government. By December 1957, these preliminaries had been completed, and the Commission was ready to begin its evaluation of "the present system and working of local government in the Greater London area."

The Commission's Study   1958–1959

During the next two and a half years, the Royal Commission held 114 meetings, seventy of which were devoted to receiving oral testimony from local authorities, private associations, and a variety of other miscellaneous bodies. In addition, the Commission spent eighty-eight days making informal visits to local authorities throughout the review area.

The Commission later published complete reports of this written evidence and oral testimony; many of these are analyzed in further detail in subsequent portions of this study. For purposes of the present summary, only three factors need be noted with respect to this particular phase of the Commission's review.

The first concerns the timing of the submission of evidence. In February 1958 the Commission sent letters to all local authorities and to a variety of private associations in the review area, inviting them to submit written evidence regarding the organization of London's government. One month later, a second letter was dispatched to all major universities, inviting their comments on this subject. The local

---

[8] Letter, R. Brain, Ministry of Housing and Local Government, to F. Smallwood, dated October 5, 1962.

authorities and private associations submitted their briefs during the summer and fall months of 1958.

By early 1959, the Royal Commission had digested these written briefs to the extent that it was ready to hold oral hearings on the evidence submitted. The first group to testify appeared on March 5, 1959. These oral hearings continued throughout the spring, with the London County Council testifying in April, the Essex County Council in late May, and the Middlesex County Council in mid-June. It was during this same month, June 1959, that one of the university groups, the London School of Economics, finally submitted a massive volume of written evidence in response to the invitation the Commission had extended more than a year earlier.

This evidence was considerably more complete than any submitted previously by the county councils or other local authorities. In addition, the majority of the London School of Economics' witnesses recommended a major overhaul in the existing London governmental set-up that went well beyond the more modest changes that had been suggested earlier by the great majority of local authorities. As soon as this LSE evidence was submitted, a second academic group, the Centre for Urban Studies of the University of London, advised the Commission that it, too, wanted to provide written evidence. The Centre's written brief, which did not appear until December 1959, represented a basic rebuttal of the LSE position. It recommended that no major changes were needed in London's governmental organization. Aside from the Centre for Urban Studies group, however, the major witnesses had little opportunity for a formal rebuttal of the LSE position. All the major local authorities, including the large county councils, had already completed their oral testimony before the LSE written evidence was received in June 1959, and it was extremely difficult for them to make any tactical adjustments in their positions at this late date in the proceedings.

The second key factor with respect to the Commission's hearings related to the relative weight of numbers of the various groups that offered testimony. As was previously noted, the Commission spent some 88 days visiting local authorities throughout the review area, the overwhelming bulk of these being the numerous second-tier units[9] that far outnumbered the six county councils in Greater London. These second-tier authorities dominated the Commission's oral hearings also. In all, 32 of the 70 days devoted to such hearings (or 45 per cent of the total) were given over to the second-tier units, with the remaining 38 days being divided between the first-tier authorities, the numerous private associations that testified, and the two university groups. Thus, during the course of its study, the Commission was quite literally engulfed with the viewpoints of the second-tier authorities.

The third factor that was significant at this stage of the Commission's hearings involved the fact that the great bulk of testimony received from all the governmental witnesses was characterized by a broad and consistent defense of the status quo. In addition to receiving local testimony from the London first-tier and second-tier authorities, the Commission heard evidence from many of the major Ministries in the central Government. The great majority of this evidence indicated a general satisfaction with existing arrangements. The Ministry of Education, in particular, expressed the view that while the local educational services were far from perfect, there was no part of the metropolitan area in which "the present system of educational administration does not work at least tolerably well."[10] Thus, the late submission of the London School of Economics' evidence took on all the more significance in light of the fact that this group did, in fact, recommend a major overhaul of the prevailing governmental system.

The Commission completed its oral hearings by receiving testimony from the Centre of Urban Studies group in February 1960. It was now ready to weigh the evidence and write up its recommendations in a final report. Both the timing of the submission of the LSE evidence and the overwhelming predominance of the second-tier testimony were destined to play a crucial role at this stage of the Commission's deliberations, a fact that became more fully apparent once the Commission had actually issued its final report in the fall of 1960.

[9] The second-tier units, and the other components of London's local government, are described in detail in Chapter 4. See especially Maps V and VI, pp. 67 and 68.

[10] Royal Commission, *Memoranda of Evidence from Government Departments*, VI (London: HMSO, 1959), 21-24.

The Commission's Report 1960

The Royal Commission issued its report in October 1960. Far from shying away from difficult issues of potential controversy, this report contained a series of far-reaching recommendations that were almost sure to set off subsequent political debate. In essence, the Commission concluded that London's existing governmental organization failed both its twin tests of "administrative efficiency" and "representative health," and that the patient's future well-being could be assured only through a program of major surgery.

As regards the first criterion—"administrative efficiency"—the Commission concluded that "with the exception of some of the environmental health services, none of [the] major functions can be discharged best by the local authorities that exist under the present structure of local government, and some of them cannot be adequately discharged at all under the present structure."[11]

Nor did the Commission feel the situation was any more encouraging when viewed in light of its second criterion. Here, after attempting to evaluate the "health" of London's representative institutions on the basis of six separate subtests,[12] the Commission once again decided that it was dealing with a rather sickly governmental creature.

[11] Rpt., Cmnd. 1164, p. 175.

[12] Rpt., Cmnd. 1164, Chapter XIII. The six "tests" which the Royal Commission felt to indicate conclusively that the present structure in the Review Area was not conducive to "the health of representative government" can be summarized as follows:

1. *Uncertainty Regarding Status.* A long period of uncertainty, especially regarding the county borough question in Middlesex, had "a bad effect . . . on the morale of local government." While the Commission did not see this as a major problem in London and Surrey counties, it classified the relationship between the two tiers as "medium" in Kent, "indifferent" in Essex, and "bad" in Middlesex.

2. *Erosion of Powers.* The transfer of powers away from local government had an adverse effect on the prestige of local government.

3. *Friction Regarding Delegation.* The system of delegation between the two tiers "over large parts of Greater London . . . is working badly and giving rise to a great deal of friction."

4. *Quality of Councillors.* The erosion of powers and the irritations arising out of delegation have "seriously lowered the status of boroughs and other county districts in the eyes of potential councillors of ability and ambition."

5. *Complexity and Apathy.* "The extraordinary complication of local gov-

As a result of this negative diagnosis, the Commission felt itself driven to the final conclusion that "judged by the twin tests of administrative efficiency and the health of representative government, the present structure of local government in the Review Area is inadequate and needs overhaul."[13]

It was not until it came to recommend the precise nature of this overhaul, however, that the political implications of the Commission's report became clear. Although the point was never spelled out fully in its final report, it is obvious in retrospect that the Commission felt the two major illnesses it had diagnosed could be isolated and remedied by separate treatment at the first-tier and the second-tier levels of government. Specifically, the Commission concluded that the first problem— that of administrative inefficiency—could be resolved through a complete overhaul of the first-tier county councils and county boroughs, while the second problem—that of the ill health of representative government—could be alleviated through a strengthening of the second-tier authorities at the local level.

When translated into concrete realities, this first-tier overhaul led the Commission to recommend that both the London and the Middlesex County Councils should be abolished completely in favor of an entirely new first-tier authority—the Greater London Council—and that significant metropolitan portions of Surrey, Kent, Essex, and (less drastically) Hertfordshire should be separated from their parent counties and should also be incorporated under the new Greater London Council. In addition, London's three existing county boroughs— East Ham, West Ham, and Croydon—should lose their first-tier status and be redesignated as second-tier authorities under this new Council. In its basic essentials, the Commission's plan incorporated the key ideas

---

ernment in Greater London is confusing to the electors, and seems to induce in their minds a sort of fatalism."

6. *Availability of Councillors.* First-tier and second-tier councils were manned, to a large extent, by councillors drawn from "different strata of the community." The first-tier county councils suffered in this regard because they held their meetings in the daytime and their councillors "must be largely drawn from people of leisure and some means."

13 Rpt., Cmnd. 1164, p. 181.

that had been presented in evidence by the majority of the London School of Economics' witnesses. With respect to the first tier, the Commission felt that administrative efficiency could be realized only through the creation of a single Greater London Council to coordinate broad programs (e.g., planning, traffic, etc.) over the entire review area (as finally defined) in lieu of the six county councils and the three county boroughs that had exercised these responsibilities previously. The first-tier authorities were to be the losers, to put it mildly, in the Royal Commission's vision of the future Greater London.

The second-tier authorities, on the other hand, were presented with quite a different alternative. Here, a major program of consolidation and amalgamation was to be undertaken in order to reduce the existing ninety-odd second-tier units into 52 new Greater London Boroughs. The purpose of this reorganization was to enable these enlarged boroughs to take on more of the powers of local government than the second-tier authorities were exercising at the time. In effect, the Commission was attempting to revitalize the health of London's representative institutions by strengthening the second-tier authorities. In the process, it was proposing to restore many of the powers the second-tier units had seen slip away during recent years.

True, the second-tier units would pay a price for such increased powers in the form of the proposed amalgamations and consolidations. These were not overly drastic, however, especially in their impact on the larger, and most powerful, second-tier units that would emerge from this ordeal virtually unscathed. In this respect the Commission had once again closely followed the majority recommendations of the London School of Economics group, with one key exception. Whereas the majority of LSE witnesses had called for the creation of a new group of second-tier Greater London Boroughs, each possessing somewhere between 250,000 and 500,000 people, the Royal Commission had reduced this population criterion to a point where each of its proposed boroughs would contain a minimum of 100,000 people. The practical consequence of this reduction was that fewer amalgamations and consolidations of existing authorities would be required to create the fifty-two enlarged boroughs called for under the Commission's plan than would have been required to create the thirty-odd still larger boroughs suggested under the LSE plan. Thus, under the Commission's proposals, the biggest second-tier units were to gain increased powers they had long been hungrily pursuing, without any drastic disruptions in their existing boundaries.

The proposed distribution of powers between the new first-tier Greater London Council and the new second-tier Greater London Boroughs is outlined in Table II, and the proposed borough boundaries are shown in Map I. While there is no doubt that the Commission provided a theoretical justification for its reorganization proposals in terms of the twin criteria it had set up in its report (i.e., administrative efficiency and the health of representative government), it is important to note the immediate and obvious political implications of these proposals. Whereas the first-tier county councils and county boroughs were to be the big losers in the reorganization process, the larger second-tier authorities were designated as the big winners. By driving a deep wedge between the first- and the second-tier units, the Commission virtually guaranteed that its recommendations would not be met with unanimous opposition. Since the Commission's proposals were obviously going to alienate one powerful tier of government (the county councils), "if the Commissioners hoped to make some impact on London government within their own lifetimes, it followed that their subsequent recommendations must gain powerful support elsewhere."[14]

The Commission's subsequent recommendations did, in fact, promise to do just this.

TABLE II

Summary of the Royal Commission's Proposals, October 1960

I. *Area*
   1. The proposed area of reorganization should be as defined in the Commission's original terms of reference, minus the local authorities deleted in Map I.

[14] D. V. Donnison, *Health, Welfare and Democracy in Greater London,* Greater London Papers, No. 5 (London School of Economics, 1962), p. 23.

2. For local government purposes, it was suggested that this area could be divided into 52 second-tier Greater London Boroughs (minimum population of 100,000) and that the over-all authority for the entire area should be a first-tier Council for Greater London.

II. *Division of Powers*

1. *General*: Statutory provision should be made for the distribution of functions between the Greater London Boroughs and the Greater London Council in the administrative discharge of their responsibilities.

2. *Concurrent Powers*: The Greater London Boroughs and the Greater London Council should enjoy certain concurrent powers in relation to parks and open spaces, main sewerage, and land drainage, plus specific aspects of environmental health and housing. Subject to these concurrent powers,

3. *Borough Powers*: The Greater London Boroughs should be responsible for:
   a. Housing
   b. Personal Health, Welfare, and Children's Services (other than ambulances)
   c. Environmental Health (other than refuse disposal)
   d. Roads (other than main roads)
   e. Libraries
   f. Local Planning Applications—and these boroughs should also have important functions with regard to the day-to-day administration of the educational services.

4. *Council Powers*: The Greater London Council should discharge area-wide responsibilities as the major authority for:
   a. Planning Policy
   b. General Educational Policy
   c. Traffic and Main Roads
   d. Refuse Disposal
   e. Fire and Ambulance Services—and the Council should also set up an Intelligence Department to collect, collate, and disseminate information regarding the performance of local government functions throughout the area.

III. *Finances*

1. The existing London "Rate Equalization Scheme" should be abolished and replaced by another of a different nature.*

2. The County Councils of Essex, Kent, and Surrey should for a

* This scheme is described in Chapter 8.

transitional period receive payment from the boroughs formerly in their counties in order to reduce the rate burden falling upon them as a result of the change.

IV. *Miscellaneous*

1. The City Corporation of London should remain unchanged geographically and should be treated as a Greater London Borough.[15]
2. The Greater London Council should be directly elected every three years, at the same time and place at which borough elections are held, with one member for each Parliamentary constituency in the proposed reorganization area.

The Government's White Paper   1961

The expected opposition to the Commission's report was forthcoming almost immediately. In late November and December 1960, the Surrey and Kent County Councils launched independent counterattacks in the form of alternative reorganization plans that were considerably more modest in their impact than that which had been proposed by the Commission. They were joined in their condemnation of the Commission's report by the London County Council and its political arm, the London Labour Party, in January 1961, and by a second group of miscellaneous private associations, most notably the London Teachers' Association, in February 1961.

Sporadic opposition to the Commission's proposals continued to appear during the winter and spring, but it was somewhat limited in intensity by the fact that the Government had not, as yet, taken any formal position on the Royal Commission's proposals. At this stage of the proceedings, the Commission's report enjoyed an advisory status

---

[15] The Royal Commission felt that the City of London should be redesignated as a new Greater London Borough, despite its small size, because "its traditions and historical ceremonial" make it "an institution of national importance." In what was destined to become a famous phrase, the Commission concluded that "Logic has its limits, and the position of the City lies outside them." This sparing of the City was one early action in which the Royal Commission most decidedly did indicate its acute awareness of political realities as they related to the realization of the reform proposals.

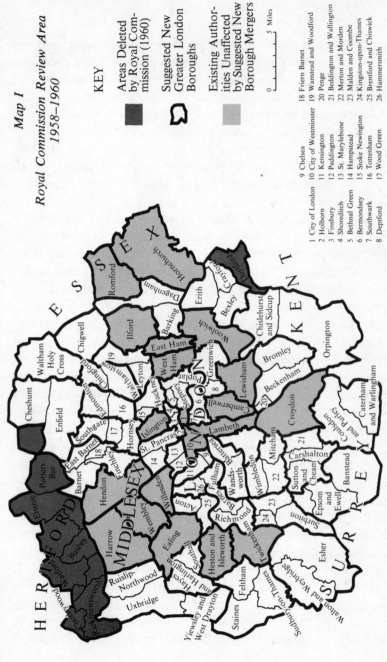

Map I

Royal Commission Review Area
1958–1960

KEY

Areas Deleted by Royal Commission (1960)

Suggested New Greater London Boroughs

Existing Authorities Unaffected by Suggested New Borough Mergers

0   5 Miles

1 City of London
2 Holborn
3 Finsbury
4 Shoreditch
5 Bethnal Green
6 Bermondsey
7 Southwark
8 Deptford
9 Chelsea
10 City of Westminster
11 Kensington
12 Paddington
13 St. Marylebone
14 Hampstead
15 Stoke Newington
16 Tottenham
17 Wood Green
18 Friern Barnet
19 Wanstead and Woodford
20 Penge
21 Beddington and Wallington
22 Merton and Morden
23 Malden and Coombe
24 Kingston-upon-Thames
25 Brentford and Chiswick
26 Hammersmith

only. It had been submitted to the Parliament as a proposed program of reform, and the Government had the option of either accepting, revising, ignoring, or totally rejecting the Commission's recommendations. Under the circumstances, the opponents of the report were reluctant to focus very much publicity on the Commission's proposals, in the hope that the entire reform program might become bogged down in indefinite delay, a fate not uncommon to a great many Royal Commission reports in the past. The more these opponents engaged in open attack, the more the resultant publicity might force the Government to take definite action.

One group that did keep up a constant barrage, however, was the London Teachers' Association. After unanimously condemning the Royal Commission's proposals at its annual meeting in February 1961, this group continued to publicize its adverse reactions by all available means, including the circulation of protest petitions to all LTA teachers in the London County area.

The Government, on the other hand, continued to remain non-committal throughout the summer and fall months, indicating in answer to Parliamentary inquiries that it was evaluating the reactions to the Commission's report that it had requested from all the local authorities in the area. Finally, in the late fall, the Government decided to make its move. In December 1961, it issued a formal White Paper, outlining its views on the Royal Commission's plan.

The Government's White Paper supported the Commission's proposals. It did, however, make two major revisions in these proposals that indicated an acute awareness of the opposition's attacks, especially that which had been launched by the London Teachers' Association. The first of these revisions related to the educational services. Here the Government rejected the Royal Commission's recommendation that these services should be split between the new Greater London Council and the new Greater London Boroughs. As is indicated in Table I, under the original Commission plan, the Greater London Council was to have exercised over-all responsibility for general educational policy throughout the entire review area, while the new boroughs were to be responsible for the actual day-to-day administration of the educational services. The Government concluded that it would be impractical to divide the educational program in this fashion, and it recommended instead that education become a primary responsibility of the new boroughs.

This first shift in educational responsibilities led directly to the Government's second major revision. The Government concluded that, if the boroughs were to exercise responsibility for the educational services, they must have greater resources (i.e., a larger population and financial base). Hence, whereas the Commission had suggested that the boroughs should have a minimum population of 100,000, the Government's White Paper raised this figure to 200,000. At this point the Government's new proposals were coming to approximate more and more closely the original majority position that had been presented by the London School of Economics witnesses. In addition, however, the Government did go off on a unique tack of its own by recommending that an entirely new, independent educational authority be created for London's "central area." Although the White Paper failed to spell out the implications of this proposal with any precision, it did indicate that this "central area" should contain approximately two million people, or roughly two-thirds of the population of London County.

In making these revisions, the Government was attempting to pacify the mounting forces of criticism, especially the objections advanced by the London Teachers' Association. Far from achieving such an objective, however, the Government's actions increased the antagonism of the opposition forces. The original opponents of the plan now began to smell blood. They were anxious to launch an even more aggressive assault in the hope of obtaining further concessions that, if serious enough, might kill the entire reform effort. In addition, many of the second-tier units that had previously supported the Commission's plan in the hope of obtaining increased powers were now becoming hostile with respect to the enlarged borough populations proposed in the Government's White Paper.

By the end of 1961 the situation had shaken down to a point where clear-cut battle lines were becoming very well entrenched.

The Opposition Intensifies   1962

Following the release of the Government's White Paper, the opposition forces began to push an all-out offensive against the entire reform program. The year 1962 was characterized by an increasingly more aggressive attack against the Government's position that eventually culminated in the creation of a specialized pressure group—the Committee for London Government—whose sole purpose was to defeat the proposed reorganization plan.

During the winter months, the Government's initial response to this intensified assault was one of rather zigzag retreat that tended to accentuate the opposition's demands for still further concessions. The Government did manage to make one shrewd tactical move during February and March 1962, when it forced a preliminary debate on the general principles of the reform program in both the House of Commons and the House of Lords. At the conclusion of these debates, the Government moved that both Houses "take note of" its White Paper, and both votes passed easily, thus providing general Parliamentary approval for the concept of reform. Further Government concessions appeared during the later spring months, however, and it was not until July 1962, when Sir Keith Joseph was appointed the new Minister for Housing and Local Government as a result of a general Conservative Party Cabinet shake-up, that the Government began to display firm resolution in its support of the reform program.

As the summer progressed, the opposition forces continued to keep up their constant fire of attack, coordinated by the newly formed Committee for London Government, which was now attempting to circulate a massive protest petition with an announced goal of 500,000 signatures. At the October opening of Parliament, the Government clarified its intention to press forward with the reform by assigning priority to this item in the Queen's Speech from the Throne. The London Government Bill was presented to the House of Commons for First Reading in November, and the Second Reading debate on the general principles of the Bill followed in early December. By late 1962, the reform program had become an issue of timing rather than intent. The Government was obviously bent on securing reform, and it possessed a large enough Conservative majority to force the Bill through Parliament. The Labour opposition was forced to fall back upon a strategy of obstruction and delay as its last hope of staving off the inevitable.

Plodding Through Parliament 1963

1963 was a year of bitter infighting over the London Government Bill in both Houses of Parliament. By the end of January, the Government had applied the guillotine to speed up progress in the House of Commons, and the Bill trudged forward against a massive weight of Labour Party amendments and debate. In February the Committee for London Government announced that it had obtained 172,000 signatures for its petition, a not insignificant total but one that fell far short of its announced goal of 500,000. By late April the Bill had moved through the Commons into the House of Lords, where it was greeted by a repetition of the Commons' delaying tactics, spearheaded this time by Lord Morrison of Lambeth, the Labour Life Peer who had built his long political career on the base of his earlier leadership of the London County Council.

The intensity of this Parliamentary struggle is indicated by the fact that more than 1,000 amendments were laid down for the Bill during the committee stage in the Commons, while the Lords dealt with no less than 303 proposed amendments during their committee stage. One Lords' session (May 13–14) had the distinction of lasting until 2:35 A.M., thereby setting a new longevity record for a single sitting (twelve hours and five minutes).

The committee-stage hearings that occupied the House of Lords during May 1963 marked the high-water point of opposition activity. They also preceded a quite unrelated episode that very nearly killed the entire reform effort.

It was in early June that Miss Christine Keeler splashed across the pages of the world's press, and in the ensuing uproar the Conservative Government tottered on the very brink of disaster. Although the future fate of the London Government Bill was hardly the *cause célèbre* of British politics at this particular juncture, there is little doubt that this Bill would have become a totally lost cause if the Conservative Government had, in fact, fallen as a result of the Profumo affair. Any new Labour Government could hardly have been expected to resurrect this legislative package as a number one post-election priority. In short, Labour's strategy of Parliamentary delay came within a whisker of paying dividends. A far distant chain of circumstances that stretched from Lord Astor's swimming pool to the inner circles of the Conservative Party very nearly added the proposed new Greater London Council to its lengthy list of mutilated victims.

The Conservative Government remained in office, however, and the London Government Bill continued its grudging forward progress. In late June it entered the Report Stage in the House of Lords where, after further debate and delay, it was finally approved before moving back to the Commons. After the Commons disposed of the Lords' amendments, the Bill received Royal Assent on July 31, 1963. The specific provisions of the new London Government Act are discussed in considerable detail in the concluding sections of this study. For purposes of the present summary, it is important to note two key points. First, while the Act that was finally approved by Parliament followed many of the broad outlines of the Royal Commission's original report, it was in no sense a perfect carbon copy of the Commission's earlier recommendations. The opponents of reorganization may not have been successful in killing the reform effort outright, but they most certainly did manage to realize some extremely important concessions as a result of their opposition stance. Second, from the time of its initial inception, the entire reform program contained a variety of highly volatile elements of political controversy.

The key question that remains is why this should have been the case. Why should a seemingly pallid program of structural reform spark off a protest drive to secure half a million signatures? produce the longest single sitting in the history of the House of Lords? involve the consideration of more than 1,300 proposed Parliamentary amendments? arouse the enmity of teachers, doctors, and a host of other professionals? and force the Labour Party to make an informal (if not, in actual fact, absolute) commitment to rescind the entire reform program if it won the next General Election? In short, why should the supposedly innocuous issue of local governmental reorganization possess such a pervasive political wallop?

The posing of such questions leads directly into the more detailed political analysis that constitutes the heart of the present study. In all, six years passed between the time of the original announcement of the Royal Commission review and the final approval of the London Government Bill. During this six-year period, many groups found themselves struggling both for and against the proposed reform. An analysis of who these groups were, what they were after, and how they went about securing their objectives poses some highly relevant lessons in the high art of metropolitan politics.

Part II

THE ARENA

"We think of politics in terms of participants inter-
acting in arenas. . . ."

—Harold Lasswell, *Politics*

The contest over the Greater London plan took place in a physical arena that had been shaped by a unique variety of historical and environmental forces.

In turn, this contest focused upon the reform of a governmental system that had been shaped by the same historical and environmental forces.

Since London's metropolitan environment, and London's governmental system, served to delineate the arena and provide the focus for the conflict over reform, it is necessary to gain a familiarity with both these elements if this conflict is to take on any significance at all.

Chapter 3 is designed to provide a brief background description of some of the major influences that have shaped the historical development of the great modern London metropolis. Chapter 4 provides a similar description of the key components of the Greater London governmental system as they existed prior to the inauguration of the Royal Commission's study in 1957.

3. London's Historical Development

In the beginning, London was the natural heir of a convenient marriage between geography and geology.

The Thames serves as the access route into the heart of southern England, but it is not until the present site of London is reached that beds of Taplow gravel, laid down on a blue clay base some 250 million years ago, line both sides of the river. This gravel base represented the lowest, and the most convenient, point at which the Thames could be forded and, in due course, bridged. As a result, there is evidence to indicate that the earliest denizens of London could lay claim to origins of considerable antiquity. "As far back as the Old Stone Age, the first Londoners were hunting mammoths in what is now known as Piccadilly,"[1] leaving as mementos a number of flint hand axes (excavated in this area in 1913) that now reside in the British Museum.

[1] R. J. Mitchell and M. D. R. Leys, *A History of London Life* (London: Longmans, Green & Company Ltd., 1958), p. 3. Other books helpful to the preparation of the general historical background in Chapter 3 included: H. M. Chadwick, *The Origin of The English Nation* (Cambridge University Press, 1924); N. Aberg, *The Anglo-Saxons in England* (Cambridge: Heffer & Sons, 1926); J. J. Clark, *A History of Local Government in the United Kingdom* (London: Herbert Jenkins, 1955); W. E. Jackson, *Local Government in England and Wales* (London: Penguin Books Ltd., new ed., 1959); K. Cameron, *English Place Names* (London: Batsford Ltd., 1961); L. Golding, *Dictionary of Local Government in England and Wales* (London: The English Universities Press Ltd., 1962); and, most especially, *The Pelican History of England,* Vols. II-VIII (London: Penguin Books), which constitutes a superb paperback bargain for any reader.

It was not until A.D. 43, however, when the Roman legions conquered the growing river settlement, that the early roots of the modern metropolis began to take shape. In addition to its ease of crossing, the geographical site of London represented the farthest inland point at which the Thames was readily navigable by seagoing vessels. The Romans, with their genius for engineering and organization, developed the community into a port and made it the central focus of a unified system of roads and communications that traversed the newly conquered island. In addition, with their talent for appropriation and adaptation, the Romans borrowed a Celtic personal name, Londinos, and called the community Londinos' town, or Londinium.

The new conquerors occupied Londinium for the next four centuries, a period of relatively quiet growth for the expanding port community. The only notable break in this early tranquility occurred in A.D. 61, when, according to the historian Tacitus, the followers of Boadicea, British Queen of the Iceni, revolted against Roman rule and invaded Londinium to sack the infant city and slaughter its inhabitants. Although Boadicea's army was subsequently crushed by the Roman legions, her exploits are still memorialized in statue, and today she can be found careening ahead ferociously on an impressive bronze chariot that is located opposite the Big Ben end of Westminster Bridge. Another modern London landmark indirectly attributable to Boadicea is the remnant of the city's old Roman wall, which was built originally to discourage further forays into Londinium on the part of any of Boadicea's overambitious successors.

Following the Roman evacuation of England during the early part of the fifth century, the Island was once again subjected to a series of external raids and was once again conquered, this time by three Germanic tribes—the Angles, the Saxons, and the Jutes. Whereas the Romans gave Londinium its original name and its start toward greatness, the Anglo-Saxons provided the early foundations for many of London's present-day governmental institutions.

The Germanic invasions were followed by a period of widespread anarchy and confusion, until gradually numerous Saxon "kingdoms" emerged, each headed by a series of petty chieftains. Modern scholarship has revealed that these ancient kingdoms were in a state of constant flux, despite earlier beliefs in a more tidy theory of Saxon administration, centering upon a convenient grouping of only seven independent regions, still known today as the "Saxon Heptarchy." It is believed, however, that many of the Saxons settled directly to the north, west, and south of the present site of London, which areas eventually assumed the present-day names of Essex (East Saxon region), Middlesex (Middle Saxon region), and Surrey (for "Suthregia," or the South kingdom of the Middlesex region). The Jutes settled in the large area stretching from the southeast of London to the English Channel, where they established a unique culture. The inhabitants of this area were known as "Cantuarii," or people of Kent. Thus, as is illustrated in Map II, these early Germanic settlements represented the rationale for a subsequent series of administrative counties that were not to acquire real governmental power until more than one thousand years later, with the passage of the Local Government Act of 1888.

Strangely, however, the former Roman cities, including Londinium, were not reoccupied immediately by the Germanic invaders, who were accustomed to building in timber and were unable to repair the crumbling stone foundations the Romans had left behind. Thus the almost eerie tone of foreboding to be found in a gnomic poem prefixed to one manuscript of *The Anglo-Saxon Chronicle:*

> Cities are visible from afar,
> the cunning work of giants
> the wondrous fortifications in stone
> which are on this earth.[2]

London's geographical site was too attractive to lie idle for any significant period of time, however, and during later Saxon times the city began to reassert itself as the leading community in Britain. The most distinguishing and, in the course of later events, the most significant aspect of local Saxon rule was the high degree of autonomy provided individual communities in the administration of two key aspects of local economic affairs—markets and monies.

[2] Dorothy Whitelock, "The Beginnings of English Society," *Pelican History of England*, II (1952), 16.

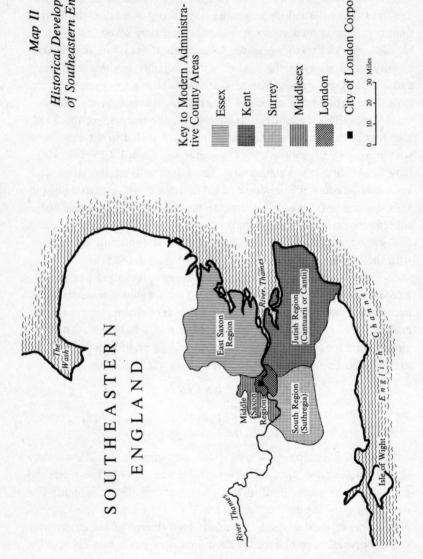

Map II

*Historical Development
of Southeastern England*

SOUTHEASTERN
ENGLAND

The
Wash

River Thames

East Saxon
Region

River Thames

Middle
Saxon
Region

Jutish Region
(Cantuarii or Cantii)

South Region
(Suthregia)

Isle of Wight

English Channel

Key to Modern Administra-
tive County Areas

Essex
Kent
Surrey
Middlesex
London

City of London Corporation

0 10 20 30 Miles

Although the rationale behind this development was quite narrowly pragmatic, the subsequent impact was to be far-reaching. During the eighth and ninth centuries, a series of ravaging raids by a new group of Danish invaders threatened the complete annihilation of Saxon culture. In responding to this threat, the Saxon kings inaugurated a "burghal" system of fortified communities that would permit the continued existence of orderly economic activities and protect the surrounding countryside against enemy attack. London became one of the key fortifications when Alfred the Great rebuilt its defenses, and in 886 he appointed his son-in-law Ethelred to be its governor, thus assuring the growing community's independent detachment from the surrounding kingdom of the East Saxons. The economic position of London was strengthened further by a later Saxon king, Athelstan (924–940), who permitted it to establish eight mints, as against six in Winchester (the capital of Wessex) and four in Canterbury.

Thus, London's early political and economic autonomy was the outgrowth of a Saxon decentralization policy that was primarily military in its motivations. The word "borough" originally meant a "fortified place," and it was only in later usage that the term came to designate any town that had been granted special privileges by means of a Royal Charter.

Although they enjoyed some degrees of local autonomy, the Saxon boroughs were in no sense completely independent of the Crown. As one observer has noted:

> In early days every borough, whether it were an ancient centre newly fortified or a new settlement on Royal land, was in a peculiar sense the King's. It was his because he had chosen to make it a borough and set it about with walls or earthworks. He wished it to prosper and he expected to share in its prosperity. Its mint was a privilege. Its market also, was a privilege granted and protected by the King.[3]

Be that as it may, the ideological consequences of this Saxon "burghal" system took on considerable importance in shaping the

[3] Doris M. Stenton, "English Society in the Early Middle Ages," *Pelican History of England,* III (1951), 167.

future development of English local government, and many of the forces set into motion at this very early date are still of basic significance. First, the establishment of the semi-autonomous boroughs fused into English political thought a strong stream of "localist" tradition which has been a potent force throughout the subsequent course of English history. Second, the Saxon policy heralded the rise of an administrative, rather than a legislative, tradition in local governmental rule, which, again, is of key importance in understanding modern English institutions. Under Saxon practice, the local communities were to administer certain functions (e.g., the minting of money, the management of markets) on behalf of the Crown. They were in no sense expected, or permitted, to establish completely independent policies by legislating in their own interests. The same general tradition remains in force today. As G. D. H. Cole has recently noted:

> Local government, as we regard it in the United Kingdom, is local self-government in the field primarily of administration, rather than in the legislative field. . . . The business of English Local Government is primarily administration—that is to say, it is concerned with the execution of laws passed by Parliament or of functions conferred by ancient Charters.[4]

Third, the early Saxon innovations established the general tradition that only the largest and most important local communities would qualify for quasi-autonomous borough status under Royal Charter. Once again, we see a very important remnant of this early tradition in the modern English practice of creating independent, all-purpose units of local government known as "county boroughs." Today, however, the criterion used in establishing these modern county boroughs has changed in theory, if not in fact, from considerations of wealth and defensive capabilities to that of population size. Finally, the early Saxon precedents established the concept of the Royal Charter as the machinery to be utilized in conferring a degree of administrative autonomy upon the local communities. For the next thousand years, the most

[4] G. D. H. Cole, *Local and Regional Government* (London: Casswell & Company Ltd., 1947), pp. 28-29.

important English cities would seek from the Crown borough status, which would permit them to enjoy some degree of independence in the management of their local affairs.

This rudimentary idealization of local autonomy that grew out of the early Saxon precedents was subjected to a direct challenge following the third, and final, conquest of England by the Normans in 1066. Understandably, the Norman French were reluctant to permit the newly conquered English communities to exercise any great degree of local self-government in the administration of their daily affairs. Instead, the Norman kings, fearful of potential revolt by the restive population, advocated a strong, centralized governmental system under the direct control of the Crown.[5] The English cities were not to be put off easily, however; and thus began a classic struggle between the forces of centralism and the forces of localism that was destined to shape much of later English history.

The first highly pragmatic, and somewhat uneasy, compromise between these two forces was the result of a financial bargaining process. The Norman kings needed money to administer the affairs of the newly conquered island, and the local communities were willing to cooperate with the Crown in return for Royal Charters of Incorporation that would recognize at least minimal guarantees of local self-government. Thus, William the Conqueror granted London a charter sometime between 1068 and 1075 which, while not conferring any new powers, did ratify the citizens' rights and privileges already in existence under the Saxon kings.

The citizens of London continued to strengthen their position under the later Norman and the early Plantagenet rulers by purchasing new immunities and further privileges from the Crown in a long succession of Royal Charters. The fragile process actually at work during this period amounted to no less than the search for a basic concept of community identity that would enjoy a standing under law. Although the

---

[5] Actually, the Normans did not weaken English local government as much as they strengthened English national government. The old Saxon government was strong in local areas, but weak in the national. The Norman government of England became stronger in both.

Saxon kings had fortified individual towns, such action had been taken solely in the name of the Crown, with the local communities possessing no legal standing of their own. The new concept now emerging was based on earlier continental precedents of corporate autonomy. Although the rudimentary concepts of corporate form had been known as early as Roman times, the Romans had never developed fully any notions of "corporate personality" as a distinct legal entity. The most immediate precedents for the newly emerging English concepts were to be found in the continental "communes" that had slowly been securing recognition from the sovereigns and feudal overlords of Medieval Europe. The English towns now grasped these continental precedents to establish the general principle that any community of persons united in a given geographical location possessed its own corporate personality and identity and was worthy of legal protection and legal perpetuation in its own right. This revolutionary concept of corporate existence was eventually solidified in a series of groping advances during the eleventh and twelfth centuries. London's whole body of citizens is stated to have confederated by 1141 to form a single community—a dramatic breakthrough in the concept of corporate personality that was destined to form a key legal precedent for all subsequent Anglo-American local governmental development. This embryonic concept of the corporate community was formalized further when John, "in the absence of Richard Coeur de Lion, acknowledged on 8 October 1191 the right of [London's] citizens to combine in sworn association, to take an oath to preserve the City and its liberties, and to be obedient to its officers. This is generally known as the granting of the 'commune' and in it may be seen the recognition of the citizens as a Corporation bound together by corporate oath."[6]

From this time forward, the development of London's government was closely intertwined with the development of the English government itself. A few weeks before he sealed the Magna Carta, King John granted a Charter to the City of London, dated May 9, 1215, which recognized the practice of the annual election of a Mayor and affirmed

[6] *The Corporation of London: Its Origin, Constitution, Powers and Duties* (London: Oxford University Press, 1953), pp. 5-6.

other basic privileges. In addition, Clause 13 of the Magna Carta assured the City of all its ancient privileges and free customs. As a result of its many centuries of evolutionary development, the historic constitution of the City of London is unique among those of British municipalities. Actually, unlike other English cities, London has no basic charter of incorporation; rather, it is viewed as being a corporation by prescriptive right. Despite its unique characteristics, however, London has served as a model to shape the local governmental development of many other English towns and cities.

During this period of early political growth, London's economic organization was also changing, and this fact was destined to have an important bearing on the City's future. For a number of years a series of "firth-guilds," or friendly societies, had been organized within the City, originally for purely fraternal and welfare purposes—to care for the aged, the needy, and the sick. Over time, these societies were amalgamated with various craft and merchant guilds to foster the objectives of particular trades. As these new guilds grew in economic power, they eventually began to seek their own Charters of Incorporation, which would provide for the legal recognition of their own corporate personalities. The greatest gains were made during the reign of Edward III (1327–1377). Edward and his immediate successors granted the guilds independent charters that gave them the right not only to elect their own wardens but also to elect the common council of the City of London, which, in turn, elected the city's Mayor and other officials (plus the members of Parliament for London). The guilds continued to exercise this complete stranglehold over London's government until the passage of the great Reform Act of 1832, and today one can still find important remnants of the original London guilds in the form of the City's eighty-two livery companies.

In addition to the emergence of the early guilds, medieval London saw the establishment of the Inns of the Court, which were to grow into four legal societies that still dominate London's legal profession. The City also witnessed the construction of the original structures of St. Paul's Cathedral and Westminster Abbey.

As London continued to develop in political and economic power, the City was subject to the same forces of catastrophe that characterized the growing pains of the English nation. In 1381, a peasants' rebellion stirred by Wat Tyler ravaged the City. A second uprising, led by Jack Cade in 1450, resulted in similar, although less damaging, results. Of more serious consequence than these political upheavals were the catastrophic plagues and fires that periodically swept the City. The Black Death of 1348 claimed some 50,000 victims, but this represented only a relatively mild foretaste of events yet to come. The most disastrous calamity to strike London was a series of double blows that took place some three hundred years later. The Great Plague of 1665, which killed more than 100,000 people, and the Great Fire of 1666, which leveled some four-fifths of the built-up City, were tragic in their impact. London managed to survive all disasters, however, continually growing in strength and power with the passage of time.

By the mid-seventeenth century, the City had developed into the cultural, as well as the political and economic, center of the English nation. The roots of London's cultural dominance reached back to Chaucer's day, although it was not until the Elizabethan Age that the City became the undisputed leader of England's Renaissance revival. During Elizabethan times, Shakespeare, Spenser, Marlowe, and a host of other creative giants drew inspiration from the diverse and vigorous elements of London. London's vibrant cultural life continued to develop in stature during the seventeenth and eighteenth centuries, until Samuel Johnson was eventually prompted to his famous observation that "when a man is tired of London, he is tired of life, for there is in London all that life can afford."

The major long-range impact of the twin seventeenth-century disasters was not to be found in any decline in the City's cultural vitality, but rather in the influence that the plague and especially the Great Fire exercised over London's rebuilding. Led by the architectural genius of Sir Christopher Wren, seventeenth-century London reemerged in a stronger position than ever before. Yet, the pragmatic aftereffects of this rebuilding process were not solely architectural. The Great Plague and the Great Fire of 1665–1666 solidified the development of two basic patterns of residential settlement that have dominated the growth of metropolitan London to the present day. The first of these was the beginning of a flight to suburbs that has continued, at an accelerating rate, into modern times; and the second was the firm establishment of a social and economic cleavage between east London and west London that, again, characterizes the residential structure of the modern metropolis.

Although the exodus to the suburbs had actually begun before the twin catastrophes of 1665–1666 struck London, both events contributed to its growing momentum. "Something like 80,000 people had fled the fire, and of these, one in four had not returned six years later. Even before the disaster there had been a tendency for craftsmen and small shopkeepers to move out into the freedom of the suburbs, away from the congestion, the trade restrictions and the high taxes of the city."[7]

The impact of this exodus was not immediately apparent, because the emerging Industrial Revolution contributed to the growth of the inner core of the central city, as well as to the continued development of the new outer suburbs, for the next two hundred years. It was not until the middle of the last century, under the stimulus of new developments in modern technology, that the population of the central city began to drop off dramatically.

During the past century, the growth of metropolitan London has paralleled that of the modern American metropolis. The key catalyst has been the development of more efficient rapid commuter transportation. The introduction of workmen's tickets, which had become general on all London railways by the end of Queen Victoria's reign, accelerated the flight to the suburbs, as did the construction of the underground tube railways that began to crisscross the famous London blue-clay subsoil.

A cry of alarm over the urban sprawl that grew out of these transportation breakthroughs was raised during the early 1900's by Ebenezer Howard and others, who urged the establishment of garden cities to preserve some semblance of natural environment in the burgeoning metropolis. It was not until the 1930's, however, under a unique ex-

[7] Mitchell and Leys, *History of London Life*, p. 151.

ample of Conservative-Labour cooperation, that major action was taken in an attempt to meet the problem. The Green Belt Act of 1938 established a ring of open space around Greater London that could not be sold or built upon without the consent of the responsible Minister and the contributing authorities. Under this Act and its subsequent modifications, some 35,500 acres of open space have been preserved from the ravages of the bulldozer.

Even the Green Belt legislation, however, could not halt the continuing outward growth of the Greater London metropolis. Between 1930 and 1960 this outward exodus reached a point where the population of the central County of London, and indeed of the entire area within the Green Belt, began to level off.

Population Growth of Greater London[8]
1931–1961

	1931	1941	1951	1961
London County	4,397,003	4,013,400	3,347,982	3,195,114
Outer Ring Counties	3,818,670	4,714,600	5,000,041	4,976,788
Greater London Total	8,215,673	8,728,000	8,348,023	8,171,902

The important figure to note in the totals above is the population decline, especially in London County, between 1931 and 1961. This decline has heralded the arrival of a third, and still dynamic, growth pattern for the outer metropolis, which characterizes Greater London's development at the present time. Whereas first the central city corporation, and next London County, stabilized in population and eventually began to drop off as newer residents located beyond their reaches, now the entire area within the confines of London's Green Belt has stabilized, and the growth of the metropolis today is leaping over, and taking place outside, the Green Belt. Map III gives an indication of the evolution of these historical patterns of population growth and notes the dates at which stabilization, or decline, occured within the inner growth areas.

It was a recognition of this new growth potential outside the Green

[8] Census 1961, England and Wales, Preliminary Report, HMSO, p. 10.

Belt that prompted the famous plans of Sir Patrick Abercrombie during World War II:

> These plans dealt with a region of about thirty miles radius from central London. They were conceived in terms of three concentric rings of declining, static and expanding population. The inner ring comprised the densely developed shell of London . . . which has in fact been losing population. . . . The Abercrombie plans proposed that this movement should be assisted and accelerated. . . . The Abercrombie middle ring consisted of outer suburbia and of the green belt which was to be created around its perimeter. The plans assumed that very few changes would occur in this suburban area. . . . The third Abercrombie ring was to be an area of expansion and development beyond the green belt. . . .[9]

While Abercrombie was correct in estimating the totality of Greater London's growth patterns, his plans did not anticipate the tremendous surge in new employment, especially commercial employment, that has taken place within the central core of the inner London region during the past twenty years. To a large extent, Abercrombie assumed that his third, outer ring, located beyond the confines of the Green Belt, would be economically self-sufficient through the creation of a series of "New Towns" capable of providing home-based employment for their residents. In addition, he assumed that London's inner core would be restricted in terms of its future population growth as part of an over-all postwar central Government plan for the Greater London area.

During World War II, London's inner core suffered from enormous damage, with the City of London alone witnessing the destruction of some 104 of its 393 built-up acres. While this destruction was tragic in its immediate consequences, it did present the potentiality of a long-range rebuilding of London's central area along carefully controlled lines. As part of its postwar planning, the Government decided to resist further population growth within this area by limiting the amount of new industrial development that would be permitted. By and large, these limitations on industrial development have been successful.

[9] P. Self, *Town Planning in Greater London,* Greater London Papers, No. 7 (London School of Economics, 1962), pp. 7-8.

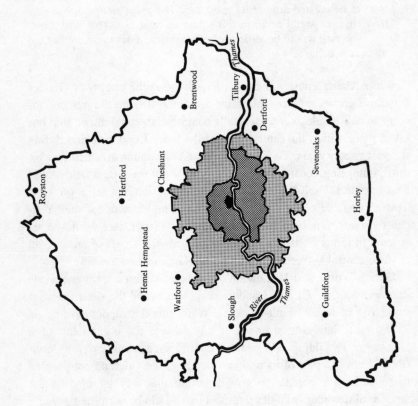

Map III

Population Growth
Greater London Area
(1850–present)

KEY

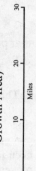

● City Corporation (Decline Began 1850)

London County (Decline Began 1930)

Suburban Metropolitan Area (Stabilization Occurred 1950)

Area Included Within 1944 Abercrombie Plan (Current Growth Area)

0   10   20   30
              Miles

Royston

Hertford

Cheshunt

Hemel Hempstead

Watford

Slough

River Thames

Guildford

Brentwood

Tilbury

Thames

Dartford

Sevenoaks

Horley

To the consternation of many, however, central London is now sprouting increasingly larger commercial buildings as the Government has relaxed restrictions on the construction of new office facilities during recent years. Hence, although new industrial development has been curbed, an explosion in commercial employment has taken place, to the degree that London faces the threat of extinction in its own growing congestion. Thus, despite a central Government concern with comprehensive planning, London's inner core has continued to explode so much during recent years that observers, such as Professor Donald Foley, are forced to conclude that "reflecting its historical significance and long evolving physical environmental setting, London strikes one as singularly unplanned."[10]

As a result of this fact, London's Green Belt, rather than acting as a check on outward expansion, now serves as something of an artificial barrier that stands in the way of new floods of exurbanites who are attempting to commute into the central city. In the words of one expert, "London is centrifugal at night and centripetal during the day."[11] The result is that local governmental authorities are caught up in an ever expanding trap, trying to move and service a population that is spilling out centrifugally at an ever expanding rate.

The crucial facts to bear in mind when viewing this historical growth exodus are twofold. First, since medieval times, London has acted as an extremely powerful magnet for the rest of the country, attracting new residents from all over England in ever increasing numbers. Second, this growth process has been characterized by a widening concentric development from one single, and common, central core.

Unlike many American cities, Greater London is in no sense a "conurbation" that has been formed from the merger of a number of independently developed cities (e.g., the Boston, Massachusetts, to Washington, D.C., "megalopolis" phenomenon). Instead, London's development is the result of an outspill from only one central focus, and

[10] Donald L. Foley, *Controlling London's Growth* (Berkeley: University of California Press, 1963), p. 3.

[11] W. A. Robson, *The Government and Misgovernment of London* (London: Allen & Unwin Ltd., 1939).

as this central area has continually enlarged in geographical size, its population has eventually stabilized, with new growth taking place in an ever widening circle.

While the mid-seventeenth-century disasters marked the beginnings of the exodus that has culminated in London's modern suburban growth patterns, they also played a crucial role in determining which people would move in which direction. Once again, the roots of this development had been formulated in earlier times, but the Great Fire and the Great Plague of 1665–1666 tended to accelerate the existing trends.

It was during the reign of Elizabeth I that the city's poor first began to drift into east London to the extent that a distinct socioeconomic cleavage between the eastern and western portions of the city began to become apparent. The immediate catalyst was the growing requirement for manual labor to work the east London docks, but once the process had begun, the effects were cumulative. As more and more of the poor crowded into east London, more and more of the wealthy moved in the opposite direction, into the growing community of Westminster and beyond. This initial movement was accelerated by a second, climatic influence that has helped shape a distinct east-west socioeconomic cleavage in so many English cities. The prevailing winds of England are westerly, and with the growth of an embryonic industrial base, the wealthy of London began to move ever further west, in increasing numbers, into these winds. The reason, in the terse if nonetheless accurate words of one early observer, was to "escape the fumes, steams and stinks of the whole easterly pyle."[12]

The basic socioeconomic cleavage between east and west London was solidified, once and for all, by the rebuilding that followed the Great Fire. East London became slum London, and west London was the province of the well-to-do. Gradually, the decay of east London spilled across the Thames onto the adjacent South Bank, and still later along an eastern industrial belt extending to East Ham and beyond.

This historic east-west socioeconomic dichotomy has remained

---

[12] M. D. George, *London Life in the XVIII Century* (London: Kegan, Trench, Trubner & Co. Ltd., 1925), p. 64.

basically intact to the present time. As Map IV illustrates,[13] the boroughs in the western portion of London County are dominated by Social Class I and II groups (i.e., professional occupations), while the boroughs in the eastern portion of the County are dominated by Social Class IV and V groups (i.e., partly skilled and unskilled occupations). This same general east-west split continues into the surrounding suburban counties, although a heavy cluster of Class I and II boroughs in southeastern metropolitan Kent County (which was not fully developed until recent years) and a scattering of such boroughs in northeastern Essex County weigh the over-all suburban balance in favor of the wealthy boroughs. This fact is of considerable importance to an understanding of the modern political alignments within the Greater London area.

Despite the existence of such internal economic variations, the concentration of goods and services that makes up Greater London, taken as a whole, represents a tremendous accumulation of total wealth. Since the early Middle Ages, London has occupied a unique position as the capital city of England. Its magnetism stems from the fact that it represents the central focus for all that goes into the making of the

[13] Map IV is prepared on the basis of data appearing in *Census, 1951, England and Wales, Report on Greater London and Five Other Conurbations* (London: HMSO, 1956), and the *County Reports for London, Essex, Middlesex, Kent, Surrey, and Hertfordshire* (HMSO, 1953). The socioeconomic groupings are based on the *General Register Office, Classification of Occupations, 1950* (HMSO, 1951). This latter volume provides five Social Class Groupings for total males (occupied and retired) age fifteen and over:

Social Class I: Professional, etc., occupations (secretaries of companies, clergymen, judges, doctors, civil service administrators, etc.).
Social Class II: Intermediate occupations (retail sales personnel, teachers, medical auxiliary and nurses, proprietors, farmers and farm managers, etc.).
Social Class III: Skilled occupations (mineworkers, transport workers, clerical workers, armed forces, etc.).
Social Class IV: Partly-skilled occupations (agricultural workers, ticket collectors, bus and train conductors, etc.).
Social Class V: Unskilled occupations (laborers and unskilled workers).

The percentages in each class for the entire Greater London conurbation are as follows: Social Class I (4.7%), Social Class II (16.2%), Social Class III (55.1%), Social Class IV (10.7%), Social Class V (13.3%). The local authorities shaded in black on the map are those in which the percentage of males in Social Classes I & II combined *exceeded* the Greater London percentage (20.9%) for these two classes.

Map IV

Socioeconomic Groupings
Greater London
(1951 Census)

KEY

Areas in which per-
centage of males 15
and over *exceeds* the
metropolitan area
average for Social
Classes I and II.

(See Footnote 12)

Areas in which such
males fall below this
metropolitan area
average.

0   5 Miles

1 City of London
2 Holborn
3 Finsbury
4 Shoreditch
5 Bethnal Green
6 Bermondsey
7 Southwark
8 Deptford

9 Chelsea
10 City of Westminster
11 Kensington
12 Paddington
13 St. Marylebone
14 Hampstead
15 Stoke Newington
16 Tottenham
17 Wood Green

18 Friern Barnet
19 Wanstead and Woodford
20 Penge
21 Beddington and Wallington
22 Merton and Morden
23 Malden and Coombe
24 Kingston-upon-Thames
25 Brentford and Chiswick
26 Hammersmith

modern nation—economically, politically, socially, culturally, commercially, and in every other important aspect of human endeavor. By 1960, the 845 square-mile area subjected to review by the Royal Commission on Local Government in Greater London contained approximately one-fifth of the total population, and one-third of the total ratable value of all the property, of England. In concrete terms, the ratable value of the property located within the Commission's review area was in excess of £205 million, or well over half a billion dollars in United States currency—a staggering figure when one realizes that the English appraise local property in terms of its rental, rather than its total market, value. As the Royal Commission noted in its report, the area of Greater London represents one of the greatest concentrations of wealth on the face of the earth, and, as the Commission observed so sagely, "the political control of London is a great prize."[14]

Thus, in many respects, both London and the modern American cities have been subject to the same forces of historical growth. The single most striking parallel between the two is to be found in the more recent impact of technological innovations, especially the development of mass transportation. As a result of these transportation breakthroughs, Greater London today is witnessing an accelerating proliferation of exurban growth that is part of the same phenomenon of metropolitan sprawl that is to be found in the United States. A second basic similarity between London and the American cities can be seen in their pronounced patterns of socioeconomic cleavage, and in the political alignments that flow from these patterns. While not all American cities adhere to London's prevailing east-west socioeconomic split, the political consequences of America's basic "central core versus suburban" dichotomy are extremely similar to those of London. In London the less wealthy inner boroughs are predominantly Labour in their political orientation, whereas the more affluent suburban boroughs are predominantly Conservative—a virtually identical match to the American division between the Democratic central cities versus the Republican suburbs.

Despite such similarities, however, there are also some notable dif-

[14] Rpt., Cmnd. 1164, pp. 21-22.

ferences between the London and the American patterns of urban development. Perhaps the most striking of these is the historical evolution of London into *the* primary English city that dominates all major aspects of national life. Whereas America's cities compete with each other for positions of national influence (e.g., Washington's political role versus New York's commercial and financial role), London monopolizes virtually all the key activities that go into the making of modern Britain. As a result, it is the focus of a sustained national attention that is without parallel in American urban experience. A second basic dissimilarity between London and its American urban counterparts is to be found in the nature, and the extent, of the efforts that have been made, albeit not overly successfully, to plan and control the future development of the Greater London area. The establishment of Green Belts, and the effort to restrict deliberately future population growth within the central London area, represent a comprehensive approach toward urban planning that is far in advance of most prevailing American practices.

Finally, despite a host of common legal precedents, the specific governmental institutions that had evolved in London were quite dissimilar from those that are found in major American cities. As a result of its tortuous, centuries-long process of evolutionary growth, Greater London's governmental system represented a highly unorthodox, if not totally unique, meeting place between the historic vestiges of the past and a more specialized functional approach that has come to characterize modern urban government. In order to evaluate the true nature of the battle over the plan that was designed to recast this prevailing London governmental pattern, it is first necessary to gain an understanding of the rather extraordinary mixture of historic precedents and more recent innovations that had combined to shape the organization of Greater London's government prior to the establishment of the Royal Commission study in 1957.

4. London's Governmental Development

London's early governmental development was shaped by a remarkable meeting of the minds between a privileged City of London Corporation that did not want to extend its historic political boundaries and a suspicious central Government that was all too willing to love, honor, and nurture the City's desire to retain a status of perennial physical adolescence.

The City of London Corporation did not want to grow because it was more interested in protecting its ancient rights and privileges than in serving the needs of a rapidly expanding urban population. In turn, the Crown had long harbored a deep mistrust of the City's political and economic position, and the early English kings were not about to force political growth upon the City Corporation if such action could possibly be avoided.

Parliament retained this attitude of underlying suspicion toward the City following the establishment of its supremacy over the Crown in 1688–1689. As Herbert Morrison has noted in a recent commentary, "for some curious reason Parliament has seemed to have a fear of order, dignity and cohesion in the government of the capital."[1] Actually, when viewed in the light of earlier historical perspective, the reason was not so curious. Like the Crown, Parliament feared the

[1] Morrison, quoted in Margaret Cole, *Servant of the County* (London: Dennis Dobson, 1956), p. 42.

57

power of London and, like the Crown, Parliament did not want to add to the strength of an already powerful urban rival.

The result was the development of a fragmented and weak governmental system for the emerging Greater London metropolis. The historic City of London Corporation, which stands at the very center of this modern metropolis, remains today a miniature monument to the pomp and pageantry of ages past. Occupying a total land area of less than one square mile, and containing a resident population of only 5,000 people, the City of London represents a historic enclave in the heart of Greater London that is unique among the great capital centers of the world.

The City Corporation was surrounded by a bewildering variety of other local governmental units that were added piecemeal through past centuries to catch up with the outward growth of Greater London's population. Once again, central Government suspicions played a dominant role in shaping these newer governmental bodies, for they were deliberately restricted in their powers in order to minimize any threat they might pose to the central authorities. Thus, for example, Westminster, located just next door to the City Corporation, "had been deliberately given a weak and divided government so that it would never develop into a strong and powerful Corporation like London."[2] In this manner, over the years, the Greater London area developed a patchwork system of local administration that was neither powerful enough nor comprehensive enough in its geographic scale to provide for "order, dignity or cohesion" in the government of the growing capital.

By the beginning of the nineteenth century, one field of local administration that demanded more unified treatment, regardless of any political sparring between Parliament and the City of London, involved the maintenance of law and order. As an angry public grew increasingly more restive in its demands for economic, electoral, and social reforms, unruly mobs and ugly riots began to crop out in many English cities, not the least being London. In 1829, under the leadership of Sir Robert Peel, Parliament passed the London Police Act, and even when

[2] J. H. Plumb, "England in the Eighteenth Century," *Pelican History of England*, VII (1950), 86.

viewed in light of modern realities, this legislation stands as a rather remarkable achievement. The Act represented the first attempt to deal with Greater London as a geographical unity by establishing a metropolitan police district extending for no less than a fifteen-mile radius from central London's focal point, Charing Cross. This original police district, as formulated in 1829, corresponds roughly to the area that is presently contained within London's modern Green Belt. To think on such a comprehensive areal scale was extraordinary in the year 1829, and the original district boundaries established at that time still serve as the basis for a highly effective system of modern police administration.

The metropolitan Police Act was not without its limitations, however, when viewed in terms of the totality of Greater London's needs, for it established two general principles that have seriously plagued the subsequent development of a coherent local governmental system for the metropolis ever since. First, it represented a specialized functional approach to the problems of London's metropolitan growth. Only one service, that of police, was picked out for comprehensive treatment, and such specialized treatment of particular services was destined to dominate later responses to the problems of Greater London's governmental development. Secondly, the historic City of London was singled out for special treatment under the 1829 legislation. It was allowed to establish its own police force for its central square-mile area—a force that is still in existence. The patterns thus established, both in isolating a particular service for special treatment and in singling out the City of London for similar special treatment, represented highly debatable precedents for guiding the future development of Greater London's governmental system.

In 1834–1835, Parliament got around to some of the broader issues of local reform that had led to much of the previous social unrest throughout the country. The Poor Law Amendment Act of 1834 was the first serious attempt to break the power of the privileged property classes over local government, by substituting elected Boards of Guardians to administer relief functions in place of the archaic, and usually self-perpetuating, parish vestries, which had been established many years before on the basis of old ecclesiastical administrative districts.

The Municipal Reform Act of 1835 went a step further by providing for elective councils to govern the affairs of all the boroughs in England. The 1835 Act applied to existing boroughs only, however, and it made little attempt to adjust the geographical boundaries of these boroughs to meet new needs, or to create new boroughs where the circumstances might have warranted it. Thus, many of England's largest cities— among them Manchester and Birmingham—were excluded from this legislation because they had never been successful in obtaining the status of boroughs via Royal Charter or other historic privilege. Further, London was again singled out for special treatment; it was excluded entirely from the provisions of the 1835 legislation. The effects of this exclusion were to prove serious; indeed, one observer has gone so far as to hold that "from this calamity, the metropolis has never recovered."[3]

It was not until 1855 that the inadequacies of Greater London's governmental needs were finally considered by Parliament; and, once again, the problem was faced on a functional basis with the establishment of a new special authority, the Metropolitan Board of Works, to handle a series of particular service needs, most notably main drainage. Nor was much consideration given to the geographical jurisdiction of this newly created Board. Its boundaries followed a rather arbitrary area that the Registrar-General had adopted from the 1851 census to issue the old "Bills of Mortality" (i.e., death registers), an anomaly that was destined to be of considerable importance to the government of the modern London metropolis.

Parliament's tendency to isolate particular functional problems for special treatment was seen again in 1870 when the London School Board was created, with its geographical jurisdiction also paralleling the curious "Bills of Mortality" area that had been used fifteen years earlier to establish the Metropolitan Board of Works. Thus, the Parliamentary response to the needs of the growing metropolis was consistent in its inadequacies. Special functions were picked out for

[3] Robson, *The Government and Misgovernment of London*, p. 21.

separate treatment, and virtually no thought was given to the desirability of adopting a unified approach to the problems of the growing metropolis, or to the desirability of establishing meaningful geographical jurisdictions to be utilized in meeting Greater London's expanding needs.

The year 1888 was a landmark not only in the development of London's government but in the evolution of the entire English local governmental system as well. Actually, London was included in the historic Local Government Act of 1888 only as an afterthought. The primary purpose of this legislation was to establish a coherent local governmental pattern for the remainder of the country.

The key provisions in the 1888 Act were two in number:

1. *Administrative Counties*—The 1888 legislation attempted to convert the ancient historic county shires, originally laid down in Saxon and Norman times, into modern administrative units, and it decreed that democratically elected county councils should henceforth discharge the administration of county affairs, hitherto controlled by justices of the peace.

Once more, however, the Act largely ignored the rationalization of geographical areas and basic resources. Although a limited number of historic county areas were subdivided, for the most part the Act merely took the preexisting historic county units and redesignated these as "administrative counties." The result was the creation of more than 50 widely varying county council areas, ranging from Rutland, with 97,000 acres, to Devon and West Riding, Yorkshire, with more than 1,500,000 acres apiece.

The Local Government Act of 1888 created only one totally new county—the County of London, which was carved out of adjacent portions of the newly established counties of Middlesex, Surrey, and Kent.

This new County of London was created because of widespread dissatisfaction with the record of the Metropolitan Board of Works, which had become involved in a series of scandals. The new county's boundaries were determined by the most expedient criterion available. That area originally utilized in 1855 to mark the jurisdiction of the Board of Works was now redesignated to constitute the jurisdiction of the London County Council. Thus, the new London County Council was limited to an area of some

117 square miles, not on the basis of any logical antecedents or analysis, but quite simply because this had been the old "Bills of Mortality" area that had served to delineate the now discredited Board of Works. As Margaret Cole was to remark many years later, "to delimit a capital city by Act of Parliament on a basis of death registers and main drainage is surely one of the oddest methods that can ever have been evolved."[4]

In addition, following well-established precedent, the City of London was not included within the jurisdiction of the new London County Council. Instead, the city continued to retain its historic identity as an independent local governmental entity.

2. *County Boroughs*—The second major provision of the 1888 Act related to the creation of a group of independent "county boroughs," which, like the administrative counties, were designated to serve as "first-tier" all-purpose authorities, responsible for the administration of all local governmental functions within their designated jurisdictional areas. These new county boroughs were to be completely independent of the newly established administrative counties. The justification for creating this second group of independent authorities was once again to be found in the ancient precedents originally formulated during Saxon and Norman times.

For a good many centuries, a number of the most important cities and towns in England had enjoyed a considerable degree of autonomy in the administration of their local affairs by virtue of the historic borough status they had won by means of Royal Charters. These historic boroughs were not now in a mood to surrender their past powers to the newly created administrative counties if they could possibly avoid such a seeming calamity. They pressured Parliament persistently, and, in the end, Parliament capitulated by specifying that any existing borough, town, or city with a population of 50,000 or more could acquire independent county borough status under the 1888 Act.

As a result, the wealthiest and most populous cities within the newly created administrative counties were immediately separated out of these counties into 61 independent county borough enclaves, including two in the Greater London area—Croydon and West Ham.[5]

---

[4] Cole, *Servant of the County*, p. 36.

[5] By 1963 there were 83 county boroughs in England and Wales, ranging in population from historic (and, hence, specially treated) Canterbury, with 30,000 people, to Birmingham, with 1,100,000 people.

Thus, the Local Government Act of 1888 created two independent systems of local authority—administrative counties and county boroughs—which were expected to operate side by side, but in mutual exclusion of each other. It soon became obvious that it would be necessary to create another group of smaller local authorities under these new administrative counties to administer local affairs on a more personalized basis. As a result, Parliament passed a second Local Government Act in 1894, which established four different groupings of smaller local authorities. In order of declining population size, they are non-county boroughs,[6] urban districts, rural districts, and parish councils. The hoped-for objective of this "two-tier" system of county administration was to provide for a general sharing of powers. Both the "first-tier" county boroughs and administrative counties were to act as the primary local governmental authorities, with the latter delegating to their smaller "second-tier" units specific functions, to be administered on a more localized basis. In this manner, the English local governmental system (outside the Administrative County of London) looked as follows after the passage of the 1894 legislation:

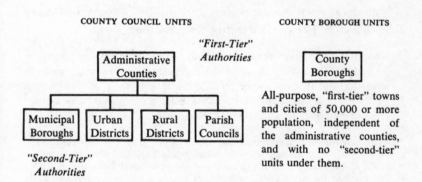

COUNTY COUNCIL UNITS

COUNTY BOROUGH UNITS

"First-Tier" Authorities

Administrative Counties

County Boroughs

Municipal Boroughs | Urban Districts | Rural Districts | Parish Councils

"Second-Tier" Authorities

All-purpose, "first-tier" towns and cities of 50,000 or more population, independent of the administrative counties, and with no "second-tier" units under them.

---

[6] Under the English local government system, those units that are completely independent of the administrative counties are called county boroughs, whereas those units subordinate to the administrative counties are called non-county boroughs. Since the logic of this terminology often escapes the foreign observer, this second group of non-county boroughs will be referred to as municipal boroughs in this study.

While this 1894 legislation provided a "second-tier" governmental structure for those portions of the Greater London metropolis lying outside the boundaries of London County (i.e., for Middlesex, Surrey, Kent, and Essex counties), it did not deal with the organization of local units within the newly created London County Council area. Parliament finally faced up to the question of the organization of second-tier government within London County by passing the London Government Act of 1899.

The result of this legislation was to depart completely from the pattern established for the remainder of the country some five years earlier, and to create instead twenty-eight unique units of "second-tier" government designated as "metropolitan boroughs." Once again, the rationale for this specialized approach toward London County's "second-tier" government was highly political in its undertones. The principle aim of the London Government Bill of 1899 was:

> . . . to undermine the interest and authority which the London County Council had aroused from its inception. . . . The Act had as its main object the establishment of centres of political opposition which would harry and frustrate the radical spirit of the London (County) Council.

Thus, local governmental powers were divided between the County Council and the twenty-eight metropolitan boroughs,[7] with

> no attempt to make them partners in the common task of governing London. [Instead] . . . each of the 28 metropolitan borough councils was to have its own mayor and aldermen, with their robes of office, gilt chains, a mace, and all the other insignia calculated to encourage the feeling of their separate civic consciousness.[8]

---

[7] Through subsequent additions and upward shifts from the boroughs to the County Council, this division of powers had reached the following stage by the mid-1950's, just prior to the inauguration of the new Royal Commission study:

The London County Council was mainly concerned with fire services, main drainage and sewerage, "overspill" housing, main highways and bridges, welfare and personal health services, education, town planning, and entertainments.

The boroughs were responsible for street improvements, public lighting, refuse removal, museum and library services, baths and wash houses, cemeteries, local parks, slum clearance, house building, local sewerage and drainage, local regulating and inspection functions, and the registration of births, marriages, and deaths.

[8] W. A. Robson, *The Greater London Boroughs,* Greater London Papers, No. 3 (London School of Economics, 1961), pp. 6-7.

In addition to creating the new metropolitan boroughs, the 1899 Act continued to emphasize the special status of the City of London. The City was not designated as a metropolitan borough; instead, it was allowed to enjoy a unique degree of partial local autonomy and to retain a unique system of local elections and governmental organization that defies easy description. Of most importance here is the simple fact that the one square mile that constitutes the central core of the modern metropolis of Greater London continued a life of political independence in many key areas.

If all this sounds somewhat confused and confusing, the simple fact of the matter is that it *was* somewhat confused and confusing. Following the passage of the 1899 Act, the outer portion of the Greater London metropolis was governed by one system of local administration that prevailed throughout the rest of England and Wales. The central County of London was governed by a second system of local administration, unique unto itself. And the central City within this central County was governed by still a third system, unique unto the face of the earth. In addition, the entire metropolitan area was subsequently crisscrossed with additional specialized functional authorities that bore little or no geographical relationship to one another. Table III and Maps V and VI on the following pages are provided in the hope of clarifying this intergovernmental maze, but if they fail to enlighten they should be discarded hastily. The important point to remember is that those who like a tidy world could find little solace in the melee of organizational anarchy that constituted London's government by the turn of the century.

The changes that took place in Greater London's government after 1900 continued to follow the earlier special authority and special functional precedents. In 1902, an independent Metropolitan Water Board was established; in 1908, the Port of London Authority was organized; in 1914, a third new independent county borough—East Ham—was created, and so it went.

By the 1920's the fragmentation of metropolitan London's governmental system had reached the special study stage of concern, the most notable study being that conducted by the Royal Commission on Local Government in Greater London, under the chairmanship of

TABLE III

Local Government Structure: Greater London Area, 1957
(Excluding Special Authorities)*

I. *Inside London County*

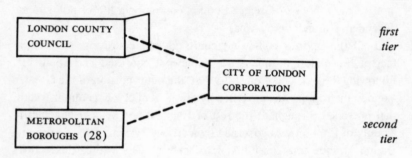

II. *Outside London County*

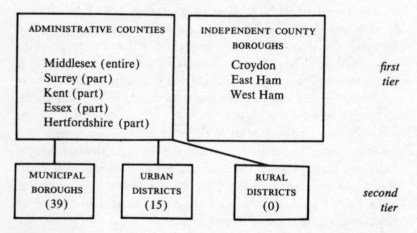

*This area covers the Greater London Council jurisdiction as finally defined in the London Government Bill (11 Eliz. 2, November, 1962). All maps from Map III forward cover this area only, unless otherwise specified.

Map V
First-Tier Local Authorities
Greater London
(1957)

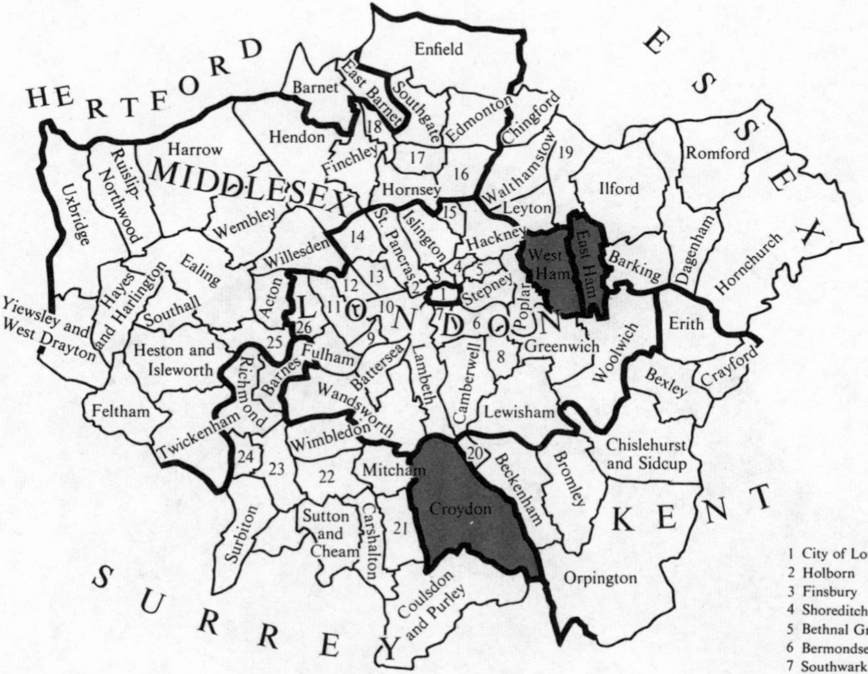

KEY

Counties (6)

County Boroughs (3)

0   5 Miles

1 City of London	9 Chelsea
2 Holborn	10 City of Westminster
3 Finsbury	11 Kensington
4 Shoreditch	12 Paddington
5 Bethnal Green	13 St. Marylebone
6 Bermondsey	14 Hampstead
7 Southwark	15 Stoke Newington
8 Deptford	16 Tottenham
	17 Wood Green

18 Friern Barnet	
19 Wanstead and Woodford	
20 Penge	
21 Beddington and Wallington	
22 Merton and Morden	
23 Malden and Coombe	
24 Kingston-upon-Thames	
25 Brentford and Chiswick	
26 Hammersmith	

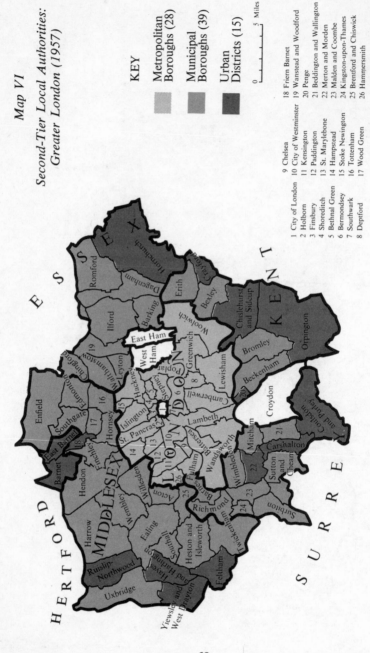

Map VI

Second-Tier Local Authorities:
Greater London (1957)

KEY

Metropolitan
Boroughs (28)

Municipal
Boroughs (39)

Urban
Districts (15)

0   5 Miles

1 City of London
2 Holborn
3 Finsbury
4 Shoreditch
5 Bethnal Green
6 Bermondsey
7 Southwark
8 Deptford

9   Chelsea
10 City of Westminster
11 Kensington
12 Paddington
13 St. Marylebone
14 Hampstead
15 Stoke Newington
16 Tottenham
17 Wood Green

18 Friern Barnet
19 Wanstead and Woodford
20 Penge
21 Beddington and Wallington
22 Merton and Morden
23 Malden and Coombe
24 Kingston-upon-Thames
25 Brentford and Chiswick
26 Hammersmith

Viscount Ullswater, which issued its report in 1923. Unfortunately, the members of the Ullswater Commission were divided in their views, and their recommendations failed to have any significant impact on the consolidation of Greater London's government. Instead, the Commission's only tangible achievement involved the establishment of still another new group, the London and Home Counties Traffic Advisory Committee, in 1924.

Although Greater London's government continued its piecemeal growth during the 1920's, this period did see the inauguration of a broader series of local governmental reforms throughout the remainder of England and Wales under the leadership of a new Minister of Health, Neville Chamberlain (the Ministry of Health was responsible for the field of local government until 1952). Chamberlain, who had begun his political career as a Birmingham City Councillor and was later Lord Mayor, held a deep interest in local government, and he was determined to carry out a comprehensive reorganization in this field. As a result, many reforms were instituted in the field of financial administration. Also, local authorities were given some new jobs to perform, such as the administration of poor relief, which the county councils took over when the old Boards of Guardians were abolished in 1929.

In addition to his concern for the administrative and functional responsibilities of local authorities, Chamberlain was interested in modernizing local governmental areas. He favored the enlargement of existing second-tier units and introduced a series of reviews, subsequently carried out between 1929 and 1938, that resulted in the amalgamation and consolidation of many of these units. As a result, the number of urban districts throughout the country was reduced by 255, and the number of rural districts, by 169.[9] Although none of the metropolitan boroughs within London County was affected by these reviews, numerous second-tier consolidations were made in some of Greater London's outlying counties, especially Middlesex.

These amalgamation and consolidation reforms coincided with the

[9] B. Keith-Lucas, Introduction to Joseph Redlich and Francis W. Hirst, *The History of Local Government in England* (London: Macmillan & Company Ltd., 1953), p. 13.

inauguration of a second basic realignment of local governmental powers that ran quite counter to the program that Chamberlain had originally envisioned. Under the impact of the Depression, a number of key functions were now taken away from local authorities and transferred to central agencies of the government. The most notable example was the administration of poor relief, which the county councils had acquired in 1929. In 1934 this function was removed from the counties entirely and turned over to a new central Unemployment Assistance Board. This realignment of local functions continued throughout the war (a key example being seen in the Education Act of 1944), and it reached its climax during the period of the postwar Labour Government from 1945 to 1951. The shift in powers that took place between 1934 and 1951 tended to have a twofold impact on local authorities. On the one hand, all levels of local government, both first-tier and second-tier, lost complete control over some important responsibilities, such as the administration of poor relief in 1934 and the administration of hospitals, which was turned over to regional boards under the National Health Act of 1946. In addition, there was a general movement of responsibilities up the ladder from the second-tier to the first-tier authorities. The most significant illustration of this latter development was to be found in the Education Act of 1944, which designated the administrative counties as primary education authorities and all but stripped the smaller second-tier units of their former educational responsibilities.

At the same time this functional realignment was taking place, a second development was occurring within the Greater London area that stood in direct contradiction to the outward and upward erosion of local governmental powers. This was the explosive population growth that was inundating London's middle suburban ring, coupled with the amalgamation of the suburban second-tier units during the 1929 to 1938 review studies. The combination of this population growth and these areal consolidations turned some of the "smaller" second-tier authorities within Middesex and adjacent counties into very sizable units that began to assume very sizable ideas about their own role in life. When this growth in second-tier ego was coupled with a withering-away of second-tier powers, the resultant uproar became clearly audible in the halls of Parliament. In essence, the suburban second-tier units were growing in population and in areal size at the very time that their powers were being drastically curtailed.

This development once again focused attention on the question of county borough status. Under the Local Government Act of 1888, any unit which had reached a population of 50,000 or more inhabitants was theoretically eligible to assume such status, thus becoming an independent first-tier authority completely free from further control by the administrative counties. Although Parliament raised the population criterion for county boroughs from 50,000 to 75,000 in 1925, a number of Middlesex and Essex County second-tier units were already well beyond this revised figure. By 1930, three second-tier units in Middlesex County (Willesden, Tottenham, and Ealing), and two in Essex County (Walthamstow and Ilford), were over the 100,000 mark in population. By 1940, ten of the twenty-six second-tier units in Middlesex County, and six of the nine second-tier units in metropolitan Essex County, contained sufficient population to qualify for the exalted privileges of county borough existence.

Some of these second-tier authorities, Ealing and Ilford in particular, began to apply direct pressure on Parliament to pass legislation recognizing their county borough ambitions. Parliament refused to act, however, for one simple reason.

Between 1888 and 1925, when the population criterion for county boroughs had been only 50,000, Parliament had created twenty-one new boroughs, in addition to extending the geographical areas of a number of those originally established by the 1888 Act. The impact of this development on the administrative counties had been far from reassuring. In concrete terms, these administrative counties had lost 23 per cent of their existing population and more than 20 per cent of their ratable value as a result of this action.[10] The counties began to complain bitterly against this loss of their most wealthy and populous urban areas, and since these counties had now been in existence long

---

[10] J. H. Morris, *Local Government Areas* (London: Shaw & Sons Ltd., 1960), p. 7.

enough to develop some political muscle of their own, Parliament was reluctant to irritate them further. In essence, the entire county borough question had turned into an unruly political power play. On the one side, the large second-tier units were desperately anxious to assume the powers and privileges of the first-tier county boroughs and to free themselves from control by the administrative counties. On the other side, the counties were extremely reluctant to lose control over their largest and wealthiest second-tier units. The situation was particularly acute in Middlesex County, which would have been decimated as an effective working unit if all ten of its eligible second-tier authorities had been turned into independent county boroughs.

The Parliamentary response to this dilemma was understandable, if not notably statesmanlike. After it had nudged up the population criterion for county boroughs from 50,000 to 75,000 in 1925, Parliament proceeded to sit back and avoid the entire problem. No new county boroughs were created after 1925. Indeed, the only direct action Parliament took on this question did not occur until 1958, when the population figure was again raised, this time to 100,000.

By the mid-1950's it had become increasingly obvious that the county borough situation could not remain in a state of suspended animation for the indefinite future. Thus, it was an occasion of more than ordinary significance when the Conservative Minister of Housing and Local Government, Mr. Henry Brooke, rose to the floor of the House of Commons, on July 29, 1957, and begged to move that "this House takes note of the White Paper relating to the Areas, Status, Functions and Finance of Local Authorities in England and Wales. . . ."

The immediate result of this White Paper was the creation of new Local Government Boundary Commissions for England and Wales (and subsequently for Scotland), which have been hard at work on a series of comprehensive reviews during the past seven years. In addition, the Minister, in his opening speech, indicated that the Government had finally decided to come to grips with the long neglected problem of the future of London's metropolitan government. In so doing, he left little doubt that the dilemma of the unresolved county borough problem in Middlesex County had served as the key catalyst in forcing this decision. Noting that the alternatives in Middlesex appeared to be either to retain the status quo by refusing to create any new county boroughs at all, or to abolish the county entirely by creating ten new county boroughs, Mr. Brooke suggested that:

> ... it may be impossible to determine what is the right structure for Middlesex, except in the context of the Greater London area. The plain fact is that Greater London needs to be looked at as a whole. . . . The Prime Minister has authorised me to inform the House that Her Majesty the Queen has been pleased to approve his recommendation that a Royal Commission should be appointed . . . to examine the present structure and working of local government in the Greater London area. . . .[11]

In all the sound and fury that was subsequently to surround this Royal Commission's work, it is important to note the underlying rationale for the original creation of this body. The Commission was established, first and foremost, because something had to be done to resolve the county borough controversy in Middlesex. In viewing this controversy, the Government made the assumption that, since Middlesex County represented an integral part of a larger metropolitan complex that presumably possessed some semblance of organic unity, it would be desirable to look at the Middlesex problem within the context of this larger metropolitan unity. Despite sometimes violent assertions to the contrary, it is difficult for this observer to conclude that the Royal Commission study was originally motivated as part of a political plot to destroy the London County Council. Indeed, London County was included within the jurisdiction of the Royal Commission study primarily because the Government felt that the county borough problems in Middlesex were inseparable from the larger problems of the Greater London metropolis taken as a whole. In essence, the Royal Commission review was forthcoming as a result of pressures exerted by the second-tier authorities themselves. Many of these authorities wanted to assume greater governmental powers by securing their status as county boroughs, and Parliament, taking the classic way out, decided

[11] Hansard, House of Commons, DLXXIV (29 July 1957), 910-926.

to delegate the entire controversy to a special review body which was somehow expected to reach a solution that would be satisfactory to all parties concerned.

The local governmental entities that were to be subject to this Royal Commission review were, in many respects, quite dissimilar from those to be found within the modern American metropolis. As a result of its singular historical, economic, geographical, and other environmental influences, the Greater London area had developed a variety of unique local governmental institutions, practices, and precedents. Note has already been made, for example, of the eccentricities that led to the stunted development of the historic City of London Corporation —a local governmental unit that certainly does not have any recognizable counterpart in the United States. In a similar vein, the English emphasis upon county boroughs and administrative counties as primary units of local administration, and upon a two-tier division of powers between these administrative counties and a variety of subordinate local units, represents a marked departure from prevailing patterns in most American cities.

Despite such divergencies, however, there was one very crucial aspect of Greater London's metropolitan governmental system that represented a virtual carbon copy of American practice. This basic similarity was, quite simply, Greater London's lack of any metropolitan government at all, at least in any formal sense of this term. As is the case with metropolitan New York, metropolitan Chicago, metropolitan Los Angeles, and America's other major urban centers, Greater London simply did not have an integrated metropolitan government at the time the Royal Commission was created in 1957. Instead, it looked to a bewildering myriad of quasi-independent, and often competing, local units—urban districts, metropolitan boroughs, municipal boroughs, county boroughs, administrative counties, special boards, special authorities, and special commissions—that were expected to be guided by some unspecified "invisible hand" in a manner that would enable them to plan and implement a coherent, comprehensive, and unified public policy for the entire Greater London metropolis.

The only difference between the governmental fragmentation that was to be found in Greater London and that which is to be found in urban America was quantitative, rather than qualitative. Whereas the New York metropolitan region is submerged under more than 1,400 local governmental authorities, and the Chicago area by some 1,000 units, Greater London relied upon something between 100 and 200 local governments to serve the needs of its growing population. Yet, despite any such numerical differences, the basic problems that grew out of this confusion of local authorities were no different in London than in New York or Chicago. Stated in the most elementary terms, all these cities have found themselves struggling under archaic governmental structures that no longer correspond to the realities of twentieth-century urban growth.

Under such circumstances, any Royal Commission review that promised to remedy the prevailing situation in London is of considerable relevance to the American observer. Such a review is relevant not only because of any potential administrative solutions it might propose, but also because of the almost inevitable necessity of its coming to grips with the problems of change as they affected the existing governmental status quo. It was hardly conceivable for the Royal Commission to deal effectively with the larger problems of London's metropolitan government needs without, in fact, upsetting the prevailing balance of governmental powers that held sway in the Greater London area. In so doing, the Commission could be expected to spark off the same brand of political fireworks that has stymied metropolitan governmental reform efforts in a host of American cities.

Thus, despite the many procedural differences between English and American local governmental experience, the particular program under consideration in this study holds a twofold significance for the American reader. Viewed in its larger perspective, the Greater London story should tell us something not only about the administrative involvements of metropolitan governmental reform but also about its broader political implications.

Part III

STAKES
AND
CONTESTANTS

"The political control of London is a great prize."
—Royal Commission on Local
Government in Greater London

Any contest needs participants if it is to be a contest at all; yet these participants will commit themselves only if some underlying incentives exist that make the game worth their effort.

The incentives that went into the making of the Greater London contest were extremely varied. They ranged from pragmatic displays of narrow self-interest to idealistic demonstrations of altruism.

Although many took the superficial view that the conflict over the Greater London plan was nothing more than a naked partisan power play on the part of London's major party organizations, the story was actually not this simple. A variety of influences, in addition to those of *Realpolitik,* were instrumental in determining the lineups for this particular controversy.

The next three chapters trace these influences in terms of power motivations (Chapter 5), professional motivations (Chapter 6), and ideological motivations (Chapter 7).

Finally, some motives, and hence some participants that an American observer might well have expected to find in a conflict over metropolitan governmental reform, proved to be conspicuously absent from the London reform struggle. Chapter 8 attempts to define these "missing" motives and to outline some of the environmental differences between London and the American metropolis that help to account for the absence of such motives from the London scene.

5. The Power Stakes

While the fight over the Greater London proposals was not solely partisan in its underlying concerns, the considerations of power politics were never far removed from the heart of this controversy.

This is particularly true if one views politics in the broadest sense of the term. In addition to its concern with parties and their attempts to elect the controlling personnel of government, politics deals with the actual distribution of governmental powers and all that this implies in the way of authority, influence, and deference. In Lasswellian terms, politics deals with "Who Gets What, When and How."

The present chapter examines the political impact of the Greater London plan within this broader conceptual framework. When related to Almond's functional analysis, it is concerned with both the "input" and the "output" sides of the ledger. In the first instance, it evaluates the impact of the plan on "interest aggregation" groups (i.e., what advantages, or disadvantages, the political parties could expect from reform). In the second instance, it evaluates the impact of the plan upon the "rule application" groups (i.e., what increase, or decrease, in formal powers the various governmental authorities could expect from reform).

The fact that these two considerations tended to cut across each other contributed to a highly unstructured political situation. As a result, much of the opening stage of the London battle was devoted to an evaluation of the precise nature of the political stakes that were actually involved in reform. It was necessary for the political parties and the governmental authorities to determine what they had to gain or lose from the reform program before they were in a position to take any definitive stand on the Royal Commission's proposals.

The Political Parties

Considerable disagreement exists over the questions of when the national parties made their first inroads into English local government and who was responsible for this development.

The Labour Party holds that the Conservatives and the Liberals bear such responsibility, and it points to history to back up this assertion.

There is certainly little doubt that the fights over the reform bills of the 1830's were highly partisan in Tory (i.e., Conservative) versus Whig (i.e., Liberal) overtones, or that, by the 1860's, both the Conservative and the Liberal parties were actually beginning to contest openly and actively for local council seats, especially in the growing industrial towns of the Midlands and the north of England.

In many of these local elections these parties did not operate under national labels, however, and this fact tended to obscure the impact of the national party organization at the local level. Thus, for example, while the London County Council was intensely political from its inception in 1888, the first battles were fought between two groups who called themselves "Progressives" and "Moderates." In retrospect, it is quite easy to identify the national political orientation of these two groups. Modern students of London politics display no hesitation in asserting that "the Liberals (then called Progressives) were in a majority for the first eighteen years of the Council from 1889 to 1907. In 1907 they were succeeded by the Conservatives (then called Municipal Reformers) who ruled undisturbed for twenty-seven years until 1934 when the present reign of the Labour Party began."[1]

It was not the success of any disguises that tended to obscure the

[1] L. J. Sharpe, *A Metropolis Votes*, Greater London Papers, No. 8 (London School of Economics, 1962), p. 1.

role of national parties in local politics, but rather the meaning of these disguises. The Conservatives now charge that, when the Labour Party openly entered local politics in the 1920's and 1930's as "the Labour Party," this did not signify any great burst of localist honesty, but rather a new national party aggressiveness toward the spoils of local politics.

Thus, the Conservatives maintain today that, whereas they have "always left full autonomy to constituency associations in local affairs," the Labour Party has "approached local government from a national political angle."[2] In support of this assertion, they point to Labour's 1930 Annual Convention, when that Party first adopted a series of "Model Standing Orders" for local councils, orders that most certainly do place some serious restrictions on the independent conduct of individual council members.

The Labourites retort that this is so much nonsense. They argue that while the Conservatives may have been considerably more shifty than Labour in entering the local political arena, it was the Conservative Party that first introduced its own brand of national policies into local elections and that this rose did not smell sweeter under any other name. The argument is of more than purely academic interest, because there is still considerable confusion with respect to the many "independent" councils that are to be found today in England. Although this term is a very slippery one, the Labourites assume for political purposes that these "independents" reside on the fringes of the enemy camp, if they do not actually possess strictly Conservative leanings.

Be that as it may, there is little doubt that today both the Labourites and the Conservatives view local government as a legitimate field of conquest, and nowhere is this fact more obvious than in London. In the words of L. J. Sharpe of the London School of Economics, "the two-party system is probably more fully entrenched on the [London County] Council and throughout the L.C.C. area than in any other local authority in the country. Both the Conservative and the Labour Parties

---

[2] G. Block, *Party Politics in Local Government* (Conservative Political Center, Local Government Series, No. 7, 1962), pp. 4, 7.

have a highly articulated party structure with a well established central organisation."[3] It is necessary to understand the basic components of, and alignments within, this party structure as they existed during the period of the reform contest if one is to understand the true nature of the contest itself.

The Conservative Party's key London spokesman was the London Municipal Society. This Society was originally organized in 1894 "to extend and complete the policy for the reform of London Government."[4] Among its early successes, the Society credited itself with saving the City of London Corporation from threatened extinction by the London County Council, and with playing a major role in the creation of the twenty-eight metropolitan boroughs in 1899. Despite these initial reform objectives, the Society was always aware of its electoral potential, and from the very beginning it began to support "Moderate" candidates, or, in its own words, "gentlemen of differing views who were mainly allied by hostility to the advanced schemes which the Progressives were adumbrating."[5]

It was not until 1906, however, when the newly organized "Municipal Reformers" swept the metropolitan borough elections, that the Society began to enjoy its first great partisan successes. The following year, the "Municipal Reform" group gained control of the London County Council, and from that time onward the Municipal Society was synonymous with Conservatism within London County. The Society officially claimed to be a "non-party," however, and one prominent Conservative, wearing a completely straight face, advised in an interview that the Society was really "an independent body that tends to look after Conservative interests in London." How he reconciled the Society's independence with its promotion of Conservative interests was never clarified.

The Society looked to a small staff and a full-time Executive Director to manage its affairs. In broad perspective it viewed its major role as providing a research and information center for Conservatives in

[3] Sharpe, *A Metropolis Votes*, p. 3.
[4] *The London Municipal Society 1894-1954* (London Municipal Society Publication, 1954), p. 5.
[5] *Ibid.*, p. 7.

London, which enabled it to serve as the spokesman for Conservative interests in the capital. Although it played a part in nominating candidates, the Society never expended its major energies in serving local Conservative constituency groups in London. Instead, it looked to the Conservative Central Office to do most of the actual campaign legwork in this area. The Central Office, in turn, relied on one of its branch arms, the London Conservative Union, to service local Conservative candidates in London County's forty-two electoral divisions.

Thus, from its earliest beginnings, the London Municipal Society's approach to the hard-core organizational aspects of London local politics was rather diffuse. It never held annual conferences; it never published membership figures; it never extended its original area of jurisdiction beyond London County, into Middlesex or other adjacent counties. As noted above, it viewed itself as the intellectual spokesman for Conservatism in London, rather than as the local party organizer.[6]

Labour's key arm in London local politics was the London Labour Party. Founded in 1914, this Party bore much of the imprint of one man—Herbert Morrison. Lord Morrison first began his long ascent up the political ladder as Secretary of the L.L.P., eventually going on to become Leader of the London Council, Deputy Prime Minister in the postwar Labour Government, and, finally, a Life Peer.

The impact of Lord Morrison's forceful personality on the London Labour Party was felt most strongly in the organizational structure that was originally built up under his leadership. The Party's approach to London's local politics was considerably more structured than was that of the London Municipal Society. To put it quite mildly, the London Labour Party has always attempted to run a very taut political ship. Its governing and policy-making body was an Executive Committee made up of top Party leaders from the London area, but each year the Party held an annual conference of divisional parties and affiliated associations to discuss local issues and lay down broad lines

[6] In this regard, it is significant to note that in 1963 the Society decided to close down its operations once the London Government Act received Royal Assent. It felt that its job was done after successfully fighting for reform (i.e., "a better deal for Londoners for nearly seventy years").

of policy. Once laid down, these broad lines of policy commanded considerable respect. Although the London Labour Party worked in close conjunction with the national Labour Party Headquarters at Transport House, it never made any bones about the fact that it considered itself to be "top dog" in the London area. On more than one occasion, the London Labour Party tended to act as a law unto itself, and its relations with Transport House were not always overly cordial.

The London Labour Party was led by a Chairman (Robert Mellish, M.P., from Bermondsey) and a full-time Secretary (Mr. Peter Robshaw). Its membership statistics were impressive. Total membership for the year 1960–1961 was 448,300, with more than 290,000 of these members being affiliated via their trade unions.[7]

Unlike the Municipal Society, the London Labour Party did not restrict its activities to London County alone. In 1951 it expanded its jurisdiction to include Middlesex County, a move which many of its adherents later viewed with considerable skepticism.

To the more organizationally minded of the London Labour Party's organization men, Middlesex represented an area of considerable confusion, if not an outright political jungle. The Party was never able to achieve a degree of political cohesion in Middlesex that was in any way comparable to its iron grip over local politics in London County. As one Party leader mused, rather forlornly, in an interview, "Quite frankly, Middlesex had always been a mess politically. When you say 'L.C.C.' everyone knows you are talking about the London County Council. But mention 'M.C.C.' and people don't think of the Middlesex council. Instead, it's always the bloody cricket club that comes to mind."[8]

In addition to their two headquarters organizations, both the Conservative and the Labour parties relied upon constituency associations scattered throughout the local authorities in Greater London's outlying county council areas. The two parties serviced these outlying constituency associations directly from their national headquarters. Re-

[7] Sharpe, *A Metropolis Votes*, pp. 3-4.
[8] MCC (Marylebone Cricket Club) is a shorthand abbreviation for the all-English cricket team that plays periodic test matches with Australia for possession of a trophy known as "The Ashes."

sponsibility for this task in the Conservative Central Office was elaborate, being split between two organizations—The Home County Southeast Area Office (i.e., the metropolitan portions of Kent and Surrey counties) and The Home County Northwest Area (i.e., the metropolitan portions of Essex and Middlesex counties). During the reform contest, the Conservatives were making plans to consolidate their separate Central Office area organizations into one new Greater London Area Office.

The Labour Party organization in the outlying counties was less elaborate and, as will be noted forthwith, Labour's hold over these outlying areas was considerably less tenacious than that of the Conservatives.

Both the Liberal Party and the Communists also found London to represent enough of a political attraction to establish independent area organizations there.

Although the Liberals had not enjoyed major political success in Greater London for many years, during the late 1950's they began to register some significant gains in the suburban fringes, especially in the Kent County district of Orpington, which they eventually captured in the 1962 elections. The Liberals' central London organization was the London Liberal Party, which, during recent years, began pushing an increasingly more aggressive campaign at the local electoral level throughout the metropolis.

While the Liberals looked with anticipation to future successes in Greater London, the Communists had enjoyed their only conspicuous successes in the past. Although they still maintained pockets of support in east London, the Communists lost strength during the 1950's. Their high-water mark came in 1946, when they managed to elect two members to the London County Council. However, the Communists still maintained an active London District Committee to service local candidates.

The offices these four parties sought throughout Greater London were contested under a rather complicated set of rules, and it is necessary to summarize the major ones quickly, because they had a definite bearing on electoral results.

The four outlying counties in Greater London were divided into local electoral districts, each of which elected only one county councillor. In central London County, however, each district elected three county councillors. In second-tier elections, the boroughs and urban districts were usually divided into wards, if their population warranted it, with each of these wards returning three members to its local council. County council elections were held every third year, in April, and county borough and second-tier elections were held, as needed, in May.

The term of office of members of all the local authorities was three years. In the county boroughs and the municipal boroughs, one-third of the members retired annually, thus assuring "scattered" elections. In the counties, and in London's twenty-eight metropolitan boroughs, however, all the council members retired together every third year. As a result, in central London an entire slate of local officers was theoretically open to contest at once, although the London County Council and the twenty-eight metropolitan boroughs did, in fact, hold their elections in alternate years.

In addition to their elected members, local authorities in England include aldermen who are named to the councils by the councillors themselves. This practice is a hangover from the early nineteenth-century reform bill days, when the House of Lords insisted that local councillors of "experience" should be permitted to name some distinguished colleagues of "experience" to prevent the untutored populace from swamping the councils with unqualified personnel. Aldermen have an advantage over councillors in that they serve for six years, with half retiring every three years. The number and strength of the aldermen is not insignificant, being one-third of the total number of councillors except on the London County Council and in the twenty-eight London metropolitan boroughs, where they made up one-sixth of the total councillors. This aldermanic process could be used to swing close elections in the favor of one party or another, and to spare top leaders from the rigors of the electoral process. Sir Isaac Hayward, the Leader of the London County Council, served as an alderman, for example, as did a number of the Council's leading committee chairmen.

The specific partisan prizes the parties fought for in the London local elections involved a welter of seats on the county councils and the second-tier authorities—some 4,300 in all in the Greater London area.[9]

Over the years, distinct geographical cleavages that dramatically affected their chances of winning these seats had appeared between the parties.

As regards the first-tier authorities, the two county councils in the southern portion of the metropolitan area displayed permanent Conservative tendencies, while centrally located London County had carried on a faithful affair with the Labour Party for more than thirty years.

Both the southern suburban counties (i.e., Surrey and Kent) were for all intents and purposes solid Conservative strongholds, and both returned overwhelming Conservative majorities in the 1961 council elections.

The Labour Party, on the other hand, had maintained a stubborn, and generally strong, hold on the London County Council since 1934, although on occasion the Conservatives managed to put up a stiff challenge. The peak of Conservative postwar strength on the LCC came in 1949, when the Conservatives elected 64 councillors, the same number as Labour. However, the Labour Party was able to maintain its hold over this council via its aldermanic advantage, and during subsequent years Conservative strength on the LCC had dwindled, reaching a low point in 1958, when the Conservatives were able to elect only 25 of the 126 councillors. The Conservatives made something of a comeback in the 1961 LCC elections when they elected 42 members to the Labour Party's 84, but this comfortable Labour lead was further strengthened by its aldermanic advantage, which gave it an over-all majority of 98 members to 49 for the Conservative minority.

Whereas Surrey and Kent stood as solidly Conservative, and London County as solidly Labour, the northern counties of Essex and Middlesex both represented contestable political areas.

[9] L. J. Sharpe, "The Politics of Local Government in Greater London," *Public Administration*, XXXVIII (Summer 1960), p. 157.

In 1958, Essex shifted from Conservative to Labour, only to swing back to the Conservatives once again in 1961. Middlesex represented another northern "swing" county, which also had shifted from the Conservatives to Labour, in 1958. The Conservatives were able to recapture control of this county, however, in 1961.

As regards the five major county councils that made up the Royal Commission's review area, then, two to the south were solidly Conservative, the central county of London was solidly Labour, and the remaining two to the north were mixed, with both voting Conservative in the 1961 elections. Thus, following these elections, the centrally located London County Council stood alone as an island of Socialism in a sea of Conservative suburbia, with four of the five major counties coming under Conservative control. In addition, the sixth county to be affected, though only slightly, by the Royal Commission's review—Hertfordshire—was also solidly Conservative, thus adding to Labour's woes at the county council level.

However, the Labour Party could gain some degree of solace from the three other first-tier authorities in Greater London, the county boroughs of Croydon, East Ham, and West Ham. Croydon was an "independent" borough, but both East Ham and West Ham were Labour strongholds. Hence, the over-all geographical distribution of strength between the parties on the first-tier authorities, following the 1961 elections, was as indicated in Table IV and Map VII on the following pages.

While it is relatively easy to trace party fortunes at the first-tier level, the great number of metropolitan boroughs, municipal boroughs, and urban districts limits analysis of the second-tier politics to a fairly general summary of over-all trends.

The first of these trends is a remarkable correlation between the second-tier authorities' socioeconomic population distributions, already noted in Chapter 3, and the actual geographical distribution of party strength among these second-tier units.

As was illustrated in Map IV (page 54), there is a distinct east-west socioeconomic population cleavage throughout the Greater London area. The percentage of population in the two upper social classes exceeded the metropolitan area average in 45 of the 83 second-tier

TABLE IV[10]

Political Control of County Councils
1946–1961

(Totals include both councillors and aldermen)

	CONSERVATIVES	LABOUR	OTHER	TOTAL
London County Council (126 Councillors, 21 Aldermen)				
1949	69	80*	1	150
1952	42	108*		150
1955	57	90*		147
1958	32	115*		147
1961	49	98*		147
Middlesex County Council (87 Councillors, 29 Aldermen)				
1949	80*	36	4	120
1952	72*	44		116
1955	78*	38		116
1958	54	61*	1	116
1961	71*	46		116
Surrey County Council (83 Councillors, 27 Aldermen)				
1949	56*	4	41[a]	101
1952	70*	4	27	101
1955	88*	8	14	110
1958	83*	21	6	110
1961	97*	10	3	110
Kent County Council (80 Councillors, 26 Aldermen)				
1949	71*	9	20[a]	100
1952	78*	6	16	100
1955	82*	20	4	106
1958	67*	36	3	106
1961	88*	18		106
Essex County Council (109 Councillors, 36 Aldermen)				
1949	37	38	47[a]	122
1952	56	70*		126
1955	68*	58		126
1958	71	74*		145
1961	84*	61		145

* MAJORITY PARTY   [a] Other groups were classified as "Independents" who eventually merged with Conservatives in Surrey, Kent, and Essex.

[10] It is very difficult to compile completely accurate and up-to-date statistics for local elections by party, since official statistics do not include party identity. The statistical data used in this chapter were taken from the working files of the Conservative and Unionist Local Government Office.

Map VII

Political Control
First-Tier Authorities
(1961 Elections)

KEY

County Council and
County Borough
Majorities or
Pluralities

Labour (3)

Conservative (5)

Liberal or In-
dependent (1)

0   5 Miles

1 City of London
2 Holborn
3 Finsbury
4 Shoreditch
5 Bethnal Green
6 Bermondsey
7 Southwark
8 Deptford

9 Chelsea
10 City of Westminster
11 Kensington
12 Paddington
13 St. Marylebone
14 Hampstead
15 Stoke Newington
16 Tottenham
17 Wood Green

18 Friern Barnet
19 Wanstead and Woodford
20 Penge
21 Beddington and Wallington
22 Merton and Morden
23 Malden and Coombe
24 Kingston-upon-Thames
25 Brentford and Chiswick
26 Hammersmith

authorities (located primarily to the west of the City of London and in southern Kent County), whereas the percentages in these classes fell below the metropolitan area average in the remaining 38 second-tier authorities (located primarily to the east of the city).

A review of voting behavior in the 1962 local council elections indicates that 43 of these 45 "upper social class" authorities elected either Conservative, Independent, or Liberal majorities to their councils, while all 38 of the "lower social class" authorities elected Labour majorities to their councils. In other words, following the 1962 elections, there were only two electoral deviations (i.e., Wandsworth Borough and Carshalton Urban District) from the underlying socioeconomic population patterns among the entire 83 second-tier authorities to be found within the Greater London Council area.

This near-perfect correlation between the socioeconomic population characteristics of the second-tier authorities and their voting habits can be seen most clearly by comparing Map IV (page 54) with Map VIII on page 93. Note that, following the 1962 elections, the Labour Party completely dominated the less wealthy east London and inner-core south London boroughs, which originally began to attract the lower income groups and the very poor some three hundred years ago. As a result of its strength in east and southeast London, the Labour Party was able to dominate second-tier politics in the inner-core area, securing majorities on 21 of the 28 metropolitan borough councils in the 1962 elections.

Outside London County, the Labour Party enjoyed enough clusters of strength in the two northern "swing" counties to control 11 of the 23 second-tier councils in Middlesex County and 5 of the 10 metropolitan Essex councils. However, Labour's second-tier strength in the southern Conservative powerhouses of Surrey and Kent counties was minimal. Hence, once again, at the second-tier as well as at the first-tier level, the Labour stranglehold over metropolitan politics was to be found in the central core area of London County.

The Conservatives, conversely, were weak in the central area, controlling only a few of the metropolitan boroughs lying just west of the City Corporation of London. The great sources of Conservative second-tier strength were to be found outside London County, especially in the south, where they engulfed metropolitan Surrey and Kent counties. In addition, the Conservatives maintained a solid band of support in central Middlesex County and shared half the 10 Essex authorities with Labour.

Thus, as regards Greater London geopolitics at both the first- and the second-tier levels, the Labourites looked to the central core area, and the Conservatives to the outlying suburban fringes, for the base of their political power.

Numerous trends, in addition to the purely geographical, emerge from the striking correlation between the socioeconomic population characteristics and the partisan affiliations of the second-tier units. Two of these were of considerable importance to further understanding of the nature of politics in Greater London, since both dealt with the intensity of the hold exercised by the parties over the second-tier authorities.

The first involved intensity in numbers—the powerful pockets of strength completely dominated by either Labour or Conservative party councillors.

This trend could be illustrated most clearly within London County itself, specifically in the east London boroughs. Here one could find a literally impregnable Labour ring circling directly to the east of the City of London.

Eight metropolitan boroughs in this area, ranging from Islington to Southwark, did not elect one Conservative to their local councils in the 1962 elections, although a scattering of Independents made the grade.

These eight boroughs, and the 1962 Labour monopolies on their councils, were Islington (97%), Hackney (100%), Shoreditch (100%), Bethnal Green (100%), Stepney (89%), Poplar (94%), Bermondsey (100%), and Southwark (100%). The only places where the Conservatives were able to make any inroads at all into this solid east London circle of socialist unanimity were the metropolitan boroughs of Finsbury and Stoke Newington, each of which elected two Conservatives to its local council. Hence, in the ten east London bor-

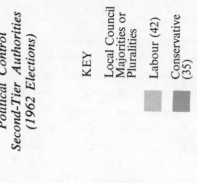

Map VIII

*Political Control
Second-Tier Authorities
(1962 Elections)*

KEY

Local Council
Majorities or
Pluralities

Labour (42)

Conservative
(35)

Independent or
Liberal (6)

0   5 Miles

1 City of London
2 Holborn
3 Finsbury
4 Shoreditch
5 Bethnal Green
6 Bermondsey
7 Southwark
8 Deptford

9 Chelsea
10 City of Westminster
11 Kensington
12 Paddington
13 St. Marylebone
14 Hampstead
15 Stoke Newington
16 Tottenham
17 Wood Green

18 Friern Barnet
19 Wanstead and Woodford
20 Penge
21 Beddington and Wallington
22 Merton and Morden
23 Malden and Coombe
24 Kingston-upon-Thames
25 Brentford and Chiswick
26 Hammersmith

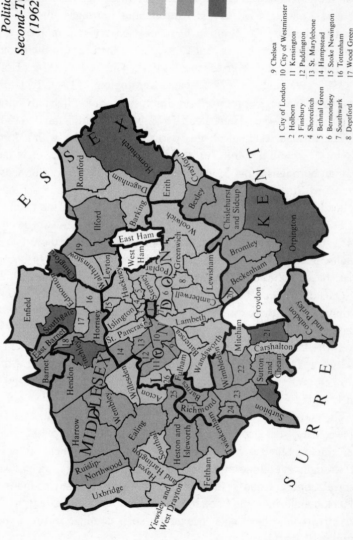

oughs taken as a whole, the Labour Party was able to capture 514 seats, or 96 per cent of the 534 total seats available, in the 1962 elections.

The Conservatives also held their pockets of numerical strength, but they were considerably less potent than the Labour majorities in east London. Five of the metropolitan boroughs directly to the west of the City Corporation had safe Conservative majorities, with each electing over 70 per cent Conservative members to their councils in 1962—i.e., St. Marylebone (84%), Chelsea (83%), Holborn (83%), Westminster (78%), and Kensington (71%). In addition, two other boroughs produced less impressive, but still safe, Conservative majorities—i.e., Hampstead (67%) and Paddington (61%).

The inverse result of all this partisan togetherness within London County's second-tier units was that very few of the twenty-eight metropolitan boroughs could be classified as contestable in any true sense of the word. In the 1962 elections, only two of the boroughs produced council majorities of less than 60 per cent for either of the two parties (Lewisham, with a 57% Labour majority, and Wandsworth, with a 54% Labour majority). It is interesting to note that these two boroughs, plus St. Pancras, represented the only metropolitan boroughs that shifted their council party majorities between 1952 and 1962.

Outside London County the situation was considerably less rigid, although again there were some pockets of numerical strength for both parties. As Map IX on page 96 illustrates, in the 1962 elections the Labour Party was able to gain more than a 70 per cent majority on 23 of the 83 second-tier councils in the Greater London Council area, while the Conservatives were able to perform this feat on 11 of these councils.

The second supplementary trend that emerges from the correlation between the socioeconomic population characteristics of the second-tier units and their party voting records is the development of "pockets of strength over time" by the two parties, especially, again, within central London County. In addition to dominating many councils with fantastic majorities, the Labour Party—and to a lesser extent the Conservatives—had been able to exercise such domination for a goodly number of years.

As was just noted, only three of the 28 metropolitan boroughs shifted party allegiance between 1952 and 1962. If one takes the entire Greater London Council area as a whole, it will be seen that some 34 of the 83 second-tier units in this area retained permanent party majorities during the entire postwar period, with these units again closely paralleling the 70 per cent-plus majority councils identified in Map III (page 50).[11]

Thus, an analysis of 1962 party preferences among the second-tier authorities indicated a number of basic trends:

First, the geographical voting patterns replicated almost exactly the socioeconomic population characteristics of the authorities.

Second, in a significant number of authorities, one of the two major parties, notably Labour, enjoyed a tremendous numerical control over the local councils.

Third, these pockets of numerical strength had been maintained over a long period of time.

Fourth, and most importantly, as a result of these socioeconomic population groupings, and the pockets of strength which they had produced, the Labour Party dominated the second-tier authorities within central London County (especially east London) almost completely, while the Conservatives' strength once again was to be found in the suburban portions of the metropolitan area.

The ultimate effect of this was that the Labour Party enjoyed a virtual political monopoly over central London politics at both the first-tier and the second-tier levels. The Conservatives, on the other hand, possessed their greatest strength outside London County, especially in Surrey and Kent, and, to a lesser extent, in Middlesex County. Thus, with relatively few exceptions, Labour represented the "party of the center" in Greater London in terms of its geopolitical strength, if not of its ideology. The Conservatives, on the other hand, were quite far out, in terms of their geopolitical strength, if not of their ideology.

When these two facts are lumped together, it stands to reason that the Labour Party would be inclined to take a very dim view of any

[11] A more detailed analysis of these permanent majorities is contained in Sharpe, "The Politics of Local Government in Greater London," pp. 167-172.

Map IX

*Party Strength
Second-Tier Authorities
Greater London
(1962 Elections)*

KEY

Areas Where Labour
Controlled 70%, or
More, of Local
Councillors

Areas Where Conser-
vatives Controlled
70%, or More, of
Local Councillors

0   5 Miles

1 City of London	9 Chelsea	18 Friern Barnet
2 Holborn	10 City of Westminster	19 Wanstead and Woodford
3 Finsbury	11 Kensington	20 Penge
4 Shoreditch	12 Paddington	21 Beddington and Wallington
5 Bethnal Green	13 St. Marylebone	22 Merton and Morden
6 Bermondsey	14 Hampstead	23 Malden and Coombe
7 Southwark	15 Stoke Newington	24 Kingston-upon-Thames
8 Deptford	16 Tottenham	25 Brentford and Chiswick
	17 Wood Green	26 Hammersmith

metropolitan reorganization plan that threatened to amalgamate the suburban forces of Conservatism with its very reliable central stronghold of Socialism.

The Governmental Authorities

In addition to its threatened impact upon prevailing party fortunes, any reform program was obviously destined to have a very decided impact on the distribution of governmental powers. This, again, was a highly potent political issue. As Bertram Gross has pointed out, government agencies themselves must be understood as "contestants, rather than as neutral referees, in the struggle for political power."[12] London's local authorities were certainly no exception in this regard. During the past quarter-century, the second-tier units had been losing their powers to higher governmental authorities, and they were anxious to see these powers restored. The first-tier authorities, on the other hand, were just as anxious to see that any such restoration of second-tier powers did not take place at their expense.

Over the years both the first-tier and the second-tier units had developed specific interest associations to protect and promote their respective positions. Five such associations had grown to a point where they played a role of considerable importance in the Greater London political scene.

The first of these was a second-tier interest group in London County, the Metropolitan Boroughs' Standing Joint Committee. This Committee was originally established in 1912 as a "defensive" mechanism to protect the rights and status of the twenty-eight metropolitan boroughs (plus the City of London) against encroachments by the London County Council. It consisted of three representatives appointed by each of its twenty-nine constituent councils, and its basic theoretical objective, as set forth in its Constitution, was "to protect and advance the powers, interests, rights and privileges of these constituent Councils."[13]

[12] Bertram M. Gross, *The Legislative Struggle: A Study in Social Combat* (New York: McGraw-Hill Book Company, Inc., 1953), p. 92.

[13] Constitution of Metropolitan Boroughs' Standing Joint Committee (4 February 1957), p. 1.

The Committee, which elected its own chairman and officers and appointed subcommittees to investigate specific problem areas, had done a great deal of useful work over the years in fostering closer administrative cooperation between the metropolitan boroughs in such matters as interborough library loans, financial analysis, and organization and methods analysis.

Despite its historical emphasis on protecting the boroughs' interests, during more recent years the Committee had begun to develop an extremely close rapport with the London County Council. The simple arithmetic of the matter was that, since the London Labour Party controlled twenty-one of the twenty-eight metropolitan borough councils, and since each of these councils appointed three members to the Standing Joint Committee, the London Labour Party controlled the Committee as well. As a result, the Joint Committee served to join the Labour-controlled London County Council with Labour-controlled metropolitan boroughs. One indication of this could be seen in the fact that the Chairman of the Committee, and its Chairman since 1949 (i.e., Mr. Norman Prichard), had served as past Chairman of the London County Council and as Chairman of the LCC Housing Committee. In Mr. Prichard's own words, it would have been "unthinkable" in past years for the Committee's Chairman to play such a key role in the LCC hierarchy.[14] By the 1950's, however, the situation was no longer unthinkable. In spite of any theoretical concerns as the protector of borough interests, the Metropolitan Boroughs' Standing Joint Committee actually occupied a strategic vantage point as a convenient meeting ground between the central London boroughs and the London County Council.

The second major local authority association that was designed to protect second-tier interests was the Middlesex Borough and District Councils' Association. This group was made up of all eighteen municipal boroughs and eight urban districts in the County. In informal terms, however, the Association was dominated by only ten of its members, the so-called Middlesex "Big Ten."

The "Big Ten" consisted of those frustrated elephantine boroughs in

14 Letter, N. Prichard to [London] *Daily Telegraph,* September 15, 1962.

Middlesex County that had theoretically qualified for county borough status but had failed to realize their county borough ambitions (see Chapter 4). These ten Middlesex units often acted in concert on many issues and virtually always acted in concert on any issues that were remotely related to their county borough aspirations. Thus, they issued a joint statement of evidence to the Royal Commission, and they were to display a high degree of cohesion in their response to the Royal Commission's report.

Unlike the Metropolitan Boroughs' Standing Joint Committee, the Middlesex "Big Ten" did not enjoy harmonious relations with their county council. Instead of serving as a potential bridge between the two tiers of Middlesex government, they were more interested in providing as much dynamite as possible to make certain that no such bridge could possibly survive in the militant intergovernmental terrain of Middlesex County.

In addition to the Middlesex "Big Ten" and the Metropolitan Boroughs' Standing Joint Committee, three national groups served as local authority spokesmen in the Greater London area. These three groups were the County Councils' Association, the Association of Municipal Corporations, and the Urban District Councils' Association. All three were virtually the same in intent and organization, although their constituencies differed. The County Councils' Association represented all major first-tier counties in England and Wales (with the exception of the London County Council, which never saw fit to join this organization). However, the CCA did represent Middlesex, Surrey, Kent, Essex, and Hertfordshire counties.

The Association of Municipal Corporations represented all the major second-tier boroughs outside the County of London, plus virtually all the twenty-eight metropolitan boroughs inside this county.

The Urban District Councils' Association served as the spokesman for these second-tier authorities and included in its membership most of the urban district councils located in the Greater London area.

Often, these Associations were subject to a tremendous amount of multi-organizational "inbreeding." Rather than following a fragmented pattern, Greater London's local governmental power structure was extremely intertwined, with the same individuals showing up on first-tier councils; second-tier councils; joint committees bridging, or separating, these councils; in Parliament; in political parties; and on the various local authority associations noted above.

To give a few examples, in addition to the case of Mr. Prichard cited previously, Lord Morrison, with his long-standing interest in the London County Council, served—for a limited period of time at least— as President of the Association of Municipal Corporations; the Right Honourable Chuter Ede, M.P., a former Chairman of the Surrey County Council, served as President of the County Councils' Association; Mr. George Pargiter, M.P., the Labour leader on the Middlesex County Council, served as Vice-Chairman of the CCA; and so forth.

These, then, were the political parties and the major local governmental interest groups that were in a position to fight for any political advantages that might result from the London reorganization plan. In final summary, exactly what were the political stakes in London all about? What partisan motivations actually drove the political parties to contest the 4,300-odd council seats in Greater London, and what power considerations tended to influence the positions of these different local councils, regardless which of the parties may have won the 4,300 seats?

The partisan motivations boiled down to two in number.

The first involved the local and national prestige and status that the political parties enjoyed by virtue of their control over the major offices of central London's government.

To use a phrase employed with quite passionate eloquence by Lord Morrison, central London is the "Crown Jewel" in English local politics, and the control of London's local government has always been of tremendous psychological and strategic importance to all parties, but most especially to the Labour Party.

Its importance to Labour stemmed from the fact that this Party had suffered three consecutive setbacks in national General Elections following its 1951 defeat by the Conservatives, and it could ill afford to lose control of the London County Council during its sojourn in the national political wilderness. As one observer noted in commenting on the 1961 LCC election, ". . . the loss of this star in Labour's political crown would undoubtedly have accelerated the party's decline."[15]

Control of central London politics was also of psychological importance to Labour because, despite its initial high hopes, the Party had never been able to achieve conspicuous success in local government elections throughout the rest of England and Wales. The control of central London's government, the "Crown Jewel" of English local politics, tended to obscure the harshness of this reality.

During the 1961–1962 local elections, the Labour Party was able to gain outright control of only 9 of England's 62 county councils. Its record in the more rural areas was woefully weak. Here it could count victories on only 72 of 317 municipal boroughs, 167 of 514 urban districts, and 33 of 473 rural districts.[16] The only really bright spots for Labour were in the larger county boroughs (where it took 42 of 83 councils), and in the central London area, where it could point to the London County Council and assert that it still had its hook in this biggest local fish of all. Likewise, it could point to central London's 28 metropolitan boroughs and show a 21 to 7 majority. The control of central London politics gave a tremendous boost to Labour's political ego.

Besides this consideration of the psychological and strategic prestige of office, there was a second partisan motivation in the control of central London's government. This, quite simply, was embodied by London's usefulness as a political laboratory in which the two major parties could bring their differing policies and philosophies to bear on such substantive issues as education and housing. As long as the Labour Party retained its control over the London County Council, it could utilize this Council to carry out specific policy experiments it felt to be important, with the realization that the impact of its actions would extend far beyond London. As already noted, London serves as a unique central focus for the entire United Kingdom, indeed the entire Commonwealth, and when new policies are instituted in this area, the pub-

---

[15] Sharpe, *A Metropolis Votes*, p. 2.
[16] *Newsletter for Labour Groups*, No. 22 (August 1962), (The Labour Party: Transport House), pp. 61-64.

licity is national, if not world-wide. The Labour Party, fully aware of this fact, was proud of the innovations it had sponsored in the London County Council, and it did not want to lose its hold over this central area authority.

It is worth taking brief note here of the partisan stakes that were not involved in the Greater London political arena. No party was concerned about gaining, or losing, political control of London's government because it wanted to exploit this government for monetary or other personal advantage. In nearly thirty years of LCC rule, the Labour Party's record had been virtually spotless in this regard; nor had the Conservative Party been involved in any major scandals or corruption in its control of Surrey, Kent, and the other outlying counties. This fact was significant with respect to the entire reorganization strategy, because it limited one of the crucial arguments that has often been utilized in the past to support local governmental reform, in both England and the United States. If metropolitan governmental change was to come about in the Greater London area, the rationale for such action would have to come on some other grounds than the old corruption arguments that had been utilized to abolish the discredited Metropolitan Board of Works some seventy-five years earlier.

So much for the partisan motivations. What of the power stakes?

The overriding consideration here was quite basic. Many of the second-tier authorities wanted to exercise more local governmental responsibilities than they were, in fact, exercising. If they could not achieve the exalted status of county boroughs, at least they could hope to enjoy a partial restoration of powers under a reform program. This feeling was pervasive and deep. It ran in, around, and between the various second-tier units with little regard for rigid party alignments.

Hence, the political motivations involved in the reform of London's government were dualistic in their potential impact.

When viewed in terms of party considerations alone, the issue was reasonably clear-cut, at least as far as the Labourites were concerned. The London Labour Party was flatly opposed to any reform that would lead to the abolition of its local political prize, the London County Council, and dilute its central area strength in a sea of Conservative suburban votes. The Conservative position, on the other hand, was not quite this precise. While many Conservatives cast covetous eyes on precisely the political prospect Labour feared (i.e., the swamping of central London's Labourites within a sea of Conservative suburbia), some of the powerful Conservative county council leaders, especially in Surrey and Kent, were adamant against any reform that would result in the metropolitan fringes of their own home counties being wrested away from their local control and turned over to a new Greater London authority.

When viewed in terms of its power stakes, the situation was considerably more confusing. The larger second-tier units longed for the increased local governmental powers. Yet, many of these units were closely affiliated with the Labour Party, and they were having a difficult time reconciling their edacious egos with their partisan loyalties.

It was obvious that if the Labour leaders (and the dissident Conservative county councillors) were to have any chance of staving off reform, they could hardly rely upon the second-tier units as a stable prop for such an endeavor. Instead, they would have to look to other groups to buttress their rather shaky position.

Fortunately for the opposition forces, such supplementary support was, in fact, forthcoming—from a variety of professional interest associations. Quite basically, these groups were haunted by one primary concern: the potential impact of any reform plan on the discharge of their individual professional specialties. They looked at the issue of London's metropolitan reform, not as the Royal Commission had done, in terms of the "health of representative government," but rather in terms of what size local governmental unit would best meet their particular professional needs. As a result, they harbored ideas that were quite different from those of the Royal Commission with regard to the intrinsic merit of revitalizing the smaller second-tier authorities.

6. The Professional Stakes

Before discussing the professional associations' reactions to the Royal Commission's proposals, it is necessary to say a brief word about the general role of interest groups in British political life.

In the words of Samuel Beer, "Pressure groups in Britain are numerous, well-organized and highly effective."[1] It is beyond the scope of this analysis to comment upon each of the various factors that contribute to this effectiveness. Of prime importance, however, is the fact that, rather than dispersing their efforts, British groups tend to concentrate on the executive arm of government. Three facts help to explain why this is so.

The first, and most basic, consideration relates to the distribution of powers within the British Government. As a result of the Cabinet tradition, the British executive branch plays the dominant role in determining governmental policy. It is here, rather than at the Parliamentary level, that basic questions of policy are really decided. All interest groups tend to move automatically toward the key centers of governmental authority, and to the British groups this means a move toward the executive arm of the Government.

The second consideration is the impact of the historic British "corporate tradition" on the political attitudes and expectations of the British public. Throughout English history different corporate bodies, such as the universities and the churches, have always played a highly

[1] Samuel H. Beer, "Pressure Groups and Parties in Britain," *American Political Science Review*, L, No. 1 (March 1956), 1.

important role in shaping general governmental policy. Largely because of this tradition, the British have been considerably more open than is generally the case in the United States in incorporating many of their groups directly into the very heart of the executive process. By means of extremely close consultation, cooperation, and even co-optation, the British interest groups provide a wide range of expertise to executive agencies, and in turn, translate the policies of these agencies to the special "publics" which they represent. This positive utilization of the interest group has become more pronounced with the development of the modern welfare state, as the bureaucracy has come to place an increasing reliance on the interest group in the performance of its daily tasks.

The third consideration represents somewhat the opposite side of the above coin, although it, too, draws heavily upon this same historic "corporate tradition." The British not only expect pressure groups to implement executive actions favorable to their cause, but they also accept the fact that such groups will block actions they find to be unfavorable. It is not at all unusual for British groups to concentrate on restraining executive action, whereas under our more elaborate institutional arrangements (i.e., federalism, separation of powers, and so on) such restraint is attempted at many points in the governmental process.

The result is that the British groups can exercise tremendous power over the executive in terms of both their positive and their negative potentialities. To quote again from Beer's analysis, "Today many groups in [British] society hold what is almost a veto over public policy in their power to refuse their work, their talents, their capital or simply their willing co-operation in carrying out public policy."[2]

Because of the crucial role that interest groups play in British political life, it was only natural that the Royal Commission (which was really acting on behalf of the executive, although it was formally reporting to Parliament) should have attempted to ascertain the professional associations' attitudes toward the reorganization of London's government and to pay careful attention to the positions these associations took on this matter.

[2] *Ibid.*, p. 15.

One issue, however, on which the Commission and a variety of key professional groups did disagree very strongly related to the seemingly neutral abstraction of the criteria to be utilized in determining the size of London's new second-tier boroughs. The major point of disagreement between the Commission and these groups grew out of their fundamentally different approaches to sociologist Otis Dudley Duncan's apparently innocuous inquiry, "What is the optimum size of a city?"

In attempting to answer this question, Duncan examined relevant data in nine different functional categories before concluding that there is no such thing as one optimum city size. Differing services pose differing requirements in terms of the population and geographical scale necessary to support their maximum realization, and what is the right scale for the discharge of one particular functional activity is not necessarily right for another. As a result, Duncan concluded that "the problem of optimum city-size originates in the realm of values . . . intrinsically beyond the scope of science."[3]

While Duncan's question is complex enough when analyzed in terms of functional criteria alone, it becomes frightfully more confusing when additional considerations are added. Each time a new variable is considered, the problem extends further beyond the realm of "organized complexity,"[4] until it finally reaches a realm of apparently irreconcilable contradiction.

The Royal Commission's consideration of the "health of representative government" represented just such an additional variable with regard to the question of the optimum size second-tier units that should be incorporated into the new Greater London government. With its apparent emphasis on intimacy and accessibility, this consideration argued in the favor of the smaller borough unit. Hence, the problem

[3] Otis Dudley Duncan, "The Optimum Size of Cities," in *Cities and Society,* ed. Paul K. Hatt and Albert J. Reiss, Jr. (Glencoe: The Free Press, 1957), pp. 759-772.

[4] Dr. Warren Weaver used this concept in a remarkably stimulating statement in the Rockefeller Foundation Annual Report, 1958. I am indebted to Jane Jacobs for first bringing this statement to my attention in her concluding chapter in *The Life and Death of Great American Cities* (New York: Random House, 1961).

facing the Commission was not only to determine the "right"-size borough to satisfy a variety of conflicting functional criteria, but also to mesh this ideal unit, if such an entity existed, with those additional criteria necessary to the realization of "healthy" local democracy.

As Duncan undoubtedly would have predicted, the response to the Commission's efforts was highly critical. It was critical primarily because the problem the Commission was attempting to resolve is "intrinsically beyond the scope of science" and, hence, cannot be answered definitely. The result was a wide-open field day for second-guessing, in which anyone and everyone was permitted to play the game, and all were permitted to play it on a relatively equal footing.

The story of the professional associations' reaction to the Commission's plan is basically a story of those groups that elected to play this particular game on the grounds that they were in a better position than the Commission to evaluate the question of optimum borough size as it related to the performance of their own particular functional specialties. Four important professional groups—the teachers, the doctors, the architects and planners, and the welfare workers—decided to play this game with an unusual display of intensity. In order to understand why this was so, it is necessary to know something about their hopes and fears concerning London's government.

The Teachers

A brief sojourn into the complicated background of the English educational system is an absolute prerequisite to an understanding of the teachers' reaction to the Royal Commission report.

Like so much else that is English, the modern educational system is a product of compromise—in this instance a terribly complex compromise that resulted in the passage of no less than ten major education acts between 1870 and 1944. The key piece of legislation that shaped the outlines of the present system is the last of these—The Education Act of 1944. Among its many provisions, this Act:

1. created a new central Ministry of Education to coordinate the Government's program in this field;
2. placed primary responsibility for the local administration of the statutory educational system on the first-tier county councils and county boroughs;[5]
3. emphasized equality of opportunity in secondary education (i.e., ages 12 to 19, compulsory to age 15) as a national policy objective.

Although the second of the above provisions has created a great deal of friction in local government, it is the third objective that has led to the most bitter political controversy—a controversy that can only be comprehended within the context of the over-all format of England's educational system.

This system consists of both a statutory schools sector (which is the primary responsibility of the counties and the county boroughs) and a sizable number of independent schools (which are free from any direct control by local governmental authorities, and which range from small private kindergartens to such famous "public" schools as Eton and Harrow).

Although both the statutory and the independent sectors feed students into England's universities, the independent schools have always held a very strong competitive position in this regard, and they continue to do so. Since there is an acute shortage of space in England's limited number of universities, the statutory schools have attempted to shape their secondary-school curriculums in a manner that will enable their very best students to compete successfully with the independent schools for these limited numbers of university places. (The famous Robbins Committee report [October 1963] recommended an immediate crash program to increase the country's university capacity, and the Conservative Government subsequently gave its full approval to such an effort.)

The essence of the statutory schools' scheme is to channel their stu-

[5] In addition, however, in order to placate the many second-tier municipal boroughs and urban districts that were losing certain prior responsibilities, the 1944 Act set up a confusing system of "divisional executives" and "excepted districts" designed to permit some of these second-tier authorities to retain certain day-to-day responsibilities in local education.

dents into different types of secondary school according to their "ability." Over the years, three distinct types of statutory secondary school have been developed:[6]

1. *Grammar Schools*—These schools handle about 20 per cent of the school population. They provide a general curriculum leading to examinations for the General Certificate of Education (GCE), which is the key to university placement. In essence, they are the schools of the "intellectually elite." They are designed to take the most able students and to prepare these students to compete for university places.

2. *Technical Schools*—Since the passage of the Education Act of 1944, these schools have handled increasingly smaller enrollments until today they cater to only about 5 per cent of the school population. They provide a curriculum directed toward some professionally oriented occupation, the most common being engineering for boys and commercial subjects for girls. Under national policy, they are expected to recruit from the same intellectual levels as the grammar schools, but this is not usually the case. However, technical schools can prepare pupils for the GCE and also for other specialized examinations that will enable them to compete for university places.

3. *Secondary Modern Schools*—These schools were created as a result of the Education Act of 1944. They now cater to approximately 75 per cent of the secondary-school population and therefore cover a huge range of ability. Although the Education Act of 1944 provided that these schools should be comparable to grammar schools in terms of faculty resources and physical plant, they are "by definition, the schools for children of relatively modest intellectual ability." Hence, they concentrate less upon academic subjects; most of their courses are vocation-oriented. Only a few of their more able pupils take academic courses leading to the GCE, and hence few go on to a university education.

In order to determine which of these schools he or she (the terms are used interchangeably throughout) is to attend, a student takes an examination at the completion of the primary phase of his education,

[6] H. C. Dent, *The Educational System of England and Wales* (London: University of London Press, 1961). The descriptions of these three types of school are taken virtually intact from Dent, p. 50.

and since he is age eleven at the time, this exam is known as the famous "Eleven Plus" examination.[7] If this examination indicates that the student has the potential to go on to a university in later years, he can hope to be placed in a grammar school. If the examination indicates the student possesses other potentialities, he can pretty well expect to be placed in a secondary modern school, or perhaps a technical school, and receive a more practical type of secondary-school education.

Many educators in England feel that this system is not only the most productive in terms of utilization of educational resources, but also the most fair and democratic that can be devised. They argue that since each student is placed in the proper stream of secondary education according to his innate abilities, each is allowed to develop his inner potential to the fullest. The essence of this argument is a seeming paradox—namely, the belief that a democratic society must segregate according to meaningful criteria (rather than by such arbitrary considerations as race or creed) in order to produce truly meaningful conditions of equality. To use an analogy from the realm of fisticuffs, no one in his right mind would expect Pone Kingpetch, the world's flyweight champion, to climb into the same prize ring with Cassius Clay, the world's heavyweight champion, and produce a fair and equal fight.[8] Utilizing similar logic, the supporters of England's present educational dichotomy argue that only by categorizing according to meaningfully observable criteria of ability (i.e., bright and not-so-bright) can meaningful conditions of educational equality be realized. In addition, this group holds that if a student initially fails to get into a grammar school but later shows abilities in this direction, he can be transferred to such a school at a future date, or he can take GCE exams directly from the secondary modern school. As a consequence, no student is automatically barred from the future possibility of a university education at age eleven.

The critics, however, retort that the present system not only is completely undemocratic but also represents a priceless waste of the

[7] In parts of London this is referred to as a "Junior Leaving Examination."

[8] A faculty colleague, Dr. Vincent E. Starzinger, first pointed out the nature of this paradox to me, but he is in no way responsible for its current restatement.

country's most valuable asset—its youth. Like the United States Supreme Court, this group holds that there are psychological influences in education that are of crucial importance. To this group, the separation of students into different educational streams at such a young age sets up patterns of "inferiority" and "superiority" that are totally detrimental to the 75 per cent of all students who end up in the secondary modern schools. Even if the "Eleven Plus" exam is completely accurate (and they would argue that when a child is eleven it is much too early to determine the future course of his educational career), these basic psychological patterns of "inequality" will continue to exist no matter how much money is poured into the faculty resources and the physical plants of the secondary modern schools in an effort to make them comparable to the grammar schools.

This attitude is especially strong within the Labour Party, many of whose members view the present arrangement as little more than a means to maintain a system of social inequality throughout the country. This argument places heavy emphasis upon environmental influences as they relate to educational achievement. It holds that children from poorer homes, and especially from broken homes or from homes in which there are basic elements of neglect and conflict, do not have the motivation to perform as well on the "Eleven Plus" examination as do children from more fortunate homes. Hence, a system of class stratification is built into the educational system from the beginning, and this stratification tends to perpetuate itself over time.

As a result of this conviction, the Labour Party has been experimenting with still another type of secondary school since the war—the comprehensive school.

Fortunately, the nature of the comprehensive school is relatively easy for the American to grasp, since this type of school is readily comparable to the average high school in the United States. Indeed, one critic of such schools advised in an interview that they were no more than "massive American sausage grinders."

The Ministry of Education has defined the comprehensive school as "one which is intended to cater for all the secondary education of all the children in a given area and includes all three elements in clearly defined sides."[9] In somewhat less eloquent language, a comprehensive school is one that places all students of all levels of ability under the same roof and then provides differing curriculum programs that veer off in different directions (i.e., technical, vocational, university) without the "stigma" of separatist facilities. As a consequence, these schools are quite large, which their supporters claim offers the opportunity for maximum utilization of plant and teaching staff with maximum returns, and which their critics claim destroys the intimacy essential to a meaningful educational experience.

The area in which the Labour Party experimented most forcefully with the concept of the comprehensive school was London County. Following the war, the London County Council adopted the London School Plan of 1947, which outlined a long-range program to create some ninety comprehensive schools, or enough to handle all LCC secondary-school needs, and some 85 per cent of all secondary students within the County. At the time of the issuance of the Royal Commission's report, this Plan was about two-thirds completed, with some sixty comprehensive schools in operation.[10]

From the start, however, the issue of comprehensive schools had been a subject of political dispute, and this issue was one of the few in which it was possible to find a clear-cut division between the two major political parties on a question of local government policy.

On the whole, the Conservatives took a rather dim view of the comprehensive school concept. There were a number of reasons for this attitude, with the major verbal Conservative criticism being that such schools represented a threat to the continued existence of the grammar schools, and that loss of the grammar schools would lead to an over-all diminution of quality throughout the secondary-education system.

At first, the Conservatives were quite open in their opposition to comprehensive schools—so much so that they used this argument as an issue in London local elections. When it became increasingly

[9] Ministry of Education Circular No. 144, June 16, 1947.
[10] In keeping with this over-all policy, the London County Council later dropped the "Eleven Plus" examination entirely. This action was taken in the summer of 1963.

obvious that more and more voters seemed to be enthusiastic about the comprehensive-school program, however, the Conservatives became somewhat less open in their opposition. Many Conservatives still harbor a deep suspicion of the comprehensive schools, nonetheless, and this bias occasionally boils to the surface under rather extraordinary circumstances.

Thus, for example, a former Conservative Minister of Education, Sir David (now Lord) Eccles, informed Commons on one recent occasion:

> I am sorry that the L.C.C. has just restated, in a slightly modified form, its 1947 education plan, which is to close county grammar schools in its area and substitute a series of comprehensive schools. It knows that this plan will not go through so long as there is a Conservative Minister of Education. In fact, we have allowed a great measure of experiment, but we cannot allow the doctrinaire destruction of good schools.[11]

It was this underlying political controversy over the comprehensive schools that constituted the key to the LCC teachers' concern over the reorganization of London's government. These teachers were totally committed to a high-quality educational system in central London, with a deep idealism that carried tremendous personal conviction. As a result, they viewed any plan that would result in the abolition of the London County Council as a potential catastrophe in terms of the threat it would pose to the future well-being of education in central London, and most especially to the well-being of London's comprehensive schools.

Their main spokesman on this issue was the London Teachers' Association, a subdivision of the National Union of Teachers, which has a membership of some 14,000 teachers in London County.

In testimony before the Royal Commission, this Association had made it quite clear that it did not want to see any changes in the organization of the London County Council. As its Executive Director, Mr. V. R. Shaw, testified to the Commission:

[11] Hansard, House of Commons, DCLIV, No. 59 (20 February 1962), 245-246.

In regard to the size of London . . . there is no particular virtue necessarily in size as size. . . . But here is an authority . . . which has now come to a state in the educational world in which all of us feel quite right to be proud. Anything which is done at this time to undermine what has been done in the past in our opinion could prove disastrous and fatal. . . . We are satisfied that the size of London is in no way detrimental to its efficiency and its good relations between the parties concerned, the parents, the children and the teachers.[12]

In all the subsequent controversy over the educational proposals in the Royal Commission's report, this basic consideration of the future of the comprehensive schools was of tremendous importance to a great majority of the LCC teachers. Any reorganization plan that would result in the destruction of the London County Council, and hence in the very possible abandonment of the comprehensive school program, was unable to win any popular support from this particular constituent group.

There are many other teaching associations within the Greater London area besides the London Teachers' Association, however, and they were stirred by a somewhat different set of fears. Specifically, the Commission's proposal that responsibility for education should be split between the proposed Greater London Council and the proposed new Greater London Boroughs stirred up a hornets' nest, both inside and outside London County.

The basic concern here was that such a system simply would not work, and critics of the system pointed to the experience with the "divisional executives" and "excepted districts" under the 1944 Act as an indication of this fact. A second concern related to the conviction that the larger the teaching area was, the more flexibility in transferring teachers between different schools according to their preferences would obtain. This flexibility, plus the potential prestige theoretically associated with working for a larger county authority, made the county educational programs more attractive to many teachers.

When all these concerns were lumped together, a number of additional groups joined the London Teachers' Association in arguing

12 Royal Commission, *Minutes of Oral Evidence,* No. 50, pp. 2,085-2,088.

against the proposed reorganization. The Surrey County Teachers' Association provided outright opposition, asserting that "the children in the county would derive no educational benefit from a change in the administration of the education service."[13] The London Head Teachers' Association, the National Association of School Masters, and the Joint Committee of the Four Secondary Associations (i.e., Headmasters and Headmistresses) also indicated dissatisfaction with the Commission's proposals.[14]

A number of specialist organizations, such as the Guild of Teachers of Backward Children and the London Branch of the Special Schools Association, expressed concern over the proposed educational powers of the new Greater London Boroughs, arguing that specialized institutions for the education of handicapped children could not be transferred from the county level to these smaller borough units and still retain their maximum usefulness. Finally, a number of religious bodies also indicated doubts about splitting educational responsibilities between the boroughs in terms of the impact such a fragmentation might have on the denominational schools—the only instance in which such a specific expression of interest in the Greater London plan was to be forthcoming from any religious or ethnic groups during the entire course of the reorganization controversy.

This is not to say, however, that all educational bodies were against awarding increased educational responsibilities to the boroughs. On the contrary, some groups favored strengthening the boroughs' educational powers even further than the Royal Commission had proposed. For example, The Middlesex Excepted Districts Association (representing the second-tier educational authorities in Middlesex) wanted responsibility for the entire local education system to be vested with

13 Royal Commission, *Written Evidence*, V, 418.

14 Some of these letter groups, however, were concerned with a set of fears directly opposite those of the London Teachers' Association. Specifically, they were worried that the new Greater London Council might extend the LCC comprehensive school program throughout the metropolitan area to the possible detriment of the independent schools' position. As the "Joint Four" Committee explained to the Royal Commission, "For efficiency, we want larger units to control general policy . . . [but] . . . we do not want too large an area of administration. We do not want the extension of the control of the L.C.C. to the Greater London area."

the new boroughs, and it received support in general principle from the South-East Regional Association of Education Officers (representing the senior educational administrators in the Review Area), which warned that the "danger in the Royal Commission's report . . . lies in the direction of giving the Greater London Council too much control of education, rather than too little."[15]

Thus, the specialist associations in the educational field looked at the Royal Commission's report and, as specialists have done since the dawn of history, they formulated precise ideas as to what they didn't want, but considerably less precise ideas as to what they did want. Some favored no change; some favored moving in the direction of larger units; and some favored moving in the direction of smaller units. None was able to state with any degree of precision what it felt was the "optimum"-size governmental unit for the discharge of educational services because all approached this question in terms of previously conceived value criteria. The London Teachers' Association was worried about comprehensive schools; the religious bodies, about denominational schools; the Excepted Districts Association, about second-tier schools; and so it went. Under the circumstances, any size unit that would fit these prior-value judgments was the right-size unit. As the London Teachers' Association testified to the Commission, "There is no particular virtue necessarily in size as size," and as Professor Duncan had asserted earlier, "The problem of optimum city size originates in the realm of values."

Indeed, about the only thing the great majority of educational associations could agree upon when they looked at the Royal Commission's proposals as they related to their particular field of concern was that they did not like what they saw.

The Doctors

Like the teachers, the doctors within London County approached the reorganization proposals from the vantage point of their own spe-

[15] "South-East Regional Association of Education Officers, Statement of Observations on the Report of the Royal Commission" (mimeographed, Winter 1961).

cialized concerns and, like the teachers, they did not care for what they saw.

Unlike the teachers', however, the doctors' opposition to the Royal Commission's report was not grounded in any deep emotional issues, such as the comprehensive school controversy. Instead, the doctors took a very practical view of the administrative implications of the Commission's proposals, and it was this consideration that served as the major source of their disenchantment.

The doctors within London County feared that the Royal Commission's plan would represent a return to administrative conditions as they had existed prior to the passage of the National Health Act of 1946. This Act, which became operative in 1948, had been so broad in its over-all implications that it resulted in a virtually complete overhaul of medical administration throughout the country. Its impact upon three particular services was especially notable.

The first factor involved was the hospital services; the central Government had taken over some 3,000 hospitals previously administered by county councils and county boroughs and had placed them under the jurisdiction of fifteen regional hospital boards.

In addition, a new National Health Program had been established for the general practitioner services under some 138 area Executive Councils, with each of these councils being advised by professional committees of doctors and other practitioners within their respective areas, such as the Local Medical Committee for the County of London.

Finally, there were the public health services, and it was here that the Act had its most pronounced impact upon the internal realignment of local governmental responsibilities.

Prior to 1948, there had been a reasonably equitable sharing of public health functions between the first-tier county councils and county boroughs, and the second-tier municipal boroughs and urban districts. The former had served as the major local health authorities, administering hospitals and having general responsibility for school health and mental health. However, the second-tier authorities also had possessed important responsibilities, including ultimate control over the domiciliary midwifery service and direct control over environmental health, maternity services, and child welfare services.

When responsibility for hospitals was transferred away from the first-tier authorities to regional boards, there was a parallel movement of other responsibilities up the ladder from the second-tier to the first-tier authorities. Specifically, the county councils and the county boroughs had taken over the domiciliary midwifery service and the maternity and child welfare services, leaving the second-tier bodies pretty much as environmental health authorities. In part this move was political, in that the counties and county boroughs had been reluctant to give up the hospitals, and they pressured the Government to give them new responsibilities to make up for their loss. In part, however, the move was also very much based upon professional considerations. Under the old arrangement it had been quite difficult, for example, for the boroughs to administer separately child welfare services and the counties to administer school health services. Under the new arrangement, this type of separation no longer existed.

Hence, most of the general practitioners had welcomed the 1948 changes on professional grounds. In addition, owing to their larger resources, the county councils were able to support more complete medical staffs than the individual boroughs had been, and this, too, met with the favor of the doctors. Finally, the 1948 arrangements were tremendously more convenient from an administrative standpoint. Whereas previously the doctors had bounced back and forth between the first-tier and the second-tier authorities, their major contacts were now restricted to the first-tier authorities alone.

In commenting on the development of England's public health and welfare services, Professor D. V. Donnison of the University of London has noted that since these services first began, "the authorities responsible for them have continually grown larger and fewer."[16] The doctors within London County had noted this trend with satisfaction, and they had no desire to see it reversed.

This was the basis for their alarm when they discovered that the

[16] Donnison, *Health, Welfare and Democracy,* p. 5. Other sources utilized for general background on the Health Services were *Health Services in Britain* (Central Office of Information Reference Pamphlet No. 20, HMSO, 1962) and *The British Medical Association and the National Health Service* (British Medical Association, September 1961).

Royal Commission was considering that the personal health services should be given back to the new Greater London Boroughs as part of a "revitalization" of second-tier government. In effect, the doctors in central London felt that the Commission, in its attempts to restore the "health of local government," would jeopardize the health of the Public Health Service, and they looked at such a development as a completely retrograde step.

Their position on this issue could hardly have been more clear-cut. Their spokesman before the Royal Commission was the Local Medical Committee for the County of London, and in both its written and its oral testimony, this group made it perfectly clear that it would view any attempts to restore powers to the second-tier authorities with grave misgivings, to say the least:

> [We] regard local government as something for the benefit of the governed, and not chiefly as either an occupation or a stimulus for the governors. . . . [Our] sole concern is to secure an administrative framework which shall ensure the best service for the patients in the area. . . . It is our experience having worked with the metropolitan borough councils before 1948, and with the County Council since 1948, that it would be a pity if the fragmentation of services that existed then should come back now.

At a later date in the proceedings, the Local Medical Committee was to state this same position in even stronger terms:

> We think the [Royal] Commission's opinion appears to ignore what the Londoner wants in local government. They have planned for him a collection of boroughs where everyone could take part in local politics. This may have been appropriate for a Greek City-State in 500 B.C.; but it is not therefore suitable for 20th century London.[17]

As was the case with the teachers, however, the London Local Medical Committee was not the only spokesman for the medical pro-

---

[17] Royal Commission, *Written Evidence,* V, 195; *Minutes of Oral Evidence,* No. 53, pp. 2,243-2,245; Statement of Local Medical Committee for the County of London on "Local Government in Greater London" (Tavistock House, March 1, 1961), p. 2.

fession in the metropolitan area, and, as subsequent testimony from other bodies began to pour into the Royal Commission, the underlying parallels between the doctors and the educators became even more apparent.

The Essex County Local Medical Committee backed the existing arrangement down the line, concluding that it had "always regarded the present basis of administration of the Health Services as being very satisfactory from the General Practitioners' point of view."[18] Similarly, the Royal College of Midwives supported the concept of the prevailing status quo, holding that the 1948 reallocation of services had been "beneficial" and that, in its opinion, "the minimum population of a Local Health Authority responsible for the domiciliary midwifery service should be 200,000 and the maximum 400,000."[19]

On the other hand, the District Medical Officers of Health Committee, representing those local medical officers who had elected to remain with the second-tier authorities following the authorities' 1948 downgrading, had completely different ideas on this question. This group held that "the main defects in the administration of the health services arise from the fact that a county is an entirely unsuitable unit for this purpose." As one example of this, the Committee argued that the London County Council had divided its Health Service into nine separate geographical divisions, and yet there still remained a "lack of local knowledge [which] is a defect of utmost importance in dealing with the 'personal health services.' "

In the opinion of this group, the size of the ideal second-tier authority could range from 60,000 to 200,000, and in no case should it exceed the latter figure. As a result, they asserted that the counties should administer "those functions which are situated in a limited area but serve the whole area, e.g., sewage disposal." The second-tier authorities, on the other hand, should be responsible for all remaining services, including environmental health, school health, and mental health.[20]

---

18 Royal Commission, *Written Evidence*, V, 120.
19 *Ibid.*, pp. 373-374.
20 *Ibid.*, pp. 99-104.

Finally, there were representatives from Middlesex County, which by now was indicating a unique ability to develop its own approach to the problems of local government, irrespective of the particular issue under consideration. In its written evidence to the Royal Commission, the Middlesex Local Medical Committee proposed that personal medical services be taken away from both the first- and the second-tier authorities and placed under a number of "Personal Services Committees" that would consist of members appointed by representatives of the public and by the various professional medical interests in the area. In its oral testimony to the Commission, the Middlesex group clarified the implications of this concept by stating, "The largest population number that one particular committee can administer personally is about 200,000, so that in an area the size of Middlesex we should require probably something of the order of ten local committees."[21]

As was the case with the teachers and the other educational specialists, there was general agreement within the medical profession as to what was *not* wanted in the way of reform, but no so general agreement as to exactly what *was* wanted. And, as the testimony grew ever more voluminous, the Royal Commission found itself facing an increasingly more complicated task. In its attempts to establish new local borough units that might be able to balance off all these conflicting functional and value criteria, the Commission was fast running out of options, if not of optimum sizes.

The Architects and Planners

The reactions of the architects and planners toward reform involved both a concern to protect something they felt to be very good, and a desire to realize the maximum potentialities from something they felt might even be better.

The chief spokesman for the architectural profession is the Royal Institute of British Architects, and its concern over the something good

[21] *Ibid.*, p. 281.

involved a deep and genuine respect for the accomplishments of the London County Council's Architects Department.

During the postwar period, this department had enjoyed extremely gifted leadership under two of the most famous of contemporary British architects—Sir Robert Matthew and Leslie Martin.

The task which faced Matthew when he took over the LCC Architects Department in 1946 was nothing short of staggering. As regards schools alone, only 50 out of the 1,200 in use in London in 1939 had escaped damage during the war. Yet catastrophe can represent opportunity, as well as destruction; and just as the opportunity had arisen for a Sir Christopher Wren to help rebuild a fire-ravaged London some three hundred years earlier, the potentialities for a second rebuilding of London were apparent in 1946.

Under Matthew's leadership, the LCC Architects Department moved into this void, and much of its work, especially in schools and housing, is now accepted as being unparalleled in Europe, if not throughout the world. In the words of one architectural critic, "The London County Council, abetted by buzz bombs, has done splendid work in creating economical new neighborhoods throughout the city. . . . Roehampton, for instance, is probably the finest low-cost housing in the world. Other outstanding LCC developments are Loughborough Estate, Brixton, Ackroydan Estate, Wimbledon Parkside, Brandon Estate, Kennington Park [and] Hillington Road."[22]

The architectural and planning associations, tremendously impressed with these accomplishments, were extremely anxious that the LCC Architects Department should not be destroyed in any governmental reorganization. At the same time, however, they realized that all was not going well with much of the postwar rebuilding, especially in central London. Forceful support, especially political support from the central Government, for a meaningful comprehensive redevelopment of London's central area had been lacking, and as a result, much of London's past greatness (including many of Christopher Wren's own sparkling churches) was being buried in an avalanche of commercial construction.

[22] G. E. Kidder Smith, *The New Architecture of Europe* (London: Penguin Books, 1962), p. 36.

Actually, the London County Council did not really bear the major responsibility for this development, since it had neither the resources nor the powers (positive or negative) to cope with the situation.

As regards positive resources, the London County Council never possessed the finances necessary to handle a comprehensive redevelopment of London's central area. Real estate in central London, as in most of the world's great cities, commands extremely high prices. Because of its limited financial capabilities, the London County Council had not been able to authorize any comprehensive redevelopment schemes in central London for a great many years. Indeed, the last such scheme to be undertaken had been the Kingsway Plan in the year 1905.

In terms of negative controls, the Council's position was every bit as difficult. The major problem here involved an obscure provision of the 1947 Planning Acts known as the "Third Schedule." This schedule permits a developer to push up the density of a redeveloped building by 10 per cent over its previous cubic area, and it was added to the 1947 legislation to avoid clogging up administrative machinery with too many minor planning applications. In 1947, there had been a number of additional safeguards to prevent indiscriminate use of this schedule; however, the more recent difficulties arose from the fact that these safeguards had been removed, while the original schedule remained intact. As a result, developers had been enjoying a field day in terms of what they could get out of this 10-per-cent density factor, especially by redeveloping central London's outmoded Victorian structures, with their outlandishly high ceiling spaces. By judicious use of the "Third Schedule," these developers could squeeze not 10 per cent, but 40 per cent more office workers into their new commercial office buildings. The only way the London County Council could prevent this was by awarding fair compensation to these developers for not building such buildings, and once again, the Council did not have the financial resources to tackle such a task.

As a result, central London has become increasingly more crowded, with all the predictable consequences. Transportation facilities are strained to the breaking point and massive amounts of new housing are needed while increasingly less space is left for such housing, and so it goes.

It was this combination of circumstances that influenced the position that the Royal Institute of British Architects adopted toward reform. While believing that "the reform of local government in Greater London is long overdue," the RIBA wanted, above all else, to see a strong Greater London Council in planning, housing, and all other fields that related to its own professional interests. It concluded that in many respects the proposed new Greater London Council would be far too weak.

Specifically, the RIBA felt that it would be desirable if the Greater London Council's geographical jurisdiction were extended beyond the confines of the Green Belt to include the newly developing fringe areas of the growing outer London metropolis. Most of the major planning organizations, including the Town and Country Planning Association and the town Planning Institute, also supported this position.

In addition, the RIBA felt that the Greater London Council should have specific powers to handle comprehensive development schemes in the central area; that this central area should be treated as an organic unity (rather than being split up between the proposed Greater London Boroughs); that the Council should be responsible for over-all planning of highways, buildings, and traffic; that its housing powers should be increased; and that a transition program should be carefully planned in order to provide minimum staff disruption in the London County Council's Architects Department, while also enabling the new boroughs to build up their own departments (at the time of the issuance of the Royal Commission's report, only eleven second-tier authorities in Greater London had independent architects' departments).[23]

Thus, the position of the architects and planners differed somewhat from those of both the teachers and the doctors in that the architects and planners were generally favorable to the concept of reform and advanced specific suggestions as to how they felt this reform should be carried out. Once again, however, there was one striking similarity between the architects' and planners' position and the positions that had been advanced by many of the educational and medical groups.

[23] The Royal Institute of British Architects, "Statement on London Government" (mimeographed; February 7, 1962).

This similarity appeared in the form of specific reservations as to how much power the second-tier authorities—the proposed new Greater London Boroughs—should be allowed to exercise under any reorganization plan.

The Royal Commission had expressed concern over the failing health of the second-tier authorities, and the immediate reaction to this concern—as an abstraction—had been generally sympathetic.

Now, however, this abstraction was being reduced to its specific realities, and the support for any major revitalization of these second-tier authorities was fast evaporating. Everybody seemed to be in favor of the boroughs doing more, as long as it was the next fellow's function, and not their own, that was involved.

In its final report, the Royal Commission proposed major new powers for the Greater London Boroughs in four basic fields—educational administration, personal health services, housing, and welfare. Thus far, the first three of these fields were being picked off one by one. All that now remained was for the Welfare and Children's Service groups to move into the picture, and these "revitalized" new boroughs could be left to enjoy a healthy life of leisurely retirement, with virtually nothing to do.

Welfare and the Children's Service

Fortunately for the Greater London Boroughs, the Welfare and Children's Service interests did not move into this picture immediately, at least not in any great numbers. Only a scattering of such organizations offered testimony to the Royal Commission, although a majority of these did indicate satisfaction with the existing performance of the first-tier authorities. Only one voluntary welfare organization—the London Council of Social Service—felt the existing plethora of local authorities made over-all coordination difficult and led to "ignorance about the provisions for many services, both statutory and voluntary" on the part of the individual citizen.[24]

[24] Royal Commission, *Written Evidence*, V, 220.

The fact that no great outburst of testimony was offered to the Royal Commission was not to imply, however, that all the welfare associations would be willing to support any major delegation of responsibilities to the proposed Greater London Boroughs. Actually, the welfare interest groups were less well organized and less outspoken than the educational, medical and architectural groups. Indeed, the most powerful spokesmen here were the government officials—the judges of the Metropolitan Juvenile Courts, the case workers on social welfare staffs— who handle day-to-day welfare responsibilities. In initial testimony before the Royal Commission, such individuals did not appear to plead their case, but this does not mean that they were not concerned with the potential impact of governmental reform upon their own professional field of interest.

Their concern was not to emerge, however, until the other interest groups, especially the teachers, had raised their voice of protest to a pitch that produced specific results in the form of concrete concessions from the Government. Once this development had taken place, the welfare, and most particularly the Children's Service, groups, let it be known in no uncertain terms that concessions were desirable in their own professional field of interest as well.

Thus, the net sum of the over-all reaction to reform on the part of the professional associations who voiced major opinions on this matter could hardly have been classified as encouraging, either to the Royal Commission or to the new Greater London Boroughs that the Commission hoped to see established.

Many of these professional groups, after evaluating the potential impact of local governmental reorganization upon their own particular functional specialties, expressed considerable doubt as to the desirability of any major reform at all. The fact that these groups possessed widespread experience within their own spheres of interest gave their testimony a degree of authority that was bound to command considerable respect, and it would have been foolish, indeed, to dismiss these opinions as just so much talk.

On the contrary, not only did most of these associations advance their convictions with a high degree of sincerity, but many employed a high degree of logic as well. Not all objections to metropolitan reorganization proposals are lacking in merit, and this very easy assumption, which is especially prevalent in American circles, should be dismissed for the fallacy that it is. The majority of the professional associations opposed to the reorganization of London's government adopted this stance because they felt they had specific, and legitimate, interests to protect in the existing system.

Yet it must also be recognized that these groups, by their very nature, approached the general problem of metropolitan reform from the particular vantage point of their own specialized concerns. There was nothing secretive or illogical about this fact, since, by definition, the groups could hardly have been expected to do otherwise. As the Local Medical Committee had explained to the Royal Commission, its "sole concern" was to secure "an administrative framework which shall ensure the best service for the patients in the area." In a similar manner, the London Teachers' Association advised that its aim was "to ascertain, represent and support the collective opinions of its members in matters affecting education and the interests of teachers." The other professional groups employed similar logic in defining, and defending, their positions.

Since the great bulk of interest organizations had approached the question of London's metropolitan needs within the restricted confines of their own professional concerns, the central Government faced the task of weighing these individual concerns against the larger realities and total needs of the Greater London area.

This obviously was not going to be an easy job under the best of circumstances. It was destined to be further complicated, however, by still another series of considerations—the ideological attitudes of the political parties toward the subject of local governmental organization—which, paradoxically, helped to clarify the Labourites' opposition stance toward the new Greater London reform proposals, while further confusing the Conservative Government's approach toward the whole subject of London's governmental reform.

7. *The Ideological Stakes*

Ideological abstractions can play a vital role in politics, serving as catalysts to spark off new political movements and providing rationalizations to reinforce previously conceived power positions.

This rationalization process, in turn, can have a twofold impact on political coalitions. Coalitions will be strengthened in cases where internal ideological unanimity exists. Conversely, they will experience severe strains, perhaps even complete fragmentation, if subjected to serious ideological disagreements.

In London, one particular ideological issue served to reinforce the Labour Party's opposition to the reform program and to fragment the Conservative Party's support of this program. The issue in question was the Royal Commission's veneration of the "health" of local government.

The Commission's concern with the well-being of local self-government brought to the fore an abstraction that has been revered, and abused, as much as any other concept in the Anglo-American political liturgy. Nowhere in the world is a more lofty degree of homage paid to the local governmental ideal than in England and in the United States, and perhaps nowhere else is this local governmental ideal treated with more underlying ambivalence, if not hypocrisy.

Political leaders in both countries, virtually without exception and regardless of party, uphold the concept of local self-government as one of the basic cornerstones supporting the entire democratic way of life. In turn, repeated protestations of support solidify public acceptance of this concept to a point where it is virtual political suicide to deny its validity. Thus, in Britain, as Professor W. J. M. Mackenzie has noted, "local self-government is now part of the English Constitution,"[1] and in America, it is necessary to look no further than to the pages of *The Congressional Record* to appreciate the political magnetism of this abstraction.

Yet, in both England and the United States, the actual treatment of local governmental institutions is often at marked variance with this more lofty ideological mystique. Time and again, local governmental units in both countries have been stripped of significant powers, or subordinated to specialized functional groupings that could hardly be classified as meaningful political communities. London is certainly no exception in this regard. In the more than one hundred years of "reform" that preceded the Royal Commission's study, little attention was paid to the establishment of viable units of local self-government. Instead, the vitality of London's local institutions was more often than not sacrificed in favor of the larger functional demands of the metropolis. The result was a hodgepodge of specialized authorities that were virtually impossible to identify, much less control.

In order to understand why this was the case, it is necessary to know something about the political parties' attitudes toward the ambiguous abstractions of local autonomy and local self-government.

The Labour Position

Historically, the Labour Party has tended to emphasize local government's role as a medium for the provision of specific services, especially those that are responsive to the needs of a socialized state.

In its earliest manifestation, this Labour Party approach was known under the hardly euphonious description of "gas and water" Socialism. Its roots are to be found in the ideologies that were developed by the Fabian Society at the turn of the century.

---

[1] W. J. M. Mackenzie, *Theories of Local Government,* Greater London Papers, No. 2 (London School of Economics, 1961), p. 5.

In 1903, H. G. Wells delivered a famous critique on "Administrative Areas" (recently republished in the United States),[2] in which he stressed the need for a functional realignment of local governmental areas to provide for the more efficient discharge of various regional services. Following the issuance of Wells's critique, the Fabians began to refine this regional approach toward local government in a group of tracts that came to be known as the "New Heptarchy Series."[3] The title of the series was adopted from a recommendation in Tract 125, *Municipalization By Provinces,* which was written by William Sanders of the London County Council.

Sanders' major proposal, which was subsequently approved by the Fabians, called for a subdivision of the entire country into seven administrative regions, which would correspond roughly to the sevenfold "heptarchy" that had supposedly characterized the ancient Saxon kingdoms. The rationale for such a realignment was that of providing for the more efficient administration of three particular services—transit, electricity, and water. In Sanders' analysis:

> . . . it will be necessary, in endeavoring to devise new authorities and new areas for their administration, to drop the idea that they should remain municipal services in the narrowest sense of the term municipal. They should not become county, but provincial services. It may be that . . . it will be found that the best administrative areas will be created by following the Hegelian historical spiral until we arrive at a stage with regard to the division of the country vertically above the period of the Saxon Heptarchy, and make a halt there.[4]

Sanders' reference to the "Hegelian historical spiral" represents a not-so-veiled attempt to provide an "acceptable" Socialist rationalization for his major thesis. In effect, Sanders was arguing that it might be desirable to turn the clock back to ancient Saxon times in order to minister to the needs of a modern Socialist state.

---

[2] Maass, *Area and Power,* Appendix, pp. 206-221.

[3] The Fabian Society's early "New Heptarchy Series" consisted of four studies: Tract 119, *Public Control of Electric Power and Transit*; Tract 123, *The Revival of Agriculture: A Policy for Great Britain*; Tract 125, *Municipalization By Provinces*; and Tract 126, *The Abolition of the Poor Law Guardians.*

[4] W. Sanders, *Municipalization By Provinces,* Fabian Society Tract No. 125 (1905), p. 8.

This early Fabian emphasis on regionalism was subsequently mollified, if not totally modified, by a number of the more practical party activists, who felt they were on the verge of local political success and were not anxious to see local powers diminished and turned over to any new regional authorities, just as they were about to gain control of local councils. As G. H. D. Cole has explained, "The New Heptarchy plan . . . was strongly opposed by a number of Labour people active in local government who hoped speedily to capture the control of their own industrial towns, just as it was coming within their grasp. I remember F. W. Jowett, in particular, met every regionalist project with the conclusive comment, 'That'd be a drag on Bradford.' "[5]

Yet, while the early Labour Party pragmatists tended partially (although not completely) to minimize this early stream of Fabian regionalist thought, they wholeheartedly embraced the Fabians' emphasis on using local authorities as a means of providing a variety of socialist services at the municipal level.

In 1918, when the Party issued its famous postwar policy statement, *Labour and the New Social Order,* great stress was placed upon the potentialities of such an approach. In addition to calling for the municipalities to discharge such basic functions as education, sanitation, police, and welfare services, and municipal utilities, *Labour and the New Social Order* urged local councils to:

> . . . greatly extend their enterprises in housing and town planning, parks and public libraries, the provision of music and the organisation of popular recreation . . . the retailing of coal [and] other services of common utility, particularly the local supply of milk, where this is not already fully and satisfactorily organised in a co-operative society.[6]

This Labour Party emphasis on both regionalism and functionalism continued to crop up during the interwar period. To cite but one example (which is of considerable interest to the present study), in 1922 the London Labour Party, when testifying before the Ullswater Royal Commission, which was studying the reorganization of London's gov-

[5] G. D. H. Cole, *A History of the Labour Party from 1914* (London: Routledge & Kegan Paul Ltd., 1948), p. 455.

[6] *Labour and the New Social Order* (London: The Labour Party, 33 Eccleston Square, 1918), p. 15.

ernment, called for the establishment of a new "Regional Authority" to encompass no less than all the "Home Counties" (i.e., all of London, Middlesex, Surrey, Kent, Essex, and Hertfordshire counties). This London Regional Authority was to be locally elected on the basis of Parliamentary constituencies, and beneath it would be a second tier of minor local units which would retain their existing geographical boundaries.

The essence of this Labour plan was a delegation scheme, in which the Regional Authority would administer "large" or "major" services while the minor authorities would handle "local" aspects of these services. Nowhere was this delegation principle more obvious than in the sphere of education, where responsibilities between the two tiers would be split on the basis of "policy" versus "administrative" considerations. In this field, it would be the responsibility of the Regional Authority to prepare a general scheme of educational services for the entire London area, including common standards of training and a uniform system of salaries and staffing, while making suitable provisions for the delegation of local educational responsibilities to the second-tier authorities.[7]

This regional approach to Greater London's government was supported by a number of influential Labour Party witnesses who testified before the Ullswater Commission, including Sidney Webb and Herbert Morrison. The latter, who appeared as Secretary of the London Labour Party and as an alderman from the Metropolitan Borough of Hackney, called for the establishment of a common Central Authority "with a margin sufficiently large to prevent, if necessary, the further growth of Greater London outwards, except on town planning lines."[8] None of this advice was heeded, however, and in the end the efforts of the Ullswater Commission came to naught.

The issue of regionalism appeared again in 1942 when the Labour Party met to draw up a new postwar policy statement, *The Future of*

[7] "The Government of Greater London" (Resolution Passed at Special Conference of the London Labour Party, March 25, 1922), pp. 24-25.

[8] Morrison, quoted in Robson, *The Government and Misgovernment of London*, p. 306. See also Cmnd. 1830, *Report of the Royal Commission on London Government* (1923, reprinted 1958), pp. 47-49.

Local Government. This policy called for the central Government to establish suitable machinery to survey the country as a whole with the aim of creating a series of "Regional Authorities" and "Area Authorities" that would be "adequate for the performance of large-scale services."

In addition, the statement turned its attention to the problems of London's government, this time, however, with considerably less precision than had been shown by the London Labour Party in its 1922 stand. The simple facts of the matter were that, in 1922, the London County Council was controlled by the Conservative Party, and the London Labourites experienced few inhibitions in recommending a radical reorganization of Greater London's government. By 1942, however, the Council was under Labour control, and this time the Labour Party experienced considerably more difficulty in taking a firm stand on the same issue.

The statement did note the facts that "built-up London has spread far beyond the Administrative County" and that within Greater London "there are far too many separate authorities whose existence must involve much overlapping and render impossible any properly co-ordinated and efficient planning of the area." As regards potential solutions, however, the statement concluded rather feebly, "whether the position can be remedied without treating London and Greater London as a whole is doubtful. The problem bristles with difficulties, but if there is a general measure of agreement under the existing local authorities, we believe that a satisfactory solution can be found."[9]

Two developments converged at this time to indicate that the regional recommendations in *The Future of Local Government* would not, in fact, enjoy much of a future. The first was the vote on the statement itself. The Labour Party adopted this new regionalist policy only after a major clash, and by a majority of only 1,542,000 to 966,000 votes—a sufficiently large opposition to indicate that no serious action would be taken to implement the plan. The second was the use of Regional Commissions by the Coalition Government during the war to

[9] *The Future of Local Government* (London: The Labour Party, Transport House, 1944), p. 11.

administer such crucial responsibilities as the distribution of food. Although these wartime Regional Commissions were appointed by the central Government and were not directly comparable to the elective bodies advocated in the Labour Party policy statement, they had established a generally bad name for regionalism in Great Britain. When the public thought of this concept, it thought of stringent rationing and a host of other emergency measures that were not designed to engender popular support. For the time being at least, the concept of regional government was a dead issue in British politics, the victim of guilt by association.

Under the circumstances, it was not surprising that when the Labor Party won the General Election of 1945, it did not make any major efforts to establish a comprehensive regional governmental organization. What it did do, however, was to place key emphasis on the second aspect of the above policy statement—the utilization of governmental units that were "adequate for the performance of large-scale services." In so doing, the new Labour Government plunged into the creation of the Welfare State with a zeal that promised to denude the local governmental authorities, especially the second-tier units, of many of their traditional responsibilities. During the period 1945–1951, the Labour Government recast the following services in whole or in part: health and hospitals, town and country planning, police, fire, transport, electricity, gas, airports, water supply, public assistance, care of children, care of the aged, ambulances, land drainage, river pollution, and valuation for rating.

Although some of the local authorities were given new responsibilities—such as the first-tier counties and county boroughs, which became primary local planning units under the Town and Country Planning Act of 1947—the cumulative impact of this realignment was quite severe. The rough "rule of thumb" was that local units were allowed to retain only those services which they could administer with maximum efficiency, but were deprived of services that could be handled more efficiently by larger national authorities. Thus, "by the National Health Service Act, 1946, local authority hospitals were transferred to the Ministry of Health; by the Electricity Act, 1947, electricity supply was transferred from local authorities to the British Electricity Authority; by the Gas Act, 1948, the functions of local authorities relating to the manufacture and distribution of gas were transferred to Area Gas Boards; and by the Local Government Act, 1948, the valuation of property for rating purposes was transferred from local authorities to the Board of Inland Revenue. The functions acquired by local authorities during this period . . . were small in comparison with the losses sustained."[10]

Many Labour leaders, including Herbert Morrison, tended to view this development with considerable doubt, if not dismay,[11] and at a later date the Labour Party itself began to wonder whether it had not perhaps gone too far in emphasizing functional criteria over all other considerations. At its Annual Conference in 1955, the Party passed a resolution noting that while the loss of local governmental powers since 1945 was "perhaps necessary to achieve efficiency," such a development "had the effect which this Party views with misgiving of seriously diminishing the sphere of local democracy."[12] The resolution went on to call for a series of area conferences to study the problem, but little in the way of positive results followed in the wake of the 1955 Conference.

The simple fact is that over the years the Labour Party had come to view local government primarily in terms of its capacity to discharge particular functional services, rather than in terms of any theoretical abstractions regarding the "health" or autonomy of local government per se, especially if such concepts tended to conflict with the primary priority of functional efficiency. This pragmatic approach which the Labour Party had adopted toward the local governmental process was destined to play a crucial, twofold role in the struggle over the Greater London reform program.

First, it served as the ideological "glue"—the central unifying concept—that pulled together the many organizational elements within the

10 Golding, *Dictionary of Local Government,* p. 160.

11 Herbert Morrison, *How London Is Governed* (London: Peoples University Press, 1949), p. 106.

12 *Report of the 54th Annual Conference* (London: The Labour Party, Transport House, 1955), pp. 189-190.

Party into one monolithic opposition force. Note was made earlier of the fact that the London Labour Party (the Labour overseer of London and Middlesex counties) and Transport House (the national Labour Party headquarters) had not always seen eye-to-eye on all issues of London local politics. Actually, five distinct Labour Party elements shared responsibilities in the London area,[13] and each of these was destined in time to play an important part in opposing the Royal Commission's proposals.

Not all these Labour organizations were motivated by cynical concerns of power politics. Not all were anxious to block reform solely because of any adverse impact it might have had on the London Labour Party's power position in central London. To the contrary, many of these Labour Party spokesmen, especially at the Parliamentary level, opposed the Greater London plan not primarily because of its political implications, but rather because they felt it would affect adversely the performance of specific functional services. In short, the strong functional orientation that had dominated the Labour Party's approach toward local government from the beginning provided the central ideological rationalization that united the Party's various wings in opposition to the Royal Commission's proposals.

In addition to forging the Labour Party into a cohesive opposition force, this same functional orientation linked the Labour opposition to the various professional groups that also feared the potentially adverse impact of the reform program on their individual areas of specialized concern. Both the Labourites and these professional associations harbored an identical approach to the question of reform in terms of their emphasis on a functional evaluation of the Royal Commission's proposals to the exclusion of all other criteria. This functional emphasis meant that neither the Labour Party nor the professional groups could really understand, much less sympathize with, the Commission's attempt to revitalize the "health" of London's local borough units. As

[13] In addition to the national Labour Party and the London Labour Party, there were the Parliamentary Labour Party, with Michael Stewart, M.P., serving as shadow Minister of Housing and Local Government; the London County Council Labour Party under Sir Isaac Hayward, the LCC leader; and the constituent Labour parties that were to be found in the metropolitan boroughs and the other local authorities.

the London Local Medical Committee had testified, it regarded local government as "something for the benefit of the governed, and not chiefly as either an occupation or a stimulus for the governors." During a subsequent Parliamentary debate, Michael Stewart, Labour's highly able shadow Minister of Housing and Local Government, was to attack the Royal Commission's plan as a "disastrous and perverse approach" on this very same ground. As Stewart argued, "the services do not exist in order to give the Councillors something to do; the authorities exist in order to perform the services."[14]

Although Stewart later went on to assert that "we should all like to see more interest taken in local government," the burden of his argument really harked back to the paper on Administrative Areas that H. G. Wells had originally delivered to the Fabian Society in 1903. In Wells's view, ". . . the whole question of the administration of any affair turns upon the question, Which will give the maximum efficiency?"[15] As regards the field of local government, this consideration of functional efficiency had been the Labour Party's ruling passion and *idée fixe* from the very beginning. Whereas the Royal Commission had spoken of the twin criteria of "administrative efficiency" *and* the "health of representative government," the Commission's opponents embraced the first of these criteria and virtually ignored the second.

As a result, the Royal Commission and its Labourite-professional association opponents eventually ended up talking by each other, rather than to each other. As time passed, they began operating on completely different wave lengths. And the particular wave length the opposition forces utilized possessed the wonderful strategic attribute of internal cohesion, if not external comprehension.

The Conservative Position

Whereas the Labour Party was unified in its opposition to the Royal Commission plan, the Conservative Party was divided in its support of the plan. This division did not center upon the same anxiety that

[14] Hansard, House of Commons, DCLIV, No. 58 (19 February 1962), 72-73.
[15] H. G. Wells, quoted in Maass, *Area and Power,* pp. 207-208.

became the overriding obsession of the Labour Party—the concern over the functional efficiency of various services. Instead, the Conservative fissure grew out of a variation on a somewhat related theme that had wracked English governmental development for many centuries. This theme was the issue of centralization versus decentralization. The Conservative variation on this theme involved the idealization of the virtues of the small local governmental unit. In short, there were elements within the Conservative Party that did pay at least lip service to the Commission's concerns over the "health" of the second-tier local borough authorities.

As Redlich and Hirst explain in their classic study of English local government, "A fundamental antithesis between centralisation and 'autonomous' decentralisation runs through the whole history of English government and its organisation."[16] Originally, this centralist-localist tension was a private struggle between a wealthy nobility who controlled local property, and hence local government, and a central sovereign who attempted to subordinate this wealth to his own interests. The nobility, in effect, represented "the obstinate provincialism of the Anglo-Saxon," and the Crown "the centralising tendencies of the Norman tradition."[17] The course of time and events tended to change the nature of the participants on both sides of this struggle.

It was the great electoral reforms of 1832, 1867, and 1884 that transformed this centralist-localist tension in English politics, in theory if not in final fact. Whereas the French, under the influence of the Bonapartist tradition and the historic legacy of the *ancien régime,* settled this issue in favor of centralism, the English, under the influence of emerging popular local democracy, settled the issue in favor of localism. As more of the population became eligible to vote in local elections, the ideal of local self-government became part of the English Constitution.[18] It was the electoral reforms of the nineteenth century

[16] Redlich and Hirst, *History of Local Government,* p. 12.

[17] *Ibid.,* p. 13.

[18] Actually, however, many of the more practical manifestations of this ideal were ignored until very recently. Prior to the enactment of the Representation of the People Act in 1945, approximately one-third of the adult British population was still denied the municipal vote, and even today, only about one-third of the local government electorate actually exercises this vote. In large

that eventually resolved this issue of localism for the English. Hence the rationale for Professor Mackenzie's pithy observation that, while the concept of local self-government is now accepted as holy writ in English politics, "nothing was heard of this ancient doctrine of the Constitution until after 1832."[19]

Yet, while the abstraction of local self-government had assumed all the trappings of the English "way of life" by the end of the nineteenth century, the political parties, especially the Conservative Party, experienced considerable difficulty in translating this abstraction into practical realities. Over time, one stream of Conservative thought converted this idealization of local self-government into a glorification of the small community—the stronghold of self-reliance, self-discipline, and all the other proper Conservative virtues.

Thus, it was a Conservative Government that passed the Act of 1899, creating London's second-tier metropolitan boroughs. In the process Lord Salisbury, the Conservative Prime Minister, delivered his famous "suicide" speech,[20] in which he attacked the London County Council as being obsessed with "megalomania"—a passion for big things simply because they were big. Salisbury then called upon the county councillors to take the "suicidal (but) . . . wise, patriotic and enlightened" course of turning over some of the LCC powers to smaller boroughs operating in more limited jurisdictional areas.

Over time, Conservative emphasis on the supposed virtues of the small local governmental unit came to occupy a central place in Party ritual. The cover of *The Councillor,* the party's monthly local govern-

---

part, this is true because many areas (especially rural areas) do not have contested elections, which certainly represent an essential prerequisite for a viable system of local democracy (See H. Whalen, "Democracy and Local Government," *Canadian Public Administration,* Vol. III, No. 1 [March 1960], 7). Despite this fact, the glorification of the ideal of local self-democracy occupies a central position in the modern English political tradition, as it does in our own tradition. For an interesting insight into some of the Anglo-American and continental differences in this regard, see the debates between Mr. Keith Panter-Brick, Dr. Leo Moulin, and Prof. Georges Langrod in *Public Administration,* 31 (1953), 25-34, 344-348, and 32 (1954), 433-440.

19 Mackenzie, *Theories,* p. 7.

20 The speech is described in detail by A. G. Gardiner in *John Benn and the Reform Movement* (London: Ernest Benn Ltd., 1925), pp. 249-251.

ment pamphlet, bristled with Disraeli's stern admonition, "Centralisation is the Death Blow of Freedom," and such eloquent Conservative statesmen as Sir Winston Churchill assured the electorate that:

> Our guiding aim will be to stimulate rather than strangle, to liberate rather than hobble, all the energies of local government, and to raise instead of diminishing the dignity and importance of the immense mass of voluntary services now given to our local institutions.[21]

In turn, when the Party issued official election directives, this fixation on the values of "localized" local government was given full play:

> The governing principle of Conservative and Unionist policy is that local government should be local, and that it should be government. That is to say, first, its units must remain within easy reach of the citizens who are affected by it. Second, these units must have adequate powers of *independent* executive action. . . . Our view is therefore in sharpest contrast with that of the Socialists.[22]

The trouble with this Conservative localist mystique was that the Party's actions were often at considerable odds with its ideological aspirations. Thus, for example, it was a Conservative minister in a Conservative interwar Government, Neville Chamberlain, who inaugurated the series of reforms in the 1930's (discussed in Chapter 4) which resulted in the consolidation and amalgamation of hundreds of England's smaller urban and rural districts into a larger and more rational local governmental structure. Again, it was a Conservative minister in the wartime Coalition Government, R. A. Butler, who authored the Education Act of 1944 that all but divested the smaller second-tier units of their prior educational responsibilities. And still again, it was a Conservative minister in a postwar Conservative Gov-

[21] Churchill, "The Conservative Aim," *Local Government Campaign Notes,* Conservative and Unionist Central Office, No. 1, (20 April 1950).

[22] *Local Government Elections Handbook* (London: Conservative and Unionist Central Office, Spring 1949), p. 2.

ernment, Henry Brooke,[23] who advised Parliament in 1957 that the assets of the New Towns would be transferred to a new central Commission (rather than to the local authorities themselves, as previously contemplated), and that the possibility of shifting to local government some of the taxes collected by the national Government was "not a prospect which attracts one."[24]

The simple point is that the Conservative Party's more pious pronouncements regarding local autonomy and the virtues of the small local community did not always coincide with its concrete actions. The difficulties the Party experienced in this regard stemmed from the fact that it had developed two internal ideologies regarding local government rather than one. One stream of Conservative thought tended to sing the praises of the small local governmental unit as an end in itself. The other stream of thought attempted to adjust this localist ideology to the realities of a twentieth-century environment.

This ideological dichotomy within the ranks of Conservatism had a dual impact on the struggle over London's governmental reform.

First, it enabled those Party leaders who were opposed to this reform to rationalize their opposition position within the broad framework of acceptable Conservative doctrine. Specifically, many Conservative leaders in the suburban powerhouse of Surrey County (and to a lesser extent Kent County) took an exceedingly dim view of the Royal Commission's plan because it called for the transfer of the wealthy metropolitan fringe areas of their counties to the proposed new Greater London Council. These leaders attacked the Royal Commission's plan, however, with the rationale that this proposed Greater London Council was "too big" to qualify as a local government. In the words

[23] The Brooke speech to Parliament represents a classic example of the dualistic ambivalence of Conservative dogma regarding local government. In the very same speech in which he rejected local control of the New Town assets and rejected the prospects of increasing local revenues by means of tax reallocations, Mr. Brooke called for "a strong and independent local government system. Freely-elected local authorities are an essential part of British democracy and a safeguard that we should treasure against the excessive use of central power. . . . Local government should as far as possible be truly local. . . . Local government means, or should mean, local responsibility."

[24] Hansard, House of Commons, DLXXIV (29 July 1957), 910-926.

of one of the Surrey County opposition pamphlets, under the Royal Commission's plan local government would become "very much less local. Indeed, in the case of the Greater London Council it would cease to be local government at all."[25] Thus it was a paradox of the reform program that, whereas the Labourites attacked the Greater London Boroughs as being too small for the efficient administration of services, dissident Conservatives attacked the Greater London Council as being too big for the health of local government. Paradox or not, however, these ideological arguments tended to forge the Labourites and the Conservative dissidents into a unified opposition force.

The second major impact of the ambivalent Conservative ideology toward local government related to the limitations it placed upon the central Government in its attempts to implement the Royal Commission's plan. Numerous examples can be cited in this regard, but only one illustration is necessary to indicate the basic thrust of this problem.

As was noted in the introductory chronological summary (Chapter 2), the Royal Commission originally recommended that the educational services should be divided between the Greater London Council and the Greater London Boroughs. This proposal raised a storm of protest, especially from the London Teachers' Association, that any such division would have a disastrous impact on the educational services. In considering alternative approaches to this problem, the Conservative Government could conceivably have done one of two things—either transfer all educational responsibilities to the Greater London Boroughs, or transfer all responsibilities to the Greater London Council. In terms of acceptable Conservative dogma, however, the second alternative was no alternative at all. It ran too deeply against the grain of the Conservative localist mystique to transfer all responsibility for local educational services to a Council which encompassed a seven-hundred-odd square-mile area and embraced over eight million people. Such an alternative was simply beyond the bounds of permissible Conservative practice, especially in light of the fact that the Surrey and Kent leaders

[25] Surrey County Council, *Surrey's Opposition to the Greater London Plan* (pamphlet, undated).

were already charging that the Greater London Council was too big and too powerful.

As a result, the educational responsibilities were transferred to the boroughs (with special treatment for a central area considerably smaller than that of the Greater London Council), with all the political consequences that followed. In order to make this transfer work, the Conservative Government felt it would be necessary to enlarge the size of the boroughs somewhat, and as soon as this was done, a new wave of protest broke out among the second-tier authorities and the dissident Conservatives who now claimed that the boroughs were going to be too big.

Because the Conservative Party's ideology toward local government was ambivalent, this ideology played a crucial role in limiting the Conservatives' effectiveness as the proponents of reform.

The Liberal Position

There are two other political parties—the Liberals and the Communists—that are active in London local politics, and although they represent something of a minority influence, their attitudes toward local governmental reform are worthy of brief consideration, if only because these attitudes point up the wild inconsistencies that exist on this subject.

During the reform contest, the Liberal Party faced the future with cautiously optimistic, if still uncertain, political expectations. What was certain was that the Liberals were hungry, and they were looking to the field of local government as the initial stepping-stone to national power.

Although the Liberals held only seven seats in the House of Commons, they occupied some 1,657 seats on local councils in England and Wales. While the Party hoped gradually to increase its numbers in Commons, it was looking to the arena of local government for its most spectacular and immediate gains. As a result, the Liberals were devoting more hard thought to the question of local governmental reform than any other British party.

The first major indication of this new Liberal interest in local government was to be found in "The Liberal Manifesto," issued shortly before the 1959 General Election. At this time, the Party called for the restoration of the powers which the local authorities had lost to the central Government and to the national corporations; the taxation of land values to widen the field from which local authorities could derive their income; the abolition of de-rating; the admission of the press to council meetings; increased expenditures on education; a doubling of expenditures on road construction; and a host of similar measures.[26]

"The Liberal Manifesto" was primarily an election document, however, and not until the appearance of a second Party discussion report, "Local Government," prepared under the chairmanship of Mr. Bryan Keith-Lucas of Nuffield College, Oxford, did the full scope of the Liberals' rethinking of local government policy became apparent.

This report proposed that all the major "conurbations" (i.e., major cities) in England should be reorganized into independent "Urban Counties," and that the existing welter of second-tier authorities under these "Urban Counties" should be amalgamated into an identifiable groups of most-purpose "City Boroughs." The report also recommended a simplification of local government structure outside the new "Urban Counties," plus a separate plan of local administration for Wales. In addition, it called for the consideration of a new group of "Urban Parishes" under the "City Boroughs," in those cases where recognizable subcommunities exist in large cities, to provide services beyond those already provided by other councils, and to preserve some semblance of local subcommunity identity for urban residents.[27]

Thus, the Liberals were laying the groundwork for what might be a highly significant approach toward local governmental reform. The highly theoretical orientation in this Liberal Party approach did not imply, however, that the Party viewed local government in a political vacuum. In the case of London, the Liberals possessed a very practical realization that any local reorganization such as that proposed by the

[26] Golding, *Local Government*, p. 221.

[27] *Local Government, A Report to the Liberal Party*, May 1962 (London: Liberal Publications Department, September 1962). The Party approved the essence of these recommendations on November 24, 1962.

Royal Commission represented not only change but also political opportunity. This fact was not forgotten in the Party's later response to the Greater London plan.

The Communist Party

The Communist Party's testimony before the Royal Commission seemed to surprise everyone, including the Commissioners themselves.

"Curiously enough," the Commission noted in commenting upon this testimony, "the views of this Party were up to a point practically identical with those of the London Municipal Society."[28] This parallel between the Communists and the London Conservatives' spokesman related to the fact that both groups emphasized the primacy of the smallest units of local government over all other considerations, and both groups argued for a revitalization of the second-tier authorities.

Yet, while the London Municipal Society represented but one of a variety of Conservative positions on this question, the Communists were advocating the heart and soul of their central ideology. The Party cell, itself, stands as the most striking testimony of the high value which the Communists place upon the small organizational unit. As the Royal Commission went on to note, this Communist bias toward the virtues of the small second-tier authority actually represented nothing more than a practical extension of "the classical form of organisation advocated by the Communist Party, who seem to find it easier to dominate a small group, than to obtain political influence through the ballot box over a larger authority."[29]

In this manner, the Communists first approached the proposed reform program in terms of their own narrow interests, and then proceeded to justify their stance by means of broad ideological abstractions that lent credence to their preconceived position. Similarly, both the Labourites and the Liberals were able to adopt consistent ideologies that added great strength to their positions on reform.

[28] Rpt., Cmnd. 1164, p. 57.
[29] *Ibid.*

The Conservatives, however, were faced with a much more difficult dilemma. Rather than meshing neatly with the Royal Commission's plan, their historic "localist" mystique (i.e., the glorification of the virtues of the small local community) cut directly against the grain of the proposed Greater London Council that was designated to serve as the new local authority for no less than eight million Londoners. On the other hand, the more practical advocates of the Conservative reform tradition (i.e., the Chamberlain-Butler-Brooke school) veered away rather sharply from much of this localist ideology.

Thus, whereas the Labourites (and others) were able to agree on a consistent ideological stance that tended to unify the various elements of the Party, the Conservatives were forced to wrestle with a much more amorphous and dualistic heritage, which tended to fragment the Party. The fact that the Labour Party was able to achieve such a high degree of ideological cohesion, while the Conservatives were much more deeply split in their attitudes toward reform, was destined to play a significant role in shaping the course of the struggle that lay ahead.

8. The "Missing" Stakes

Two American political scientists have recently made observations on the dynamics of political conflict that are particularly relevant to the Greater London reform contest.

The first, Professor E. E. Schattschneider, advises watching the size of the crowd in order to understand the development of the battle. "The outcome of every conflict is determined by the *extent* to which the audience becomes involved in it."[1] The second, Professor James S. Coleman, examines some of the fundamental transformations that take place during the course of conflict. The translation of specific issues into general issues and of initial disagreement into subsequent antagonism are among the key transformations that Coleman identifies.[2]

Each of these observations sheds light on a fundamental, if somewhat paradoxical, truth of politics. The apathetic spectator—the nonparticipant—can play a crucial role in shaping the end result of any political contest. As Schattschneider explains, if these nonparticipants can be induced to enter the fray, they can exercise a profound impact in tipping the balance of power one way or the other. This is especially true, of course, in electoral contests. The Conservatives, for example, had a 1.5 million margin over Labour in the 1959 British General Election, while the Democrats had only a 120,000 margin over the Republicans in the

[1] E. E. Schattschneider, *The Semisovereign People* (New York: Holt, Rinehart & Winston, 1960), p. 2.
[2] James S. Coleman, *Community Conflict* (Glencoe: The Free Press, 1957), p. 10.

1960 American Presidential election. Despite these numerical disparities, the final results could have been quite different in both elections if the 21.3 per cent of the nonvoting British electorate, or the 35.5 per cent of the nonvoting American electorate, had actually exercised its franchise. Hence the rationale for Schattschneider's second observation, "The most important strategy of politics is concerned with the scope of the conflict."[3]

The Coleman analysis, in turn, indicates one of the major ways in which the scope of conflict can be enlarged—by transforming specifics into broad-based generalities. One of the simplest means of doing this is to convert technical issues into emotional issues. In the process, initial disagreement usually degenerates into antagonism. "Sometimes consciously, often unconsciously, the opposing forces attempt to reach new people through this means, drawing more and more of the community to their side by creating personal hostility to the opponent."[4]

This strategy is especially appealing to those who are losing the battle at any given point, since it is in their interest to woo new participants into the arena in the hope of upsetting the prevailing status quo. Such a strategy became extremely important in Greater London, and it is analyzed in considerable detail in the next section of this study. Before any such analysis can be undertaken, however, it is necessary to know who was missing, as well as who was present and accounted for, at the time the Greater London contest began to unfold.

The study to date has indicated that three major groups—the political parties, the local authorities, and a variety of professional associations —were ready to do battle over the proposed Greater London Plan. Each of these groups harbored certain interests, ideologies, and objectives that were worth protecting, or advancing, through the defeat, or the realization, of this plan.

American experience in such cities as St. Louis, Cleveland, and Miami would tend to indicate that there are many other interests, animated by motives beyond those already identified in London, that are ready to struggle over the issue of metropolitan governmental

[3] Schattschneider, *Semisovereign People*, p. 3.
[4] Coleman, *Community Conflict*, p. 11.

reform.[5] On the basis of such American experience, it would seem that a number of potential participants had not as yet declared themselves on the Greater London Plan.

The primary explanation for this is to be found in a variety of fundamental environmental and procedural factors that distinguish London from the typical American city. Such factors should not be ignored, however, simply because they are different. In any comparative analysis, differences can be as significant as similarities. Indeed, they can tell us a great deal about the most important aspects of the political process. Hence, it is certainly worth considering what motives, and what participants, were missing in London, compared with those which have been found in the United States.

Although it is possible to identify these missing motives under a wide variety of classifications, they can be summarized quite readily in terms of two basic headings—economic stakes and public stakes.

As is the case with any such summary appraisal, each of these headings contains a host of underlying cross-currents that are worth evaluating in some further depth.

The Economic Stakes

Efficiency *and* economy represent two of the cornerstone arguments used by the proponents (and often by the opponents) of metropolitan reform schemes in the United States.[6] Yet, while the Royal Commission paid due homage to the first of these criteria, it virtually

[5] An Advisory Commission on Intergovernmental Relations study, for example, lists the following groups as generally favoring, or commonly opposing, metropolitan reform programs: *Favoring*—metropolitan newspapers; League of Women Voters; central city commercial and real estate interests; banks; radio and television stations; academic groups; utilities; manufacturing industries; civic research agencies; central city officials and homeowners. *Opposing*—farmers and rural homeowners; county and fringe-area local government officials and employees; suburban newspapers; and suburban commercial interests (Advisory Commission on Intergovernmental Relations Report M-15 [May 1962], p. 13).

[6] The Advisory Commission on Intergovernmental Relations study mentioned in note 5 indicated that the financial implications of reform plans were an important basis for opposition arguments in sixteen of the eighteen cities investigated (*ibid.*, p. 9).

subordinated all considerations of economy to an entirely different second criterion—the health of local government.

In its 257-page report, the Commission devoted only one chapter, eight and one-half pages in length, to the question of local government finance, and at no point did it advance any real claims that its proposed reorganization plan would result in major savings for the ratepayers (i.e., taxpayers) of Greater London.[7] What factors prompted the Commission to so underplay this consideration of economy?

Obviously, a number of influences were at work here, but two basic assumptions the Commission made regarding finances stand out as being of particular importance.

The first of these was the belief that Greater London, taken as a whole, was wealthy enough to handle the costs of any reasonable local governmental burden it might be required to bear. Here is an area that contains one-third of the total ratable value of all property in England. In the Commission's eyes, there was no question that this area could carry its fair share of local governmental costs. The only real problem the Commission felt it faced with regard to finances was the question of the way in which financial resources and burdens should be distributed among the local governmental units that it recommended in its reorganization plan.

Here the Commission made its second assumption, and it is at this point that one finds a very fundamental difference between local government finance as practiced in London and local government finance as practiced in the United States. What the Commission assumed in this second instance was that some type of selective scheme of rate equalization, similar to that which had been used in London County for a great many years, could be applied throughout the new Greater London Council area as a whole.

The history of rate equalization in London County goes back almost a century, to the time the Metropolitan Common Poor Fund was introduced in 1867. Although there have been many variations in the

[7] Rpt., Cmnd. 1164, Chapter XVIII. The Commission also included some financial data in two appendixes—the first, a listing of some financial statistics on the local authorities in the area, and the second, a memo on the effect of the proposals on rate burdens in Greater London.

specific formulas utilized since that time, the basic principle underlying the different equalization schemes has remained intact. The objective of the rate equalization idea was to have all the twenty-nine second-tier units in London County (i.e., the twenty-eight metropolitan boroughs plus the City Corporation) pool a percentage of their expenditures and then reallocate this pool between themselves in order to achieve a more equitable uniformity in the individual rate burden that each unit was forced to levy on its own ratepayers. In short, through the pooling process, the richer boroughs helped the poorer boroughs pay for their costs of local government. Under the revised equalization scheme, approved by the Government in 1959, 70 per cent of the expenditure incurred for their own purposes by these boroughs was pooled,[8] with this pooled expenditure being met by ratable contributions levied over the entire area of London County.[9]

While the Royal Commission did not propose a specific rate equalization formula for the new Greater London Boroughs, it did provide a general outline of a scheme that would:

> provide that Boroughs whose rates, without any form of equalisation, would be below a certain minimum would contribute the amounts required to bring their rates [up] to this minimum ... while ... Boroughs whose rates without equalisation would be above a certain maximum would receive contributions sufficient to reduce their rates to this maximum. ...

The Commission then suggested, ". . . on the limited information available to us," that this minimum-maximum rate variation should not exceed five shillings (70 cents) for each pound ($2.80) of assessed valuation in each of the proposed new boroughs in the Greater London Council area.[10]

Since the Commission assumed that some general type of rate

[8] In addition to receipts from this pool, the poorer metropolitan boroughs received direct help from the central Government in the form of rate deficiency grants.

[9] Golding, *Local Government.*

[10] Rpt., Cmnd. 1164, p. 245. The Commission actually suggested that a balance could be achieved by a minimum level of 16 shillings ($2.24) and a maximum level of about 21 shillings ($2.94) for each pound ($2.80) of assessed valuation.

equalization plan could be applied to each of the new Greater London Boroughs, it felt that its task of making any detailed analyses of the individual needs and financial resources of these proposed new boroughs was reduced considerably. The result was that the Commission tended to minimize the economic stakes of reorganization throughout its study, although it did harbor the general hope that a more efficient coordination of London's government would result in the realization of some meaningful, if unspecified, economies.

Yet the fact that the Commission minimized the economic aspects of reorganization does not imply that such considerations were non-existent.

To the contrary, the rate-equalization idea that was used within London County represented a rather unique, if not revolutionary, approach to local government finance as practiced throughout the remainder of the Greater London area, and throughout the remainder of England as well. Certainly not all local ratepayers are enchanted with the idea of bearing the costs of services for their more distant neighbors. The history of political conflict in England, in the United States, and anywhere else for that matter, indicates that economic altruism is not an overriding virtue of political man.

Under the circumstances, one certainly might have expected to see a variety of local ratepayers' and business-oriented interests warn the Commission against the "dangers" of extending any such radical equalization approach to local government finance beyond the confines of London County and into the outer fringes of the proposed new Greater London Council area, which would encompass, among other things, themselves.

The simple facts of the matter are, however, that no such interest groups appeared. The most obvious groups that might have been expected to voice an opinion on the issue of local government finance declined to offer any testimony to the Royal Commission at all, even after being formally invited to do so.

In sum total, only nine local ratepayers' associations throughout Greater London offered any written evidence to the Commission, and none of these followed up this evidence with any oral testimony.

Of these nine groups, six were very small organizations located on the far fringes of the Review Area.[11] The seventh group was the Federation of Ratepayer and Kindred Associations of Middlesex (FORAM), which represented the large Middlesex second-tier authorities. This group came up with the understandable concept (in terms of the Middlesex situation) that all the county councils should be abolished entirely and replaced by one-tier "all-purpose" authorities (i.e., county boroughs). The final two associations to offer written evidence to the Commission represented smaller Middlesex boroughs, each of which objected strongly to this FORAM proposal.[12]

Certainly more significant, in terms of potential power and prestige, were the groups who did not, rather than who did, appear before the Commission. The following organizations declined a direct invitation to offer any testimony to the Royal Commission at all, either written or oral: The Association of British Chambers of Commerce, the Federation of British Industries, the Holborn Chamber of Commerce, the London Chamber of Commerce, the National Federation of Property Owners, the National Union of Ratepayers' Associations, and the Westminster Chamber of Commerce.

In addition to the nine local ratepayers' associations noted above, only three metropolitan borough chambers of commerce—those of St. Marylebone, St. Pancras, and Stepney—offered written evidence to the Commission, and only one major business organization—the National Chamber of Trade: Greater London Area Council—presented both written and oral testimony.[13]

With the exception of the above groups, the Commission's study apparently did not possess enough of a political, or an economic, kick to excite the imagination of either the ratepayers in general, or the businessmen in particular, in the Greater London area.

As a result, the only major economic considerations that did create any controversy growing out of the Commission's recommendations

---

[11] Each of the six groups argued against any incorporation of its localities into Greater London at all, primarily on the grounds that such a move would destroy the virtues of the "unspoiled" village life the groups presently enjoyed.

[12] R. C., *Written Evidence*, V, 121-122.

[13] *Ibid.*, p. 324.

were those relating to the separation of the metropolitan fringes of Surrey, Essex, Kent, and Hertfordshire from the rest of these counties, in order to incorporate these severed fringes under the proposed new Greater London Council.

The potential losses to these four counties as a result of this proposal were considerable:

	Loss in Population	Loss in Ratable Value	Loss in Area
Surrey	62.6%	66.1%	22.4%
Essex	54.5	58.6	7.4
Kent	30.4	33.0	5.6
Hertfordshire	9.7	10.0	2.3

The Commission recognized the severity of this recommendation but felt that these counties would still be financially viable despite the losses. In order to ease the shock, however, the Commission did suggest that some transitional arrangement should be made whereby the former "lost boroughs" would make financial contributions to their truncated county parents for a limited period of time.[14]

The net result of the Commission's economic proposals, then, was quite simply to reinforce further the already apparent hostility of the first-tier counties to the reorganization plan. The counties were singled out as being the big potential losers from reform, not only politically, but economically as well.

With the exception of the embattled counties, no other groups seemed to be overly concerned with the economic impact of the Royal Commission's plan. In effect, economic considerations had a nonexistent influence in terms of activating either further support for, or opposition to, the reorganization program.

The Public Stakes

While it is difficult to account for this all-pervading silence in the economic area, several explanations can be advanced that help to

[14] Rpt., Cmnd. 1164, pp. 246-247.

explain some of the general public apathy that greeted the Royal Commission's study.

At the outset, it must be noted that certain public groups did display an active interest in the London reform program. The two most notable examples were local residents' associations and academic spokesmen. Some sixteen residents' associations offered evidence to the Commission, in almost all cases on their own initiative and without direct Commission invitation. In addition, the Commission invited all the major universities in England to assist in its study, and four responded, one of them—the London School of Economics and Political Science —providing a massive amount of written evidence.

Hence, a limited number of similarities such as these was evident in the public response to the London plan as compared with the public response that has greeted metropolitan reform proposals in the United States. On the whole, however, the public response in London was quite dissimilar from that which has taken place in the typical American city on this issue. At least two considerations—the first environmental and the second, procedural—can be utilized to explain partially why this was the case.

As regards environmental factors, a number of considerations in London tended to neutralize the impact of key groups whose counterparts have been quite vocal on the issue of metropolitan reform in America. Significantly, for example, racial tensions, which have often played havoc with this issue in the United States, were not of any major consequence in shaping the response to the London plan. It is impossible to obtain precise figures in this regard, but experts on the subject advise that the Negro community makes up no more than 3 per cent of the total Greater London population. What is certain is that this community is not large enough to play a crucial role in Greater London politics.

Similarly, issues involving ethnic and religious groups are not a significant factor in London local politics and, with the exception of the denominational school question, such issues were totally absent from the London reform contest.

Another key environmental difference between London and the

American city is to be found in the utilization of the "political spokes-men" principle in English politics. In many American cities, for example, labor unions have played an active role in metropolitan reform contests, usually on the opposition side. In London, no such open union activity was evident. The Trades Union Congress, for instance, was another in the long list of organizations that declined to offer any testimony to the Royal Commission, even after being specifically invited to do so. The apparent reason for this was to be found in the fact that the political parties—in this case the London Labour Party—with their affiliated union membership, served as the unions' spokesmen on local issues of this type.

These, then, are some of the environmental considerations that help to explain a certain degree of the disparity between the experience of London and that of American cities.

A basic procedural consideration can also be utilized as a possible explanation of such disparity. The specific consideration here is the very fundamental difference in the method of approval of metropolitan reorganization proposals. In the United States, this issue is generally decided by public referendum. In England, on the other hand, the issue is resolved by a higher authority—the central Government and the Parliament. In actual practice, a Royal Commission is not created to prepare a report for the general public, although its findings hopefully do perform a public education role through their later dissemination. Instead, a Royal Commission is a body whose members are appointed by the Crown (on behalf of the Government) to inquire into matters of general legislative importance. In effect, a Royal Commission's role is similar to, though presumably it has less partisan implications than, that of the Congressional investigating committee in the United States.

How much of an impact this very basic procedural difference may have contributed to general public disinterest in the Royal Commission's study is, of course, a matter of speculation, but presumably this factor was of considerable importance.

As a result, it is difficult to evaluate the significance of the fact that, in response to a general press release and advertisement of its interest in obtaining public comments on the reorganization of London's government, the Commission received a total of 174 individual communications on this issue. Was a response of 174 people out of the more than eight million inhabitants of Greater London significant, or was it not?

Those who emphasize the group approach to politics might well hold that such a response was all that could be expected—that we look to the individual to express himself through the larger association on an organizational issue of this type. If this is the case, the question remains as to what significant public groups—besides the business, labor, racial, religious, ethnic, *et al.* associations already noted—failed to make any commitment on the issue of London's reform?

At least three additional groups that might have been expected to take a stand on this issue failed to speak out with any real degree of conviction.

The first were the general civic organizations—the so-called "good government" groups—that often play a leading role in advocating governmental reforms in America. This omission was especially notable with respect to women's associations.

The League of Women Voters, for example, has rarely failed to show an active interest in the question of local reform in the United States. In London, however, there was widespread apathy among somewhat comparable organizations. The Commission invited testimony from the National Women Citizens' Association, but this group failed to respond with either written or oral evidence. The same lack of response characterized the position of the National Association of Women's Clubs, the National Union of Towns-women's Guilds, the Women's Voluntary Service, and a host of similar groups. For better or for worse, the distaff portion of the Greater London populace displayed no marked interest in the future shape of London's local government.

A second missing element was the organized local bureaucracies. Here there were two major groups—the National and Local Government Officers Association (NALGO) and the London County Council Staff Association. In one sense, "missing" is perhaps not the proper term to describe the nature of their response, since both groups were physically present to give written evidence and oral testimony to the

Commission. What was missing was that high intensity of feeling, predominantly negative in tone, which has characterized much of the response to change on the part of local bureaucracies in the United States.

The NALGO group was in a peculiar position in this regard, since a number of influences tended to neutralize its position. First, as a national body, it faced the difficult problem of reconciling any position it took on London's reorganization with the interests of its members outside the Greater London area. This tended to blunt the potency of any stand it might have taken on the issue. Second, its membership was drawn from both the first-tier county units and the second-tier local authorities, some of whom presumably stood to lose, and some to gain, from any potential reorganization plan. Third, the Association has traditionally viewed itself as a local government trade union, more interested in securing pragmatic benefits for its members than in taking policy positions on potentially controversial political issues. As its Constitution states, its major object is "to improve the conditions and protect the interests of [its] members by collective bargaining, agreement, withdrawal of labour, or otherwise."[15] Today, NALGO is, in actual fact, the seventh largest trade union in the country, with a total membership of just under 300,000 drawn from local governmental offices; New Towns; national health, electricity, gas, and water supply services; road passenger transport; and inland waterways. Finally, since the political aspects of any reorganization proposals cannot be completely ignored, the reform of London's government represented a potential opportunity of considerable attractiveness to NALGO. Specifically, the Association virtually blanketed the local government offices on both the first- and the second-tier authorities throughout England—with one very notable exception. The London County Council had its own staff organization, originally organized in 1909, some four years after NALGO was founded, and NALGO had long cast covetous eyes in the direction of the LCC. When the Royal Commission decided to recommend the abolition of the LCC in favor of a larger Greater London Council, NALGO was presented with a golden opportunity to organize the employees of this new Council.

[15] National and Local Government Officers Association, *Constitution*.

The second major employees' group, the London County Council Staff Association, was also a registered trade union, having a membership of some 10,000 administrative, professional, technical, and clerical personnel of the LCC.

The testimony which this body offered to the Royal Commission can only be classified as remarkable in terms of its restraint. The essence of the Association's position was an outline of the advantages of the "large-scale organization," with this argument, quite obviously, being designed to provide concrete support for the retention of the LCC along its existing lines. This, of course, was a perfectly defensible and understandable position. What is difficult to understand is the high degree of thoughtfulness and moderation that characterized the Association's stand in this regard.

As was noted in the previous analysis of the professional associations' reaction to the plan, the Local Medical Committee for the County of London had accused the Royal Commission of ignorance of Londoners' desires when it attempted to apply the concepts of "Athenian democracy to twentieth-century London." The LCC Staff Association, in testifying on this very same point, used a considerably different emphasis in tone:

> As a simple political ideal there is much to be said for a form of authority in which the elected representatives are physically able to keep in close touch with those whom they represent. Doubtless the Greek city government in which all enfranchised citizens could be present at the taking of political decisions approached most closely the ideal form of administration. But such simplicity is now outside the realm of the practical because of the sheer number of citizens. Primitive democracy has become a utopian dream; the practical issue is how far we are compelled to depart from it.

The Association then went on to present a defense of the advantages of the "large-scale organization" (i.e., the existing London County Council organization) as the best way to meet the needs of modern London government.[16]

This display of reasoned restraint was to characterize much of the

[16] R. C., *Written Evidence*, V, 224-233.

LCC Staff Association's response throughout the remainder of the controversy. This is not to say that the Association did not protest, often vigorously, against various aspects of the reform program. Its monthly periodical, *London Town,* often bristled with indignation over certain aspects of the plan, but it is significant to note that the very first issue of this publication to comment on the Royal Commission's report did so in depth, summarizing a wealth of helpful background information that explained what the reorganization proposals were all about, and including articles by advocates, as well as opponents, of these proposals.[17]

It is always difficult to explain why any organization deviates from an anticipated course of action, and there is no easy answer here. Yet the fact remains that the LCC Staff Association's response to the Royal Commission plan was a unique example of articulate opposition, despite the fact that it stood very close to the top of the list when one counted the potential losers under the reform proposals. Perhaps the most significant explanation of the Association's reasoned restraint was to be found in the caliber of its leadership, particularly its Secretary, Mr. Laurence Welsh, who possessed a more thorough grasp of the realities of modern London life than a great many of the highly placed political leaders who were destined to lock horns over the future of London's government.

The third significant missing element in the public response to the Royal Commission's plan was the press. Once again, care has to be exercised with respect to the use of the word "missing" because, once again, the press was physically present, at least in part. However, with very few exceptions, the press did not attempt to exercise any significant leadership initiative.

If one studies the increasing volume of literature on metropolitan reform proposals in American cities being developed by Edward Sofen, Henry Schmandt, and others, a reasonably precise pattern of press response to such proposals appears to be emerging. On the one hand, most of the larger metropolitan dailies—the Miami *Herald* and the Miami *News,* the St. Louis *Post-Dispatch,* and the St. Louis *Globe-Democrat*—are attempting to provide positive support for such

[17] *See* "London Town," *LCC Staff Gazette,* December 1960.

schemes, whereas most of the suburban and neighborhood weeklies are displaying a general opposition stance. (In their study of St. Louis, for example, Schmandt, Steinbicker, and Wendel note that 22 of 29 such suburban papers in the area opposed reform, while the others remained silent.)[18]

No such clear-cut pattern emerged in London on either side of the ledger. Although the majority of the large dailies generally favored the Royal Commission's plan, outright expressions of editorial support came in inverse ratio to circulation figures, with very few of these papers attempting to provide any real leadership on this issue. The editorial stance of the major London papers was as follows (circulation figures and political affiliations of the dailies are indicated in parentheses):[19]

I. *Daily Newspapers*
  1. *The Times* (253,441, Independent)—Initially hailed plan as a "Bold Reform," and provided consistent support throughout, although it attempted to make constructive criticisms of plan from time to time.
  2. *The Guardian* (245,056, Liberal)—Experienced considerable difficulty making up its mind on the plan, and often printed columns on its editorial page (i.e., "London Letter") that cast doubt as to the wisdom of the whole idea. When the London Government Bill entered the final Parliamentary debate stage, however, the Guardian supported it "in broad principle as a rightly conceived and necessary measure."
  3. *Daily Telegraph & Morning Post* (1,248,961, Conservative)—Supported the plan in principle from the beginning, although its attitude became somewhat more hesitant as the battle unfolded.
  4. *Daily Herald* (1,394,919, Labour)—Took no editorial position on the plan until just before the Parliamentary debates began, when it dropped something of a bombshell by announcing its support under the heading, "YOU CAN'T STAND STILL."
  5. *The Evening News & Star* (1,458,553)—General sympathy for the

---

[18] Henry J. Schmandt, Paul G. Steinbicker, and George D. Wendel, *Metropolitan Reform in St. Louis* (New York: Holt, Rinehart & Winston, Inc., 1961), p. 41.

[19] The circulation figures utilized in this table are obtained from *Advertisers' Aid* (London: The Newspaper Society, April 1962), p. 67. Specific editorial comments in quotations are from the following sources: *The Guardian*, December 12, 1962; *The Evening News and Star*, February 19, 1962; and *The Observer*, December 9, 1962.

plan throughout on the grounds that after "the inevitable teething troubles [are] overcome, it can hardly fail to work more efficiently than the present unruly complex of boroughs."

6. *Daily Sketch* (1,000,000, Independent Conservative)—No editorial position.
7. *The Daily Mail* (2,610,487, Independent Conservative)—No editorial position.
8. *The Daily Express* (4,328,524, Independent Conservative)—No editorial position.
9. *The Daily Mirror* (4,561,876, Independent Labour)—No editorial position.

II. *Sunday Newspapers*
1. *The Observer* (715,238)—Reluctant support on the grounds that "if a choice is to be between [reform] and no change at all, with the prospect of reform postponed perhaps for decades, then the measure deserves support despite its weaknesses."
2. *The Sunday Telegraph* (688,770)—No editorial position.
3. *The Sunday Times* (967,060)—No editorial position.

If one speculates as to the reasons for this general display of apathy, especially among the larger papers, two considerations are of special importance.

The first relates to nothing less than the geography of England. The geographical compactness of the British isles induces the major London papers to strive for a national, rather than just a local London, circulation.

The papers' news and editorial coverage tend to reflect this fact.

Typical of the responses received in regard to this question were the following:

> *Daily Mail*— . . . As a national newspaper our editorial position does tend to be stated on national and international affairs, rather than on the affairs of a particular city.
>
> *Sunday Telegraph*—In spite of the metropolitan importance of London, its municipal government is really a local issue which the London Evening and Weekly papers discuss most fully.[20]

[20] Letter, E. V. Matthewman, Managing Editor, *Daily Mail*, to F. Smallwood, dated August 23, 1962; letter, D. Brown, Assistant Editor, *The Sunday Telegraph*, to F. Smallwood, dated August 23, 1962.

This national orientation of the metropolitan press is reflected most clearly by the fact that the major dailies do not employ what could be classified as full-fledged London government reporters. While most papers have journalists who are knowledgeable on the general subject of London's government, they do not devote full-time coverage to metropolitan developments. In this respect, London stands unique, perhaps, among the great cities of the world in the lack of emphasis which its daily newspapers place upon the governmental affairs of the metropolis. Indeed, if one wants to find the most thoughtful and provocative analyses of such issues as the Greater London plan, the best sources are not the London papers, but rather such weekly periodicals as *The Economist* (strong initial editorial support which gradually gave way to increasing disenchantment over modifications in the plan) and *The New Statesman* (some highly thoughtful and persuasive articles in opposition to the plan). Thus, it is a paradox, but nonetheless a reality, that the national weekly periodicals are willing to comment upon the very local London issues that the London daily papers tend to feel will alienate their potential national audiences.

The second consideration that governs the dailies' coverage of London's governmental affairs relates to the always difficult question of news priorities.

Not only do many of the daily papers tend to minimize London governmental news because they feel it is of little interest to a national audience, they tend to minimize it also because they feel it takes second priority to other news values of more interest to London readers. There is always a host of stories competing for attention; therefore, some value judgement has to be made as to what will be emphasized under these circumstances. The fact that *The Daily Express,* for example, failed to take any firm editorial position on the Greater London plan can hardly be classified as surprising in light of Lord Beaverbrook's overriding obsession to keep England out of the Common Market. In terms of the priority of its interests, by the time *The Daily Express* had completed its daily diatribe against the perils of European economic integration, there was literally no space left in the paper for editorial comment on either the perils or the benefits of London's local integration.

Although the *Express* stood somewhat unique in its Common Market bias, other large London papers had other priorities that they felt to be more important than the issue of London's governmental reform.

Thus, on the day the London Government Bill received its First Reading in Parliament (November 22–23, 1962) this story made the first page of *The Times*, *The Guardian*, and *The Telegraph*, but it was relegated to page 13, and beyond, in the mass-circulation dailies in favor of such more newsworthy stories as:

1. Conservative Party defeats in two Parliamentary by-elections ("Tories Reeling").
2. Speculation that the Prime Minister was about to confer with President Kennedy ("Mac To U.S.?").
3. A fight between two pushcart vendors ("Man Goes Beserk in Hot Dog War").
4. Settlement of a factory labour dispute over how much time female employees could spend "off the job" during company time ("200 Girls End Strike Over 'The Ladies' ").
5. Various local tragedies ("Boy Dies in Fire—Sister Toddles to Safety," etc.).
6. And articles stating that there were only 32 more "slimming" days to Christmas.

At the top (if not the first) tier of London's press coverage, the response to the Royal Commission's plan was hardly stimulating.

The response at the second level of coverage—the community and suburban press—was considerably more muddled. Among the nearly one hundred local weeklies in the Greater London area, some papers did take forceful positions on the proposed reorganization, and unlike the St. Louis papers, they argued on both the pro and the con sides of this issue. *The Croydon Advertiser* and *The Kentish Times Series*, for example, provided significant editorial support in favor of reorganization, whereas papers such as *The South London Press* and *The Surrey Comet* fought the plan tooth and nail.

Taken as a whole, however, the response of the suburban press to the Royal Commission plan was primarily one of indifference.

The very evidence that serves to support this finding also represents the most significant explanation for its unexpected appearance. A great many of the London suburban newspapers are consolidated under a number of sizable advertising "chains," and they do not view their mission as that of providing vigorous editorial leadership in local affairs.

Two such chains, for example, are the *South London Advertiser* Newspapers and *South London's Suburban Group*, covering over ten separate weeklies in metropolitan Surrey and northern Kent counties. Neither of these chains took any position on the reorganization plan.[21] A similiar chain, *The Middlesex Advertiser Series*, provides coverage to a portion of the northwest corner of the Greater London area, and it, too, failed to take any position on the reorganization issue.[22] Since most of these local newspaper chains are consolidated primarily for advertising purposes, they tend to view their primary roles as those of basic informer on local events (i.e., births, marriages, deaths, movies, etc.), and provider of sales media for the local community. In very few cases do they attempt to provide any forceful, independent editorial comment on local developments.

When this localized editorial apathy is coupled with the predominantly national orientation of London's larger daily papers, a significant void appears with respect to local governmental coverage in the Greater London area. Not only does this void account for a good part of the dispassionate public response to the reform program, but it also offers a new insight into that deeper preoccupation of the Royal Commission —the supposedly sickly state of local government in the Greater London area. Certainly, the least that can be said is that, if London's local government really does experience poor health, this is not owing to the fact that it is being choked to death by publicity.

The television and radio media were not in a position to remedy this situation.

Somewhat surprisingly for a metropolis of eight million inhabitants, Greater London was serviced by only two television stations—B.B.C.

---

[21] Letter, N. Hird, News Editor, *South London Advertiser* Newspapers, to F. Smallwood, dated August 23, 1962; letter, R. Exton, Managing Editor, *South London's Suburban Group*, to F. Smallwood, dated August 23, 1962.

[22] Letter, H. Tilley, Editor, *Middlesex Advertiser and County Gasette*, to F. Smallwood, dated August 23, 1962.

and an independent group known as Associated Rediffusion. Under such circumstances, the competition for time was intense, especially during prime viewing hours, and neither station was able to devote any major emphasis to the problems of London's government. In addition, both stations were national in outlook, since they were tied into a network system that covers the entire country. Although they did occasionally shift off into programs designed for more localized audiences (i.e., Welsh-speaking, B.B.C. Scotland, etc.), their basic orientation was not local in outlook. The same condition held true with respect to radio coverage.

These major stations did provide some spot coverage of local London events following the early-evening news commentary, and on limited occasions they even provided forum-type discussions on immediate issues of local concern (e.g., they allotted five minutes to a commentary on the Greater London plan the day after the Bill was presented for First Reading in Parliament). However, such spot commentary was in no way designed as a substitute for more comprehensive press treatment, but rather as a supplement to such treatment. If the press did not provide the leadership initiative in covering London's governmental affairs, neither television nor radio could fill the void.

While it is difficult to evaluate all the ultimate implications of this void, it does help to explain a great deal about the widespread mass apathy that characterizes the Londoners' approach toward local government in general, and the Royal Commission's plan in particular. Indeed, it brings to the forefront that always intriguing, if terribly murky, problem of the sequential relationship between cause and result. One very knowledgeable London journalist, when asked why the great majority of papers underplayed local government to such an extent, explained quite matter-of-factly, "It isn't news." Yet, such an answer only begs the further question as to why the news potentialities of this subject appear to be so minimal. Is general public apathy toward London government primarily an excuse for a widespread lack of newspaper leadership on this subject, or more accurately, is public apathy in large measure the end result of poor coverage?

The extent to which such general public apathy actually is prevalent in London is the subject of a more detailed examination in a concluding chapter of this study. For the time being, suffice it to say that there was little indication that the general public was enthralled with the issue of London's governmental reform. On the contrary, many significant groups—business, labor, civic, and otherwise—were very much out of this particular picture. As a consequence, the contest over the reorganization of London's government promised to be very much a private, if nonetheless a potentially bitter, affair confined in large measure to the three groups already noted—the local political parties, the various professional associations, and the local governmental authorities involved.

Under such circumstances, it was only natural to expect that these groups, especially those which opposed reform, would attempt to increase the intensity and the visibility of this issue in a manner that would tempt the apathetic to commit themselves on the question of London's governmental reorganization. Indeed, those who were losing the reform contest could only hope to reverse this losing trend if such additional outside help were forthcoming.

Part IV

STRATEGIES AND RESULTS

"The most important strategy of politics is concerned
with the scope of the conflict."
—E. E. Schattschneider, *The Semisovereign People*

Although any conflict is bewildering in its apparent surface complexity, most contests can actually be reduced to a relatively few simple elements of underlying strategy.

The next four chapters attempt to identify the key strategic elements that characterized the conflict over the Greater London plan. These strategic considerations were four in number:

First, there were the preliminary maneuvers, in which the participants attempted to evaluate the potential conflict situation before making their initial commitments to position (Chapter 9);

Second, once these initial commitments were made, the participants attempted to concentrate their resources in an effort to operate from maximum positions of strength (Chapter 10);

Third, the participants who were operating from disadvantageous positions attempted to open up the scope of the conflict by inducing new participants to join them in battle, while those who were operating from strong positions attempted to make concessions that would contain the scope of the conflict (Chapter 11);

Finally, when the end resolution of the conflict was in sight, the losing side was forced to engage in a series of tactical forays that were designed to salvage as much as possible for their cause (Chapter 12).

The above four elements represent the essence of the perplexing variety of strategic currents and cross-currents that made up the melee of confusion over the Greater London plan.

If the reader keeps these four themes in mind, he should find it considerably more comfortable to traverse the bumpy terrain of detail that lies just ahead.

9. The Preliminary Maneuvers

It is an easy luxury to evaluate the wisdom of strategies and tactics after their subsequent effectiveness has become fully apparent, and a considerably more difficult challenge to formulate such strategies while their future implications are still very much unknown.

In retrospect, it is obvious that the opponents of reform in London made some very serious miscalculations during the original period of Commission testimony, before the reorganization battle was actually joined. The most lax parties here were the county councils and the other witnesses who favored the status quo. Their key miscalculation was to limit their sights quite severely with respect to the existing realities and needs of Greater London. As the Royal Commission noted, these authorities, with very few exceptions, confined their attention to the narrow areas delineated by their own geographical boundaries, and in so doing they placed themselves in a very awkward position in which later to comment upon the much broader reform proposals that were actually recommended.

The Commission itself attempted to explain the authorities' parochial approach toward reform in terms of both "defensive tactics" and "a genuine lack of understanding of the needs of London as a whole."[1]

To the extent that this was, in fact, a tactical maneuver, its wisdom was highly debatable.

Yet, in fairness to the "defensive" authorities, and most especially

[1] Rpt., Cmnd. 1164, pp. 43-45.

171

to the county councils, it must be recognized that these groups were operating under a number of distinct disadvantages at the time they originally presented their testimony to the Royal Commission.

In the first place, as is true in any investigatory process, most of them had no real idea of the specific program that the Commission would ultimately recommend. They had certain feelers out in this regard, but on the whole, they were testifying in the dark. The reform of London's government did not really come into sharp focus until the very last group of witnesses to appear—the London School of Economics—had offered its evidence to the Royal Commission. Only then did the full implications of reform take on concrete significance, and by this time the various authorities had already locked themselves into specific policy positions on the matter.

Second, and somewhat more relevant to the peculiarities of London itself, the counties were subject to a considerable degree of restraint with respect to how comprehensive they should be in their approach to the question of reform. This restraint grew out of the fact that the local governments in London had to exercise a high degree of interdependence with respect to the cooperative implementation of a number of joint projects. To give but one example, approximately half the London County Council's housing estates were located outside its own boundaries, within the borders of the adjacent boroughs and counties of Greater London. Under these circumstances, it was essential for the LCC to maintain good working relationships with these neighboring authorities, and such a fact tended to blunt any desire, if such a desire had existed in the first place, for the LCC to advance recommendations that would have threatened in any way the sovereign prerogatives of these neighbors.

In addition, each of the local authorities was subject to a considerable degree of confusion as to what was wanted in the way of evidence. Here, the Royal Commission itself must bear the major portion of the blame. Although, in its final report, the Commission repeatedly criticized the local authorities for being too narrowly parochial in their grasp of the problems of Greater London, a great deal of this parochialism can be traced back to the original directive that the Royal Commission sent to these authorities when it first requested their views on this issue.

The key document was a letter from the Commission's chairman to the authorities, dated February 17, 1958. There is no doubt that the over-all tone of this letter was extremely restrictive in its outlook. In essence, the Commission picked out six particular services—education, environmental health, housing, personal health and welfare, town and country planning, and traffic—and asked each of the local councils to provide a description of the present arrangements, and any defects experienced, in carrying out these functions "within the Council's area." The local authorities were further advised that "an outline only is asked for at this stage." Only once in its two-page directive, and this was buried at the end of a sentence, did the Commission refer to the "organisation of local government in the area," and at no point did the directive refer to the problems of Greater London as a whole.[2]

Subsequent documents make it clear that the Royal Commission was working under a false illusion with respect to the type of information it thought it had actually requested from the local authorities. For example, in a letter to the central Government ministries, dated March 4, 1958, the Commission advised these ministries that it had already written to the local authorities, "inviting them to submit evidence . . . generally on any aspect of local government in Greater London."[3] The actual facts of the matter are, however, that it had done no such thing. On the contrary, its basic inquiry to the local authorities had been quite narrowly conceived in its general frame of reference.

This may seem to be beating a rather small, if not perhaps quite dead, horse, but the initial misunderstanding that took place here was destined to have a decided impact upon the subsequent development of the entire reorganization struggle. In this particular instance the Commission did not ask the right questions in terms of what it later indicated

---

[2] Rpt., Cmnd. 1164, pp. 270-271.

[3] R. C., "Memoranda of Evidence From Government Departments," *Written Evidence*, IV, 1.

it had hoped to elicit in the way of substantive information, and its criticism of the local authorities' parochialism was hardly justified under the circumstances.

When all this is admitted, however, it still remains highly doubtful whether the local authorities might have been more comprehensive in their approach to reform even under the most forceful of Commission directives. In addition to the inhibiting factors already noted, there were two further influences—this time somewhat more political in their implications—at work.

One was the example of precedent. Royal Commissions represent a somewhat curious phenomenon in English Government in that they are often appointed with the intent of sidetracking a problem rather than solving it. This is, of course, a part of the mystique of the study group in any society. No one knows quite what to do about a particularly difficult issue, with the result that it is often relegated to a study committee to get it out of the way. To a certain extent, there was a somewhat glib underestimation of this particular Royal Commission from the very beginning, and many of the witnesses failed to take its study seriously. The most disastrous precedent the Commission had to overcome was the dismal fiasco of the Ullswater group, which had produced virtually nothing during its 1923 study of London's government. Since that time, the general problem of reform had been largely ignored, if not totally avoided, primarily because no one knew how this particular conundrum could be resolved. As a result, many of the local witnesses adopted the highly mistaken attitude that this Royal Commission would eventually come to naught, as its predecessor, the Ullswater inquiry, had done before it.

The second more politically oriented consideration was the timing of the study. The Commission began work in early 1958, and it was common knowledge that a General Election was not far off. Following the Suez debacle of 1956, the Conservative Party had begun to look rather ragged at the edges, and Labour had made a very good showing in local elections, especially in London. As a consequence, much of the smart money was predicting a Labour victory in the 1959 General Election, with few realizing the Party was actually about to go down to its third successive defeat. This optimistic appraisal of the future tended to lull some of the Labour-oriented local authorities into a sense of false security in the belief that the new Labour Government, shortly to be elected, would not be inclined to move very quickly on any London reorganization proposals growing out of the work of a study group established by its Conservative predecessors, especially if such proposals might have an adverse impact upon Labour's political position in the central London area.

It was this complicated combination of factors—and it is impossible to separate them—that served as a partial explanation of the narrow attitude which many of the local authorities, and most especially the London County Council, adopted toward the reform of London's government. As a result, most of these local authorities failed to offer anything very helpful in the way of imaginative proposals to the Royal Commission during the preliminary stages of the reform effort.

The County Councils

The preponderance of evidence offered by the county councils was overwhelmingly negative with respect to the need for any change in the structure of existing institutions, most particularly the counties themselves.

The most negative group of all was the London County Council. The only substantive problem this authority could find in the whole of Greater London was a minor mixup in the allocation of responsibilities for the control of water courses. The Council advised the Commission that there was "a lack of definition in the division of responsibilities among the authorities concerned with the tributaries (particularly the Wandle) and of the Thames (other than the Lee) and of the Ravensbourne." Other than this, "no major defects of structure or organization exist. . . . On the whole, the present system is workable and its patent merit is the fact that it works." The LCC did feel that there were some minor defects in the distribution of functions between itself and the twenty-eight metropolitan boroughs, but here it advised the Commission that it had been working since 1955 on a new delegation plan which was designed to remedy this situation.

Taken as a whole, the LCC's attitude toward reform can best be summed up in the words of Sir Isaac Hayward, the Council's leader, who advised the Commission that "the whole trend of our evidence is to try to prove to you that change is not necessary."[4]

The Essex County Council also held that "it is clear that the present Local Government system . . . has withstood successfully the heavy burdens imposed upon it . . . [and] . . . this system having been tested by actual experience . . . should not be abandoned unless it can be shown conclusively that alterations will result in something which is clearly an improvement in the services to the general public."[5] Like the LCC, this Council was willing to review the delegation of functions between itself and its second-tier authorities, but this was about as far as it was prepared to go.

The burden of the Kent County Council's position was to prove that "continued association of Metropolitan Kent with the rest of the County would, particularly economically and administratively, be of greater advantage both to the metropolitan area and to the County as a whole, than would its severance." This Council went somewhat further than London or Essex in that it considered four alternative arrangements for the government of Greater London, before concluding that none of them would be as satisfactory as the present system. In addition, this Council's testimony tended to indicate strongly that it was misled by the Commission's original February 17 directive to the extent that it deliberately restricted its comments quite severely and declined to offer views on any of "the functions which are the responsibility of its Borough or District Councils."[6]

The evidence offered by the Middlesex County Council indicates that this body also was thrown completely off course by the Commission's February 17 directive, in light of the information the Commission

[4] *Statement of Evidence by the London County Council*, July 1958, pp. 16-17; R.C., *Minutes of Oral Evidence*, Nos. 11-12, p. 384.

[5] R.C., *Minutes of Oral Evidence*, No. 18, p. 629.

[6] *Outline of Evidence on Behalf of the Kent County Council*, 24 July 1958, pp. 1-2, 11.

later indicated it had hoped to obtain from the local authorities. Middle-sex opened its statement by first quoting directly from this directive and then explained quite succinctly, "The County Council is not at this stage adducing evidence or advancing arguments outside the terms of reference of the Commission's letter. In particular it is not at this stage making any proposals for, or endeavoring to meet any proposal that may be put forward for, a change in local government structure either within the County Council's area or within the Greater London review area as a whole."[7] The Council then went on to offer an extremely thorough factual description of the six functional services, as they related to the County itself, without attempting to elaborate on this description in terms of the larger needs of Greater London.

Rightly or wrongly, much criticism was to be leveled at the Middle-sex County Council during the subsequent course of the reform effort; yet on this particular occasion the dictates of fairness require a sympathetic appraisal of the attempt the County Council made to follow the narrow lead which had been formulated by the Royal Commission. The Middlesex evidence represented a conscientious effort to follow the guidelines the Commission had formulated, and under the circumstances it is extremely difficult to criticize the Council for being too parochial in its outlook at this point in the proceedings.

The Hertfordshire County Council, being the least affected by the Commission's review, took a somewhat different stand from the other counties. The entire tenor of evidence advanced by this body was to prove that "Hertfordshire is in a very different position from any of the other counties." The Council argued that the only portions of Hertford-shire under review were low-population-density fringe areas, which were not part of Greater London and should be "dealt with in exactly the same way as the rest of the country."[8] In other words, Hertford-shire wanted to be excluded from reform from the very beginning, on the grounds that it had been a mistake to include any portions of its jurisdiction within the Commission's general frame of reference.

The final county to offer testimony, Surrey, also adopted a defensive

[7] *Outline of Evidence by the Middlesex County Council,* June 1958, p. 5.
[8] R.C., *Minutes of Oral Evidence,* No. 25, p. 964.

attitude, its position being that none of the defects which might exist in local government were of "fundamental importance or significance . . . [or] . . . of such a character as to justify a prima facie view . . . that any change was necessary or desirable." The key difference that tended to distinguish Surrey's testimony from that of its county neighbors was the fact that its key spokesman, Sir Cyril Black, advanced the germ of an idea that was destined to become of considerable significance in the counties' later approach to the Commission's report. This was the suggestion that the County would be in favor of establishing "a joint advisory committee to deal with major planning in the whole of the London area" along the lines of a recommendation that had been advanced previously by a group known as the London Planning Administration Committee. In 1949 this group, under the chairmanship of Mr. Clement Davies, M.P., had proposed a joint planning effort between the different Greater London counties for an area well beyond the Green Belt and comparable to that covered in the Abercrombie Plan of 1944. However, its proposal had been ignored. Now, Sir Cyril Black advised the Royal Commission that Surrey "liked the 1949 recommendation, we said so then, and we have consistently adhered to that view."[9]

Thus, Surrey became the only county to advance at least the nebulous outlines of a possible solution to the broader needs of Greater London, at any rate in the field of planning. The only other county to consider these broader needs was Kent, which had rejected any alternative schemes in favor of the status quo. The counties of London, Essex, Middlesex, and Hertfordshire, on the other hand, had not really gone into the questions of Greater London's needs at all.

The final expressions of opinion to come from the counties were to be found in the evidence offered by the County Councils Association, the Minority (i.e., Conservative) Party of the London County Council, and by one Labour member of the London County Council, Mr. Hugh Jenkins.

The County Councils Association agreed with the previous county council witnesses that the existing two-tier system represented the most satisfactory form of local government for Greater London. The only

9 R.C., *Minutes of Oral Evidence*, Nos. 43-44, pp. 1,821, 1,834-1,835.

real difference between its testimony and the county councils' previous testimony was to be found in the quality of presentation. In the Commission's words, the CCA's arguments were "able, powerful, reasoned and temperate." Yet, this was really a difference of style, rather than of substance. Like the county councils, the CCA looked at the problems of Greater London "through the eyes of the existing counties,"[10] and the result was, in essence, another defense of the status quo.

The Minority (i.e., Conservative) Party on the London County Council differed completely from the other county representatives by arguing that the problems of London could not be met under the existing governmental structure. Instead, the LCC Conservatives testified that "there ought to be some form of Greater London Authority; that it ought to extend further than the present Administrative County of London; [and] that it ought to have far fewer functions than the London County Council and the other town councils in our area have at the present time."[11] Thus, it is interesting to note that the LCC's Conservative minority adopted a position almost exactly parallel, in terms of areas if not of powers, to that which the LCC Labourites had recommended to the Ullswater Royal Commission some thirty-five years earlier, when Labour had been the minority power on the London County Council.

The testimony offered by Mr. Hugh Jenkins, a LCC Labour member from the Metropolitan Borough area of Stoke Newington and Hackney North, was remarkable on a number of counts, not the least being its high degree of creative ingenuity. At the outset of his oral testimony, Mr. Jenkins attempted to establish three criteria to serve as guidelines for any reform effort. First, "the governed [should] be able to comprehend the system under which they are governed." Second, "the areas covered [should] be reasonably related to the functions to be administered." Third, "the governors [should] be a reasonable cross-section of the governed."

Mr. Jenkins then went on to suggest that the Commission should approach the problem of reform as a two-stage operation. First, it should

10 Rpt., Cmnd. 1164, p. 48.
11 R.C., *Minutes of Oral Evidence,* No. 50, p. 2,097.

establish a new top-tier authority for that portion of Greater London roughly covered by the London postal area. Then, at a later date after this new authority had been firmly established (Mr. Jenkins suggested the possibility of a twenty-year waiting period), a second Commission could be created to consider the further question of the larger regional reorganization of Greater London.

Mr. Jenkins' proposals were based upon some highly interesting speculations. The London postal area is larger than London County, but somewhat smaller than the inner Green Belt area that the Commission was actually reviewing. It represented something of a halfway house between the two. Mr. Jenkins selected this area, first, on the grounds of "metropolitan identity." He felt that residents within the postal area might well have some semblance of Greater London consciousness, since they daily came into contact with communications that were addressed to them as Londoners. In Mr. Jenkins' words, "the London postal area really is London." The second rationale was strategic. Mr. Jenkins felt that a reduction in over-all size of the review area would reduce the potential scope of opposition to reform by those outlying authorities who would be, at least temporarily, excluded from reorganization. Again, in Mr. Jenkins' words, "I believe that this area is one in which change could be made without too much opposition. . . . This particular bite of cherry is as far as one can go without risking the possibility of doing more harm than good."[12]

Thus, it was one individual Labour member of the London County Council, rather than the LCC Labour majority, who attempted to provide the Commission with some creative thinking as to how the reform of Greater London's government might proceed. Like the Council's Conservative Minority, Mr. Jenkins harbored some recognition of the potentiality that all might not be perfect with the existing status quo; but Mr. Jenkins' stand, unlike that of the Conservatives, cannot be explained in terms of potential partisan considerations. His testimony represented the most refreshing example of original thinking to be advanced during the entire course of the county councils' testimony.

Taken as a whole, however, the testimony of the counties, and that

[12] R.C., *Minutes of Oral Evidence*, Nos. 48-49, pp. 2,033-2,035, 2,041.

of the County Councils Association, was overwhelmingly defensive in its tone.

In effect, the counties took a look at themselves as they presently existed, and they very much liked what they saw.

The Second-Tier Authorities

The weight of numbers makes it impossible to analyze the testimony of all the second-tier authorities in any great depth. Certain general trends emerged in this testimony, however, that give at least an impressionistic picture of the second-tier position on reorganization. Two of these trends are of particular significance.

First, the great majority of these authorities, when testifying as individual units, followed the county councils' lead in adopting a restrictive interpretation of the Commission's February 17 letter. As a result, few of them commented on the desirability of any major structural reforms in Greater London's government; instead, they concentrated upon the considerably more restricted objective of arguing for an increased delegation of responsibilities from the county councils to themselves.

In all, only six of the nearly one hundred second-tier authorities in the Commission's original Review Area—Westminster, Chelsea, Fulham, Hampstead, Kensington, and Twickenham—urged that the Commission take a dramatically new approach to the problems of London's local government. "The proposals of these authorities differed quite widely from one another in detail but had two common features. These were . . . [first] to confer most local authority functions on enlarged and strengthened boroughs, and [second] to give other functions which could not be dealt with on a purely local basis to some new authority covering the whole of the Review Area or substantial parts of it."[13]

The reasons for which these six authorities took this initiative varied, although in most cases the lead could be traced to in-

[13] Rpt., Cmnd. 1164, p. 45.

dividual councillors who had adopted a larger conception of Greater London's needs than was characteristic of the general second-tier authority attitude. It is interesting to note also that five of these six units were controlled by Conservative councils. The only exception was the Metropolitan Borough of Fulham, which was unique among the Labour strongholds in its advocacy of reform from the very beginning. More will be said of this later because the Fulham position was to take on more than local importance. This borough made up part of the home Parliamentary constituency of Michael Stewart, M.P., the Labour Party's shadow Minister of Housing and Local Government, who was destined to lead the Labour opposition to the reorganization plan in the Commons.

On the basis of their individual testimony, the great majority of second-tier authorities did not display any more initiative than the counties did in arguing for major change in the status quo.

Many of these authorities also testified as members of larger group associations, however, and here one finds the second, and somewhat different, general trend with respect to their position on reform.

Four second-tier authority groupings made major representations to the Commission, and the essence of their positions was the same in each case. All four felt that the second-tier units should have vastly increased powers at the expense of the first-tier county councils.

The Metropolitan Boroughs' Standing Joint Committee took the mildest stand on this question, largely because the twenty-eight London boroughs had never really enjoyed any great powers in the first place, and, hence, were less affected by the postwar erosion of powers than were the other second-tier units outside London County. While expressing unanimous agreement on the "desirability that the borough councils should be the main organs of local government in London," the Committee felt that "the present two-tier structure should be retained . . . [and] . . . so far as boundaries are concerned, we see no reason to justify the upheaval which an extension of the [LCC] County boundary would cause." Thus, from the very beginning, the Metropolitan Boroughs' Standing Joint Committee stood behind the London

County Council in its plea for the retention of the status quo with respect to the preservation of its existing area of jurisdiction.[14]

The "Big Ten" boroughs in Middlesex also stood behind their county council, but in a manner that threatened to denude it of any meaningful existence at all. What this group really argued for was the creation of ten independent Middlesex county boroughs, namely themselves. Emphasing that their "joint statement in no way derogates [the] individual statements" they had already offered, "the Ten Boroughs contend that . . . they are fully competent and fully equipped Local Government Units to have directly conferred upon them by Parliament the additional local government functions, and greater local autonomy, which they seek in the interests of the inhabitants and to secure effective and convenient local government." In all, these boroughs indicated they would like to take over no less than twenty-two new local government functions, among them education, personal health services, town and country planning, highways, welfare, and "any other services which are not mentioned above and for which non-county boroughs are the local authorities."[15] As a result, Middlesex County would be limited to such services as ambulances, main drainage, and civil defense in the areas of jurisdiction covered by these ambitious separatist boroughs.

As the Royal Commission noted in its report, the attitude of these large Middlesex boroughs toward the Middlesex County Council reminded them of the verse, "Thou shalt not kill; but need'st not strive officiously to keep alive."[16]

The third second-tier group to offer testimony consisted of a number of northeast Essex County authorities, including the Municipal Borough of Ilford, which, like its large Middlesex counterparts, had long sought county-borough status. As was the case with Middlesex, these Essex authorities also argued for the creation of independent

[14] R.C., *Minutes of Oral Evidence*, No. 1, pp. 3-5.

[15] Joint Statement of Evidence, submitted jointly on behalf of the borough councils of Edmonton, Enfield, Harrow, Hendon, Heston & Isleworth, Hornsey, Tottenham, Twickenham, Wembley, and Willesden, all in the County of Middlesex, January 1959, pp. 5, 9-12.

[16] Rpt., Cmnd. 1164, p. 43.

county boroughs to cover their areas of jurisdiction, although "their attitude towards the Essex County Council was much less hostile than the attitude of the larger Middlesex boroughs to the Middlesex County Council. These [Essex] authorities hit upon the brilliant tactical device of attracting to their group the [already existent] County Boroughs of East and West Ham, and the obvious inference . . . was . . . that they would be at least as viable as county boroughs as either of the two Hams."[17]

Finally, the Association of Municipal Corporations, the major national spokesman for the local borough units, also wanted to strengthen the second-tier authorities. The major argument of this body was "the thesis that the best form of government for Greater London would be a series of county boroughs with no counties over them." This argument was based on the assumption that any area-wide problems could be resolved by means of joint committees with consultative powers, or by joint boards bridging the newly proposed county boroughs. Unfortunately for the Association, at a meeting of the boroughs within the Review Area, only twenty-two constituent members supported the Association's position, while thirty-six rejected it.[18] These second-tier units were generally in favor of assuming more powers, but not all of them, and especially not the Labour metropolitan boroughs, wanted to see their county councils abolished completely via their own amalgamations into new county boroughs.

The emphasis of each of these four second-tier groups, then, was not so much to concentrate on any comprehensive reform of Greater London's government taken as a whole, but rather to pursue practical objectives that were designed to enhance their own powers and status.

Thus, on the question of comprehensive reform, there was not very much difference between the first-tier and the second-tier authorities. The great majority in both groups indicated general satisfaction with the prevailing situation, with the single crucial exception that most of the second-tier units were very hungry to increase their functional re-

17 Rpt., Cmnd. 1164, p. 43.
18 Rpt., Cmnd. 1164, p. 49.

sponsibilities within the framework of the existing governmental structure.

The Central Government Departments

The third level of governmental authorities to present testimony to the Royal Commission comprised eight ministries of the central Government.

The testimony of these Whitehall spokesmen was not so important for what they did say as for what they did not say. Most of these ministries looked at the present operations of local government in the Greater London area and indicated general satisfaction with the existing governmental setup. Hence, their testimony was destined to have an important bearing on the development of subsequent strategies, especially where it supplied ammunition to the arguments of the opposition forces, which were dead set against any major changes in the status quo.

Five ministries—Agriculture, Health, Labour, the Home Office, and the Board of Trade—felt that, with the exception of some minor procedural problems, there were no significant defects in the existing arrangements. A number of important services—among them the children's service, the fire service, weights and measures, youth employment, and personal health services—were encompassed under this generally clean bill of health.

A sixth department, Education, was also very generous in its appraisal of local administration, and since the issue of education was to become a very key point of controversy in the ensuing struggle, the highlights of this testimony are worth pointing out in at least a summary fashion.

Over-all, the Ministry of Education found the Greater London area to be "an efficient local education authority." As regards the counties, it felt that the London County Council was "particularly successful in those parts of their work which require a high degree of professional skill or which raise problems of great complexity." The Middlesex County Council did "very good work," and its "general education standard is high." The four other county councils—Essex, Kent, Surrey, and Hertfordshire—each "provide a satisfactory service." In addition, the three county boroughs (which also served as first-tier educational authorities) received generally high marks from the Ministry of Education. Croydon's service was "fully adequate," East Ham's "quite effective"; and while West Ham did "not [enjoy] a very high reputation as a local education authority . . . there are signs of some improvement."[19] Thus, as far as the Ministry of Education was concerned, "there is no part of the [Greater London] area in which the present system of educational administration does not work at least tolerably well," although there were procedural defects in many parts of the area, especially as they related to the delegation of educational functions to the second-tier "divisional executives" and "excepted districts."[20]

The two other Government departments to testify—The Ministry of Housing and Local Government and the Ministry of Transport and Civil Aviation—also provided a generally favorable appraisal of the existing local services, although each suggested specific reforms in certain of these services.

In the field of housing, the Ministry of Housing and Local Government provided quite lavish praise of the London County Council, although it did admit that "the very multiplicity of authorities in Greater London is, in the absence of co-ordinating machinery, an obstacle to [the] effective handling of London's housing problems." The same held true in the field of planning, which was generally good, but again there

---

[19] Subsequent statistics have revealed that the London County Council was the top county council in the country in terms of educational expenditures. It spent an average of £133 ($372.40) per child. Middlesex ranked fifth in the country with an expenditure of £124 ($347.20) per child, and Hertfordshire sixth with £120 ($336.00) per child. East Ham was the top county borough in the country with £129 ($361.20) per child, and Croydon tied for fourth with £118 ($330.40) per child. The lowest county average in the country was Rutland (with £97, or $271.60, per child), of which more is said in Chapter 13 (*The Times* Sunday Magazine, November 10, 1963, p. 11).

[20] R.C., *Memoranda of Evidence from Government Departments*, IV, 21-24.

was a "question of whether some machinery is not required for continuous review of the whole region, and perhaps also for carrying through some of the work needed to implement planning. The major failure of planning in Greater London has been in dealing with problems of traffic congestion."

Despite these rather modest hints that further coordination might be desirable in housing and planning, the Ministry did not propose any specific alternative reforms to replace the existing governmental structure. The only area in which it actually went out on a limb and came up with a concrete recommendation was the field of refuse collection. Here it felt there was a pressing need to establish "a central organisation . . . to take charge of the collection and disposal of London's refuse [with] its scope not . . . necessarily limited to the L.C.C. area."[21]

The Ministry of Transport was the most outspoken—indeed, really the only outspoken—Government ministry of the eight to testify before the Royal Commission. This group stated the desirability of setting up an entirely new local structure for the management of highways and traffic, indicating that it would like to see the establishment of a revised pattern of local highway authorities throughout Greater London. Since the basic aim of this proposal was to reduce the number of local authorities responsible for this activity, the Ministry suggested that a population of 200,000 should be the minimum for each such authority. It then included a "specimen Organisation" in the Appendix to its written evidence, which suggested the establishment of twenty-two independent highway authorities, each having an average population of 400,000 people.[22]

Thus, with the exception of the testimony offered by these latter two ministries, the Government departments' general appraisal of the prevailing situation in Greater London was quite favorable, and even these latter two proposals were certainly not totally radical in their implications.

Yet, an indication of the degree of resistance to change on the part of the local authorities can be seen in the hostility of their reactions to

[21] *Memoranda of Evidence*, pp. 105-124.
[22] *Ibid.*, pp. 162-187.

these two suggestions. The position taken by the Metropolitan Boroughs' Standing Joint Committee represents a classic case in point. In its oral testimony before the Royal Commission, spokesmen for the Joint Committee classified the proposals made by the two ministries as being nothing less than "monstrous." As regards the suggestion by the Ministry of Housing and Local Government that something might be done to improve the refuse collection service, the Joint Committee commented, "We are staggered that the Ministry—which we consider to be our Ministry—could have made such a proposal." The Committee then went on to explain (presumably with a straight face), "The collection of refuse is . . . the service above all others which brings the [local] authority into closest contact with its residents and ratepayers."

The Joint Committee's castigation of the Ministry of Transport was even more scathing. Here it concluded that the Ministry's suggestion regarding the establishment of the twenty-two new highway authorities could "be summed up in one sentence as a root and branch attack on local democratic government as we now know it."[23]

This adverse reaction on the part of the Metropolitan Boroughs' Standing Joint Committee serves as a fitting commentary on the general position that the great majority of governmental authorities at all levels—first-tier, second-tier, and central ministries—took on the question of reform. With only minor exceptions, these authorities failed to advocate any basic changes in the existing organization of Greater London's government. On those few occasions in which specific proposals for change were advanced (i.e., refuse collection, highways), the hostility to these proposals was so rigid as to border on the ludicrous.

The great mass of evidence that all three levels of government advanced to the Royal Commission amounted to a basic defense of the status quo. If the Commission was to look for support for a comprehensive reform of Greater London's government, it would have to turn to some group other than the governmental authorities to find the motive power for such an effort.

[23] R.C., *Minutes of Oral Evidence*, No. 1, pp. 5-6.

The Political Parties

The attitudes the political parties adopted toward the Commission's review fell into three distinct categories—defense of the status quo; advocacy of minor procedural change; and advocacy of major change. The Labour parties occupied the first camp; the Liberals, the second; and the Communists and the Conservatives, the third.

The London Labour Party did call for a devolution of more responsibilities from the county councils to the second-tier authorities (specifically suggesting the personal health services in this regard), and it also indicated a willingness to see some "minor county boundary alterations." The essence of its argument, however, was to oppose any major changes in the existing governmental system.[24] While it admitted that the "present system of local government may appear to be untidy," the London Labour Party held that "any large-scale cutting up of local government boundaries and functions will inevitably serve to break up a well established system," and it was especially concerned that "the unitary education system of the County of London should be retained undisturbed."[25]

Similarly, the Essex Federation of Labour Parties came to the defense of the Essex County Council when it was attacked by its second-tier authorities, who wanted to secure county-borough status. In addition, the Federation expressed strong opposition against establishing any first-tier authorities that might have their members appointed by the councils of constituent units. It viewed the directly-elected councillor as "a safety valve" in local government, commenting that "we have, in too many parts of the world in recent years, seen the rights of the voters whittled away [and] we would not like to see the tendency growing here."[26]

[24] In line with the earlier ideological analysis (Chapter 7), it is interesting to note that the London Labour Party dropped the criterion of "convenient" local government entirely and argued in its testimony that the existing system provided for a high degree of "effective and efficient" local government.

[25] R.C., *Written Evidence*, V, 252-254.

[26] *Ibid.*, pp. 116-118.

The Liberal Party's testimony serves as a unique illustration of just how much this body did recognize the fact that change can represent opportunity. Although the London Liberal Party did not offer evidence to the Commission, the Liberal Party organization did speak out. Its major criticism of local government in the London area was founded in the argument that there was difficulty in securing good candidates for local elections. The root problem here was one-party domination of local councils, especially in the metropolitan boroughs, which made "a travesty of the idea of local government by publicly elected representatives." The remedy which the Liberals suggested to cure this disease was a new type of "preferential voting system" (in lieu of the "block" vote), along the general lines of the proportional representation idea.[27] As is well known to political analysts, and presumably to the Liberal Party as well, any such voting system tends to provide a boost to third and fourth parties in elections, by cutting into the strength of the major parties.

The London District Committee of the Communist Party, along with the various Conservative Party organizations, argued the case for major structural reform in Greater London. The District Committee offered some thoughtful written evidence to the Royal Commission and backed up this evidence with some highly impressive oral testimony. The essence of the Communists' plan was to establish a completely revised two-tier approach to Greater London's government, the new top level to consist of a "Council of London" which would be responsible for overall policies throughout the area, and the second level to comprise a new series of local "District Councils," each containing approximately 200,000 to 250,000 people. Thus, the basic plan that the Communists recommended closely paralleled the final proposals that were subsequently advanced by the Royal Commission.

The reason the Royal Commission expressed skepticism regarding these Communist Party proposals in its final report related to the emphasis which the Communists placed on "the Development of Democratic Control" over these two new tiers of local government. This control was to be achieved by carving up the two tiers into the smallest

[27] *Ibid.*, pp. 182-183.

possible electoral districts, especially at the second-tier level. On their proposed second-tier "District Councils," the Communists favored "the development of small electoral areas, with one member for each polling district of about 2,000 electors. We oppose the present tendency to expand the size of the electoral area with a large number of members to be elected on a single list."[28] Hence, the rationale for the Commission's comment that the proposals advanced by the Communist District Committee represented "the classical form of organization advocated . . . by [a Party] who seem to find it easier to dominate the small group than to obtain political influence through the ballot box over a larger body."

Be that as it may, the Communist Party's position was forwarded in a highly articulate manner, with the Commission itself noting that these views were "very ably presented and argued."[29]

The same cannot be said of the two Conservative Party groups to appear before the Commission, both of which experienced considerable difficulty in formulating any precise recommendations regarding reform, although both indicated such reform was highly necessary.

The first of these Conservative bodies, the Bow Group (an independent research organization of young Conservatives), criticized "over-centralisation" in the existing local governmental structure and called for a two-tier concept similar to that advocated by the Communist Party. At the second-tier level this Group wanted to establish some forty-five "most-purpose" boroughs, containing from 125,000 to 250,-000 persons each. The Bow Group was considerably more confused as to what kind of over-all organization it favored at the top tier, however, suggesting that this might be one directly-elected "County" authority, a series of three or four counties, or possibly some further degree of central Government coordination.[30]

The London Municipal Society, the Conservatives' spokesman within London County, was even more fuzzy than the Bow Group in its initial evidence. It, too, was very strong on the necessity for reform,

---

[28] *Ibid.*, pp. 234-244.
[29] Rpt., Cmnd. 1164, p. 57.
[30] R.C., *Written Evidence*, V, 66-70.

attacking the London County Council as being too big and characterizing the existing London governmental system as "top-heavy." However, the Society confined its conclusions to a description of three different alternative plans of reorganization, and it failed to advance any final recommendations as to which one of these it felt would be desirable.[31]

The Society was later to submit "Supplementary Evidence" to the Commission, and on this second go-around it very definitely did advance a concrete plan of reorganization. It did not do so, however, until the final group of witnesses to testify had already formulated such a concrete plan. The London Municipal Society's later stiffening of attitude regarding the reorganization of Greater London's government came only after someone else had already provided the initiative in this area, and only after the obvious partisan implications of such a plan had become fully apparent.

As such, the Society's position serves as an apt commentary on the political parties' general attitudes toward the Royal Commission's study. Like the local governmental authorities, all the political parties were opportunistic in their desire to derive specific tactical advantages from reform. As a result, the only clear trend that emerged from the parties' testimony was that the Labour spokesmen did not want to upset the strong partisan position they already enjoyed in central London (and hence were opposed to any major reorganization at all), while the three other parties felt they had more to gain than lose from reorganization (and hence supported the general concept of reform). Yet the Liberals' approach was very narrow, and the Conservatives' position, highly obscure. Only the Communists presented their case with conviction, and this was hardly the party to engender widespread support for any major reform program.

Thus, in terms of the over-all testimony the Commission had received, the situation looked rather desperate for any comprehensive overhaul of the existing London governmental system. Well over one hundred witnesses had appeared before the Commission, and most of them were solidly opposed to major change. The great majority of pro-

[31] *Ibid.*, pp. 255-265.

fessional associations, the Labour Party, the first-tier county councils, the first-tier county boroughs, the majority of the central Government ministries, and even many of the second-tier local councils had all indicated a general satisfaction with leaving things as they were. It was now June 1959, and time was running out, both figuratively and literally. The Commission had been receiving evidence since early 1958, and the over-all impact of eighteen months of testimony was almost totally defensive in tone.

Only one further group had indicated a desire to offer written evidence to the Royal Commission, and if this last group failed to advance a powerful argument in favor of a comprehensive reform effort, it was highly doubtful whether the Commission would be able to come up with anything major in the way of a meaningful reorganization program.

The Academic Spokesmen

The entire situation changed quite drastically and dramatically when the last group to appear—the academic spokesmen—presented their case to the Royal Commission.[32]

The evidence submitted by the London School of Economics in June 1959 was assembled under the direction of a special study committee, known as the Greater London Group. This Greater London Group, in turn, presented three different positions to the Royal Commission.

One member of the Group, Professor J. A. G. Griffith, felt that only two services—planning and highways—were so broad as to require

[32] In all, four different universities accepted the Commission's invitation to present testimony on the reorganization of London's government. Representatives of two of these universities—Professor H. Myles Wright of Liverpool University and Dr. Peter G. Richards of Southampton University—had presented testimony to the Commission earlier. Both these witnesses had offered highly useful, but somewhat restricted, evidence on their particular fields of specialized interest—planning, and the utilization of delegation schemes in local government. It was the third group of academic witnesses—from the London School of Economics—that did not appear until June 1959. In turn, the LSE group was followed by a rebuttal from the Centre of Urban Studies, University of London, which submitted its written evidence in December 1959.

centralized treatment over the whole of the Greater London area, and he recommended that both these services be taken over by appropriate central Government ministries. Otherwise, he did not feel any major changes were necessary with respect to local government reorganization.

The two other positions were advanced by different LSE teams, with both of these advocating no less than grand strategies for the complete reorganization of local government in Greater London. They were presented to the Commission under the titles of Scheme "A" and Scheme "B."

Scheme "A," which was formulated by a team under the direction of Professor William A. Robson, recommended a revised two-tier system of government along the following lines: [33]

1. A new, directly elected "Greater London Authority" should be created as the top-tier government and should assume only those functions required to be dealt with over the Review Area as a whole.
2. The primary units of local government should be a series of revitalized second-tier "Greater London Boroughs," which should, through extensions and amalgamations, have average populations between 250,000 and 500,000.

Scheme "B," which was presented to the Commission by an LSE team under the leadership of Mr. Peter Self, called for an even more dramatic revision of the existing governmental structure: [34]

1. There should be a Greater London Authority covering the entire Review Area to deal with a few limited problems requiring central treatment.
2. The primary units of local government should be an entirely new series of five or six "most-purpose" counties, radiating out from one central core county that would coincide roughly with the existing London County area. These five or six new counties should each contain a population of roughly one and a half million, while the central core county should contain a population of approximately one-half million.
3. Some form of "Urban Parish" with limited powers should be created under these new counties for purely local functions.

[33] R.C., *Written Evidence*, pp. 464-492.
[34] *Ibid.*, pp. 493-519.

Thus, Scheme "A" represented a more comfortable (if nonetheless dramatic) reconciliation with the existing organizational structure, in that, while the existing first-tier counties would disappear, the second-tier units would retain the essence of their present identity. Scheme "B," on the other hand, represented a complete overhaul of both the first-tier and the second-tier units. In terms of the practicalities of future political implementation, Scheme "A" was considerably less radical than Scheme "B."

Here, for once in its report, the Commission openly indicated its acute awareness of political realities. It rejected Scheme "B" with the comment, "It may well be that if one were starting afresh in London with no history and no existing institutions, one might devise a scheme of government of this kind."[35] The problem was, however, that there was an existing history, and there was a host of existing institutions that could hardly be expected to welcome the complete obliteration that Scheme "B" promised. The Robson scheme, on the other hand, would undoubtedly meet with resistance from the county councils, but it held out the very real possibility of eliciting considerable support from the second-tier authorities, which, through amalgamation and extension, were destined to become the primary units of local government in the Greater London area.

In its final recommendations, the Royal Commission accepted a modified form of the Scheme "A" concept, the most significant revision being that it called for Greater London Boroughs of only 100,000 to 250,000 population, in lieu of the 250,000 to 500,000 that the Robson scheme had suggested.

In terms of its over-all implications, the key significance of Scheme "A" lay not so much in any sweepingly original concepts contained in the proposal itself. Actually, the essence of such a plan had already been suggested by the six second-tier boroughs—Westminster, Chelsea, Fulham, Hampstead, Kensington, and Twickenham—and, in modified form, by a number of other minor groups. Indeed, Professor Robson had long been openly advocating such a comprehensive reorganization of London's government, ever since he had written his major study, *The Government and Misgovernment of London,* in 1939.

[35] Rpt., Cmnd. 1164, p. 190.

What was really of importance here was the fact that the London School of Economics testimony offered the Royal Commission the very thing it so desperately needed if it was to advance any comprehensive reform proposals at all: namely, a solid base of support upon which it could plead its case. The entire reorganization study, which had been floundering upon an amorphous mixture of parochial, opportunistic, and contradictory testimony, came into clear focus once the LSE group had presented its evidence. The Royal Commission finally had a peg upon which it could hang its reform hat, and it was a particularly valuable peg for a number of reasons.

First, this testimony had been offered by an academic group which had no particular ax of its own to grind. Unlike virtually all the other witnesses, the LSE spokesmen had no immediately direct interests to protect, or advance, in the local government arena. Hence, not only did this testimony carry the prestige generally associated with academic analysis, but it bore the mark of objectivity and impartiality as well.

Second, the Greater London Group provided the Commission with a great wealth of factual data that was highly useful to its study. In all, the LSE written testimony covered more than two hundred pages. This testimony not only provided the Commission with much valuable background information, but it also served to reinforce the impression of objectivity and impartiality noted above.

Finally, there was a political overtone involved here, which, while completely fortuitous, was also destined to have a major bearing on subsequent events. This is the fact that testimony which was obviously going to be distasteful to the London Labour Party, and to Labour's stronghold, the London County Council, was advanced by an academic body that had enjoyed long historic ties with the Labour movement. The London School of Economics and Political Science was originally founded on the inspiration of the Webbs, most particularly Sidney Webb. Its faculty, which has included such figures as Harold Laski, has hardly been regarded as a spokesman for Conservatism in England. Professor Robson himself had formerly served as the head of the Local Government Bureau of the Fabian Society. It is difficult to imagine any group that could have offered testimony to the Royal Commission which would have been less liable to the charge that it was politically motivated to serve the Conservative cause.

Once the London School of Economics evidence was presented to the Commission, the handwriting was very much on the wall. A variety of other groups now understood very clearly what the central target of reform was all about, and they moved in either to support or to oppose the LSE concepts with a totally new display of realism.

The Conservative London Municipal Society, for example, was now able to make up its mind with respect to the precise kind of reorganization it favored. Surprisingly enough, this was a carbon copy of the LSE two-tier system—the top tier to consist of a Greater London Authority, and the second tier to consist of a revitalized grouping of County Borough Councils which, through extension and amalgamation, would average 250,000 in population.[36] In advancing this scheme, the Society hardly needed to emphasize the fact that it would be necessary to abolish the Labour-controlled London County Council in order to create the new Greater London Authority.

On the opposition side, the University of London's Centre for Urban Studies decided to present to the Commission evidence that finally appeared six months later, in December 1959. The formal leadership for this group was provided by Sir William Holford, Professor of Town Planning and a leading London architect, but most of the basic research was prepared under the guidance of Mrs. Ruth Glass, the Centre's Director of Research.

The essence of the Centre's argument was that "we are not aware of any necessity for a radical re-organisation of the local government structure in Greater London . . . [and] . . . we are convinced that the status, functions and boundaries of the London County Council, in particular, should be maintained."[37] Like Professor Griffith of the London School of Economics, the Centre's witnesses argued that, while there was a need for more effective coordination and control of some services, especially planning, by central Government departments, the existing local government machinery was adequate to perform the great

---

[36] R.C., *Written Evidence*, V, 266-268.
[37] *Ibid.*, pp. 64-99.

majority of local services. Hence, the Centre's spokesmen did not recommend the creation of any new ministries for Greater London,
although they did call for the establishment of a regional research and
information agency.

The Royal Commission characterized the Centre's presentation as
constituting a "sociological approach" to the problem, and the average
American academician would probably classify it as being the most
"behavioral" in orientation of any of the evidence presented to the
Commission. Among other things, the Centre attempted to provide the
Commission with a wide range of data on population trends, socioeconomic groupings, demographic influences, and voting trend analysis.
In so doing, it offered much of the most originally creative research
analysis received during the entire course of testimony, and also much
of the most potentially useful analysis.

By and large, however, this analysis did not appear to make any
significant impression on the Commission, at least in terms of persuading the Commissioners that a major reorganization of London's local
government was unnecessary. Instead, the Commissioners had already
caught a glimpse of their potential New Jerusalem in the form of LSE
Scheme "A," and a revised version of this scheme was to represent the
essence of their final recommendations. As noted, however, the Commission did make one important population change in the LSE plan,
and this in turn led to one important functional change. The Robson
group had recommended Greater London Boroughs of 250,000 to
500,000 population, indicating that considerations of educational administration "have carried great weight in determining the size of
[these] second-tier units." In short, the LSE group felt their new boroughs would be large enough to handle both primary and secondary
education in a satisfactory manner. When the Royal Commission proposed that these boroughs should be reduced to a population range of
100,000 to 250,000, it also made a corresponding change in the educational services. Whereas the LSE Scheme "A" witnesses had proposed
that education should be a borough responsibility, the Commission
proposed that education should be a concurrent responsibility, to be
split between the Greater London Council and the new London bor-

oughs, with the former handling over-all policy and the latter covering day-to-day administration.

Hence, in the end, the Royal Commission did favor a comprehensive reorganization of London's government, but it was a reorganization designed to be even more attractive to the second-tier authorities than the LSE Scheme "A," since it called for even fewer disruptions in existing second-tier boundaries (through amalgamations and consolidations). In effect, the Commission's proposals were bound to have tremendous appeal to the second-tier units, which would enjoy significantly increased powers at a very modest cost.

It was now completely obvious that the major opposition to the Commission's proposals would come from the first-tier county councils and from the London Labour Party.

The major support for the Commission's plan, on the other hand, was to be found in the London School of Economics group, the central London Conservative organizations (i.e., the London Municipal Society, the LCC minority), and, most probably, in the second-tier authorities.

Yet, second-tier reaction remained the one big question mark, and this question mark was destined to shape the immediate strategies of the opposition forces more than any other single factor. It took little insight to realize that the second-tier authorities now constituted the key to the entire reorganization program. Somehow, the county councils would have to hold these second-tier units in line if they were to have the slightest chance of defeating the Royal Commission's proposals. If these second-tier authorities broke away *en masse* from their first-tier county councils, the balance of forces would shift to a degree which would render any effective opposition impossible. Above all else, the counties had to solidify their second-tier support, and then attempt to provide a united front of opposition to the Commission's plan.

Obviously, this was not going to be easy. For one thing, the Royal Commission had thrown out some very tempting bait (in the form of increased powers) to the second-tier authorities. For another, the counties had already seriously miscalculated their position in their initial testimony to the Royal Commission. The narrowly parochial attitude they had adopted toward the Commission's study was hardly of a nature to engender support from their second-tier units.

Hence, the counties had to make a very "agonizing reappraisal" of their position, and they had to make it very quickly. Unless they could come up with an approach that was a great deal more imaginative than any they had displayed to date, their chances of successfully opposing the reorganization scheme were nil.

10. The Opposition Consolidates Its Forces

Following the old military adage that "there is no more important . . . law for strategy than to keep your forces concentrated,"[1] the county councils used three different approaches in an effort to line up their second-tier units in opposition to the Royal Commission's plan.

The first was a positive appeal to symbols of allegiance and loyalty; the second, the employment of direct political pressure; the third, a counterattack in the form of an alternative plan.

The Surrey County Council was able to protect much of its local support through use of the first and third techniques, and the London County Council consolidated its position through primary reliance on the first and second techniques. Neither the Middlesex, Essex, or Kent councils, on the other hand, enjoyed much real success with any of the three approaches, and as a result the effectiveness of their own opposition to the reform effort disintegrated rapidly, and finally virtually disappeared.

Hertfordshire, the sixth county to be affected by the plan, played a somewhat different game from the outset. This county viewed the Commission's recommendations in terms of what might have been, and on these terms it had gotten off very lightly.

Originally, nine of Hertfordshire's second-tier units had been in-

[1] Karl von Clausewitz, *War, Politics and Power* (Chicago: Gateway, 1962), Chapter XXIV.

cluded in the Greater London review area, but in its final report, the Commission recommended that only three of these units should actually be placed under the jurisdiction of the proposed new Greater London Council. Since one of these three units, East Barnet, was generally favorable to this proposal, "the County Council's opposition was only to the inclusion of the [other two] Urban Districts of Barnet and Cheshunt in the Greater London area."[2]

In its attempts to spring these two units free from the future rigors of a Greater London existence, the Hertfordshire Council decided that discretion represented the better part of valor, and it spoke very softly with respect to any outright criticism of the Royal Commission's report. Although it did meet with the other county councils at strategy sessions, its role in these sessions was minimal; no further major reference will be made to this council's activities during the remainder of this study.

The real story of the counties' opposition to the reorganization plan is to be found not in Hertfordshire, but rather in Surrey and London counties. The deftness with which these two bodies employed the techniques of second-tier consolidation, and the corresponding failure of their Middlesex, Essex, and Kent counterparts to do the same, represents an intriguing study in the art of political infighting.

Symbols of Allegiance

"There are people who would still prefer to be called men of Kent, rather than men of Greater London."[3]

Such was the hopeful clarion call sounded by one of the Kent County aldermen in an attempt to rally his second-tier legions to battle against the Royal Commission's plan. Yet, the simple facts of the matter were that the local authorities in metropolitan Kent County did not care to partake of this particular fray, nor were their Middlesex or Essex coun-

[2] Letter, Neville Moon, Clerk of the Hertfordshire County Council, to F. Smallwood, dated December 3, 1962.

[3] The remark is that of Kent County Council Alderman H. N. Breecher Bryant, quoted in *The Times*, March 2, 1961.

terparts any more anxious to demonstrate patriotic fidelity to their home counties.

Actually, when it came to the question of second-tier allegiance, Middlesex County was in the most desperate shape of all. It had literally nothing going for it, and virtually everything going against it, in this particular area.

MIDDLESEX COUNTY

When London County was originally created in 1888, a good chunk of its territory had been carved out of the ancient area of Middlesex. This surgical severance had created something of a physical freak as far as the remainder of Middlesex was concerned. To mention but a few of the resultant anomalies, the Middlesex Guildhall (i.e., the seat of its county government) was left in London County. The county's law courts and archives were likewise left in London County. The county's Cricket Club played at Lords in London (i.e., Marylebone); the Middlesex Hospital is in London; and even Middlesex Street, the site of the famous Petticoat Lane Market, is located in London (as the geographical border between the City of London and its most easterly neighbor, the Metropolitan Borough of Stepney).

About all that Middlesex received back for this bounteous display of external generosity was the London Airport, which is located in Middlesex County. Indeed, historically, Middlesex was the victim of the most basic *non possumus* in English local mores—it had never even built its own cathedral. In essence, the county had no central core and little ideological coherence. It was, in the words of one observer, "a county without a county town, a torso with its head adrift in alien fields."[4]

Yet, the real difficulty in Middlesex was to be found, not so much in this outward dissemination of symbolic attachments, as unorthodox as it may have been, but rather in the form of some very serious glandular disorders within. The key difficulty here, of course, was the county borough problem, and the living manifestation of this problem was the so-called Middlesex "Big Ten." As has already been noted,

[4] Lena M. Jeger, "Old Middlesex," *The Guardian,* December 11, 1962, p. 5.

these ten Middlesex second-tier giants, each with its 100,000-plus population, had long clamored for independent county borough status, and the resultant relationships between the county council and these boroughs was, to put it mildly, disastrous. It is difficult to place categorical blame for this deterioration of relations on either party. Instead, it was an inevitable offshoot of two independent forces—the historic growth of the borough's population and the division of the county into large geographical borough units during the 1930 local government reviews that later proved to be too large for the county's own good.

As regards population growth, throughout most of its long history, Middlesex had served as the breadbasket for the City of London. In 1132, Henry I granted "Middlesex to my citizens of London to farm for 300 Pounds to them and their heirs," and it was not until some 750 years later that these farms began to disappear when the suburban population moved in *en masse*.

By 1930 many local areas in Middlesex, Ealing and Hendon being two notable examples, had already passed the 100,000 mark in population and had theoretically qualified for independent county borough status.

This situation was aggravated further by the local government reviews in 1930, when new chunks of territory were added to the already large second-tier units. Between 1930 and 1940, Ealing acquired Manwell, Greenford, and Northolt and jumped by 50,000 in population. Hendon picked up the district of Edgeware, and with it 30,000 more people. Harrow was consolidated out of Pinner, Harrow Weald, Great Stanmore, Little Stanmore, Wealdstone, and Harrow-on-the-Hill and soared from 96,000 to 190,000 in population. Wembley absorbed Kingsbury and increased from 65,000 to 121,000, and so it went. These consolidations may well have made for a more tidy local governmental structure, but they also played havoc with the future relations between the county council and its growing children.

As a result of these growing population pressures, coupled with an inverse erosion of the second-tier authorities' powers, there was very little prospect for anything but bad relations between the Middlesex County Council and its local units, regardless of any good work either may have done. Actually, in a great many respects the Middlesex County Council was a very fine local authority. The Ministry of Education credited this body with "very good work" in the educational field, but its terms of praise might well have been even stronger than this. Among its many achievements, Middlesex County had the highest figure throughout England and Wales for the proportion of children staying on in school after the optional dropout age of fifteen, which many experts think is "the most telling litmus paper of all."[5]

Yet, regardless of any good work done either by the County Council or by its second-tier units, relations between the two were bound to be strained. In actuality, Middlesex had no chance of holding these larger units in line once they had savored the hitherto forbidden fruit of increased powers implicit in the Royal Commission's proposals. Even if meaningful symbols of allegiance had been located inside, rather than outside, the county's boundaries, there was little hope that Middlesex could have persuaded many of its larger second-tier authorities to oppose the Royal Commission's plan.

ESSEX COUNTY

Essex County also had some sizable second-tier units, the most notable being the municipal boroughs of Ilford (178,000), Romford (115,000), Walthamstow (108,000), Dagenham (108,000), and the Urban District of Hornchurch (128,000).

As was the case in Middlesex, the relationships between the Essex County Council and these units were not overly cordial. The Royal Commission described these relationships as being "indifferent," but in many cases they were quite poor. A number of the Essex second-tier units felt the County Council had been much too stingy in delegating meaningful responsibilities to them, and once again, they were much bedazzled by the tempting bait of increased local powers which the Commission had dangled before their eyes.

A second factor that complicated the Essex situation was the political dichotomy between the largely Labour-controlled metropolitan units

[5] Lena M. Jeger, "A Human Awful Wonder of God," *New Statesman*, April 27, 1962, p. 586.

in the urban portion of the county, which were directly affected by the Commission's plan, and the Conservative-oriented, rural units located in the eastern edges of the county, which were unaffected by the plan. In terms of geographical size, Essex was a fairly impressive county, eight times larger than Middlesex. In total area, it ran from London County on the west to the coast bordering the North Sea on the east. This eastern coastal area is dominated by two municipal boroughs, Colchester and Harwich. The relations between these two eastern communities and their more westerly metropolitan neighbors were quite distant in terms of mileage and, very often, in terms of attitude as well. As a result, there was a considerable display of sympathy among some of the eastern Conservative spokesmen to let the Labour units in Metropolitan Essex be transferred outright to the new Greater London Council without further ado. Indeed, one slogan utilized in eastern Essex County to dramatize this attitude was the hardly subtle phrase, "Kick the Cockneys Out."

This internal division within the Essex County Council compounded the issue of allegiance considerably, and it most certainly tended to blunt any feelings of second-tier loyalty that may have existed at the time. On the one hand, there was a strong segment within the Essex Council that argued vehemently against the proposed reorganization, holding that the loss of 54 per cent of the county's population and 58 per cent of its ratable value would be disastrous. This was the group which had originally testified before the Royal Commission. Yet, there was also a second, more rurally oriented Essex contingent, which was quite willing to see the Labour-dominated metropolitan fringe separated from the remainder of the county.

Hence, a recurrent question in Essex was not only whether the second-tier authorities would remain loyal to the county, but whether the county would remain loyal to these second-tier units. Under the circumstances, it is hardly surprising that many of the metropolitan Essex authorities bolted away from the County Council and supported the Royal Commission's plan. This loss of second-tier strength, coupled with its own internal ambivalence, tended to reduce the over-all effectiveness of the Essex County Council as a serious opposition force.

KENT COUNTY

The position of the metropolitan Kent County authorities—for which the county alderman had harbored such high-flown hopes of pious parochialism—was a curious one. It was curious for two reasons. First, unlike Middlesex and Essex, Kent did not have any potential county boroughs in its metropolitan area. Its largest second-tier authority was the Municipal Borough of Bexley, with only 90,000 persons. Second, Kent is quite an attractive "status" area in terms of suburban prestige. Although not perhaps quite as fashionable as Surrey, metropolitan Kent ranked well ahead of most of London, Essex, and even Middlesex counties in terms of social appeal.

Under these circumstances, it was reasonable to guess that many of the Kent authorities would have resisted any submersion into the Greater London area, that they would, in actual fact, have preferred to remain "Men of Kent." Yet, in the final analysis, seven of the eight second-tier Kent authorities affected by the Royal Commission's plan decided that they wanted what the Royal Commission had offered. The eighth authority—Bromley—was not in outright opposition to the reorganization plan, but rather remained neutral on the matter.

The primary reason for which these second-tier Kent authorities deserted their County Council was basically similar to the position taken by the Middlesex and Essex units. The Kent authorities had long disagreed with their County Council over the delegation of powers. In its report, the Royal Commission described the relations between the Kent County Council and its second-tier units as "medium"—behind Surrey but ahead of Essex and Middlesex. Actually, there was a tremendous amount of ill will between the local Kent units and the County Council with regard to the issue of delegation. The Kent County Council ran a very tight and tidy shop, retaining highly centralized control over many functional activities, most especially the health services. The local authorities had long sought increased powers, and as was the case in both Middlesex and Essex, these units were tremendously impressed with what the Royal Commission had to offer in this respect.

A second factor that tended to influence the local Kent units to support the Royal Commission's plan was a fortuitous distribution of partisan political power as it related to the suggested Greater London Borough groupings which the Royal Commission had outlined. The Commission had suggested that metropolitan Kent could easily be divided into three new Greater London Boroughs. One of these would consist of two Conservative strongholds, plus the tiny Urban District of Penge, which was hardly a political power at all. The second would again consist of two Conservative authorities (although one of these was destined later to go Liberal). The third would contain two Labour units, plus a Conservative borough, but one with a strong Labour minority. Hence, in terms of practical partisan politics, the Commission's suggested new borough groupings were attractive to the Kent local politicians. If this was all that was necessary to restore the health of local government, it represented a pretty easy pill to swallow.

In addition, the factor of administrative precedent and convenience was a consideration that helps to explain further the willingness of the metropolitan Kent authorities to support the Royal Commission's plan. In many of the counties, the new Greater London Borough groupings suggested by the Commission threatened to cut across current service patterns quite severely. In Kent, however, these proposed borough groupings promised to provide only a minimal disruption of existing services. Again this was a fortuitous accident, since the existing administrative service divisions in metropolitan Kent just happened to coincide quite closely with the proposed borough groupings the Commission had outlined. Hence, whereas in some of the counties the proposed Greater London Borough groupings promised to fragment existing service patterns quite brutally, in metropolitan Kent these groupings coincided very closely with such existing patterns.

Finally, there was the consideration of County Hall accessibility. In both Kent and Essex, the seat of county government was quite distant from the metropolitan authorities; indeed, in both cases the Green Belt served as a natural buffer separating these authorities from their County Halls. This was perhaps not a major problem with respect to the promotion of second-tier loyalties, but it is interesting to note that Surrey and London—the only two counties in which the County Hall was located within convenient reach of the second-tier units affected by the Royal Commission's plan—were also the two counties that enjoyed the most success in holding these second-tier units in line.

SURREY COUNTY

The major reason Surrey County was able to consolidate its local support was certainly not County Hall accessibility, however, but rather a careful cultivation of second-tier loyalties over a great many years. The Royal Commission classified the relationships between the two tiers as being "good" in Surrey, and indeed, they were very good. In large measure this resulted from enlightened county leadership at both the staff and the elective level.

The staff leadership had been inaugurated originally by Mr. Dudley Aukland, who had placed great emphasis on a partnership concept between the two tiers during his service as Clerk of the Council from 1927 to 1950. This cooperative leadership tradition was continued under Mr. Aukland's successor as County Clerk, Mr. W. W. Ruff. In turn, the cooperation promoted at the staff level was reinforced by a number of strong County Council Chairmen, among them The Right Honourable Chuter Ede, M.P., former Home Secretary of the postwar Labour Government (Surrey, unlike other counties, elects its chairman as the Chief Executive Officer, regardless of Party); Sir Cyril Black, M.P., a formidable figure in Surrey local politics and a fabulously successful London business executive (he is a member of the boards of more than fifty business enterprises); and Sir John Wenham, a distinguished lawyer and former President of the Guildford Conservative Association.

The degree of good will which these men built up between the Surrey County Council and its second-tier authorities can be illustrated by the manner in which the county spokesmen presented their testimony to the Royal Commission. One of the key points which Sir Cyril Black emphasized in this testimony was the fact that the County Council had reviewed its evidence with all its local authorities before it presented its position to the Royal Commission. Hence, he was able to assert that "by and large, the County Council's view is endorsed and supported by every concerned organized body of official opinion in the county."[6] None of the other county witnesses could make such a claim before the Commission.

In addition to a policy of enlightened leadership, it must be admitted that the Surrey County Council had a number of other factors going for it when it attempted to convince its second-tier authorities to back its opposition stance against the Royal Commission's plan.

First, none of the county's second-tier units approached the population figure of 100,000 theoretically necessary to qualify for independent county borough status. The largest second-tier authority in metropolitan Surrey was the Municipal Borough of Sutton and Cheam (79,000), and most of the second-tier units here were well under 70,000. Hence, unlike Middlesex and Essex counties, Surrey had never been plagued with the county borough controversy.

Second, in Surrey the proposed Greater London Borough groupings suggested by the Commission threatened to cause serious disruption in existing service patterns, and this was a relatively easy threat to illustrate. For example, the county had built some 120 new schools since the Second World War, but unlike those of Kent, these schools had not been planned to coincide with the metropolitan portion of the county. Instead, they had been built on a county-wide basis, without regard for any potential future separation of the metropolitan fringe from the rest of the county. Thus, for example, all during the controversy over the reorganization plan, the new Kingston Technical College was rising just opposite the County Hall. This facility was designed to serve the needs of the entire county, yet it was being built in an area that would soon be separated out of Surrey (as would the County Hall, itself) and turned over to the Greater London Council. Concrete physical aberrations such as this served as a daily reminder of the potentially severe impact of the proposed reorganization plan.

Third, Surrey is a very rich county, but one that would be tremendously hard-hit by the Commission's proposals, losing some 63 per cent of its population and some 66 per cent of its ratable value. This

[6] R.C., *Minutes of Oral Evidence,* Nos. 43-44, p. 1,832.

consideration not only tended to stiffen the county's opposition to these proposals, but it also helped to explain a good part of this opposition. Surrey's wealth made the county one of the most desirable prestige residences in the entire Greater London area. Status symbols were very powerful here, because to many of its residents Surrey implied "class," whereas Greater London implied what they thought they had left behind when they moved to Surrey. The pride and prestige of the Surrey name helped to explain a great many of the strong ties of loyalty that were apparent in this county.

When all these factors are lumped together, it is quite possible to understand why the Surrey County Council was able to obtain strong allegiance from its second-tier units in its battle against the Royal Commission's plan. Yet, in actual fact, this support was not quite as strong as the Surrey County councillors liked others to believe. The county spokesmen always tried to illustrate the depth of this support by quoting figures for all the second-tier units in Surrey—for those inner boroughs that were earmarked for incorporation under the new Greater London Council as well as for the more rural units that would remain under the jurisdiction of the Surrey County Council. On the basis of this analysis, these spokesmen argued that twenty-six of the thirty-three second-tier units in Surrey were opposed to the reform proposals. Yet, when this analysis is extended to include only those metropolitan units actually affected by the reorganization, as it was finally delineated by the Government, these units split quite closely on this issue. Originally, seven of these affected second-tier Surrey authorities opposed the reorganization effort, while five supported this effort.

Hence, in the final analysis, Surrey did not receive overwhelming allegiance from the most crucial second-tier units of all. What is of most importance, however, is the fact that it received enough second-tier support to justify its continued opposition to the plan. Although Surrey's second-tier flank may have been somewhat shaky, it did not, like those of Middlesex, Essex, and Kent, collapse completely. As a result, the Surrey County Council was able to keep up a constant drumbeat of opposition against reorganization throughout the entire reform contest.

LONDON COUNTY

London County was the most controversial of all when it came to a question of second-tier loyalties. There were many who would argue that no real loyalties existed here, that the metropolitan boroughs' support of the London County Council was nothing more than an automatic submission on the part of these boroughs to the dictates of the London Labour Party. This, most certainly, is the simplest explanation of the situation, but it is not necessarily the most accurate one.

There is considerable evidence to indicate that the factor of allegiance and loyalty was not totally absent from London County's second-tier authorities, especially as regards the Labour metropolitan boroughs. In its oral testimony before the Royal Commission, the Metropolitan Boroughs' Standing Joint Committee had emphasized that whereas it "was first set up to combat certain policies and trends of the London County Council . . . in later years the hostility which was present at that time has given way to mutual trust and respect."[7] This statement was, perhaps, a bit stronger than circumstances warranted, yet there is no doubt that a considerable degree of underlying loyalty did exist between the boroughs and the LCC.

The most significant indication of this fact was to be found in interviews with various leaders of the boroughs. In no case, in either conservative or Labour boroughs, did any of the elective or staff leaders indicate a complete antipathy toward the London County Council, although some of the Conservative borough spokesmen did support the reorganization plan. Rather, in all cases (including those of the Conservative boroughs), the leaders indicated genuine respect, bordering on admiration, for the achievements of the LCC. In the case of some of the Labour boroughs, this feeling was extremely strong, often approximating reverence. Part of this attitude can be explained by the existence of strong physical symbols which tended to accentuate the boroughs' respect for tangible LCC achievements. This was especially apparent in the east London boroughs, many of which had been virtually leveled during the war. Here the LCC Architects Department had been highly instrumental in rebuilding new housing projects and

7 R.C., *Minutes of Oral Evidence*, No. 1, p. 3.

schools, which served as highly visible reminders of the LCC's relationship to the local councils. In the east London Borough of Stepney, for example, an old Town Hall, located next door to a completely bombed-out public library, stands just across the street from a new LCC housing project that contrasts sharply with this wartime devastation.

How much these physical symbols may have meant to the man on the street is a matter of debate. One local Labour leader complained that as soon as the citizenry began to get new housing and the other physical facilities they had wanted, many of them had become complacent toward the local authorities that had provided these amenities. There is a considerable body of precedent to indicate that he may well have been right on this. Public interest in government, be it national or local, seems to thrive most successfully under the stimulus of unmet need and unresolved conflict, and to drop off rapidly once these problems are resolved. Yet, the fact remains that the Labour borough councillors in London County had not become complacent about the LCC, even if segments of the local public may have lost interest. The bonds that had been forged between these councils and the London County Council on the basis of tangible physical achievements alone exerted a very strong pull.

Nor were the considerations here entirely those of physical symbols, for personal factors entered into this equation as well. One of the major arguments the proponents of reform advanced was that the London County Council had become so large as to lose contact with its constituents. Again, this may well have been a point of legitimate debate as far as the general public was concerned, yet it is highly doubtful whether it held true with respect to the elected local councillors. On many separate occasions, borough leaders advised that the great strength of the London County Council was to be found in its easy accessibility. How does one analyze seeming contradictions such as this?

The apparent reason for such confusion is to be found not so much in the question whether any basic loyalties existed between the two governmental tiers in the LCC area as in whether these loyalties

were so strong as to justify the subsequent extremist position the Metro-
polian Boroughs' Standing Joint Committee was to take on the question
of reorganization. Before the reform battle was over, this Committee
was destined to adopt an opposition stance of total obstinacy, matched
in intensity only by the position of the London County Council. Since
the voting patterns that supported this extremist stance almost exactly
paralleled the Labour-Conservative split on the Committee (with the
sole exception of the Metropolitan Borough of Fulham, which refused
to join the opposition forces from the beginning), many quite naturally
assumed that the entire question of second-tier loyalties in the LCC
area was nothing more than a naked political power play. Actually,
however, the situation was not quite as simple as this. Indeed, the most
basic finding that emerged from the entire analysis of local authority
reaction to the Royal Commission's report was that the political parties
were severely limited in the extent to which they could dictate to their
constituent local authorities on the question of reform. Such dictates
were consistently rejected unless there was an underlying base of loyalty
and allegiance between the two tiers of government.

These limitations in the application of direct political pressure were
obvious throughout the Greater London area.

Direct Political Pressure

The difficulties that the county party organizations faced in their
attempts to pressure the local authorities were nowhere more apparent
than in the Metropolitan Borough of Fulham.

The independent stand which the Labourite Fulham Council took
against the London Labour Party on the question of reorganization was
a highly interesting one. This borough was somewhat unique in that it
was one of the relatively few Labour strongholds located to the west
of the City Corporation of London, but its Party majority (39 Labour
—7 Conservative) was extremely powerful, and indeed, Labour had
been in continuous control of the Borough Council since 1933. Like
every other unit of local government in London, Fulham had some

strong historical forces working on its behalf. "Its history as a Local Government area dates back to 691 A.D. when a Charter was granted to Earconwald of the Manor of Fulham."[8] Earconwald was then Bishop of London, and since that time (with a few minor exceptions), Fulham had served as the official residence of the Bishops of London, and as the home of Fulham Palace.

The borough was not notably wealthy, ranking nineteenth out of the twenty-eight metropolitan boroughs in total ratable value as of April 1, 1962,[9] but it did harbor a strong tradition of local public service. Harold Laski served as an alderman in the borough before his death; Baroness Summerskill, P.C., the former chairman of the national Labour Party, represented West Fulham in Parliament from 1938 to 1955; and Michael Stewart, M.P., Labour's shadow Minister of Housing and Local Government, occupies the Fulham Parliamentary seat at the present time. In addition, the borough's voting participation record in county council elections was quite strong. In the 1961 London County Council election, Fulham polled a vote of 47.3 per cent, well over the county area average of 36.4 per cent, and in 1952, Fulham West achieved the highest LCC vote in the entire postwar period, reaching 59.9 per cent on this occasion.[10]

It was in the local borough elections, however, that the Fulham vote was lowest, generally falling about 10 per cent under the County Council turnout, and averaging in the vicinity of 35 per cent to 38 per cent. This fact dramatized much of the disagreement between the London Labour Party and the Fulham Borough Council, and in turn, it helped to explain the borough's position on the reorganization plan.

For a number of years dating back to the early 1950's, Fulham had argued that it was necessary to increase the functional responsibilities of the second-tier units in order to stimulate more public interest in local affairs. As such, the Fulham Council had been a leading advocate of an increased delegation of powers from the London County Council to

[8] The Metropolitan Borough of Fulham, *Official Guide* (undated), p. 15.

[9] *The Municipal Yearbook and Public Utilities Directory* (London: Municipal Journal Ltd., 1962), p. 786.

[10] *General Election of County Councillors 13 April 1961* (London County Council, June 1961), pp. 2, 7.

the metropolitan boroughs, and it was this borough that had been most highly instrumental in convincing the LCC and the London Labour Party to consider the 1955 delegation scheme. Hence, for many years a strong faction on the Fulham Council had been highly sympathetic to the "health" of local government criterion as this was later developed by the Royal Commission, and, as previously noted, Fulham was one of the six local authorities within the Greater London area that advocated a comprehensive reform program with this end in mind, during its testimony before the Royal Commission.

While the Fulham councillors were not unanimous in their view, a majority of them continued to support the reform program, despite their Labour leanings and despite very strong pressure to reverse their stand—pressure emanating from the London Labour Party, and subsequently from the London County Council and the Metropolitan Boroughs' Standing Joint Committee.

The fact that the London Labour Party was not able to alter the Fulham position serves as one indication of the limitations of directly applied Party pressure even in a highly organized political arena such as central London. A second indication of similar Labour Party unrest became evident in the Metropolitan Borough of Hackney (a 100-percent Labour-controlled council) shortly after the Royal Commission issued its report. Just one month after this report appeared, the Ministry of Housing and Local Government, by letter dated November 28, 1960, asked all the London local authorities for their reactions to the Commission's proposals. Like Fulham, the Labour-controlled Borough of Hackney indicated general sympathy with the Greater London Council concept, although its support was somewhat ambivalent. Instead of supporting the Commission's plan outright, the Hackney Council advised the Ministry that it favored the general idea of the directly elected council, but it felt that "the whole of Greater London is too large an area for effective administration and true democratic representation."[11]

[11] In this regard, the Borough of Hackney agreed with Mr. Hugh Jenkins (the Labour LCC representative from Hackney North and Stoke Newington) that the proposed Greater London Council area was too big, but unlike Mr. Jenkins, Hackney did not recommend a specific alternative (i.e., the London Postal District) to serve as a halfway house.

It was outside, rather than inside, London County, however, that the breakdown in Party discipline became most apparent. As the Ministry of Housing and Local Government received comments on its inquiry during the period from January to March 1961, it became increasingly more obvious that neither the Labour nor the Conservative Party was going to be able to hold its second-tier units in line outside the LCC area. In Labour-controlled Middlesex County, all four of the "Big Ten" boroughs which had Labour council majorities broke with the Party to support the Royal Commission's plan in its basic essentials, although two of these boroughs disagreed with specific portions of the plan. In Labour-controlled Essex County, two of the five key Labour boroughs supported the Royal Commission plan outright, and a third reserved judgment on the matter but indicated considerable sympathy with the general position the Commission had taken. In Conservative Kent County, four of the five Conservative authorities affected by the plan indicated outright support for the Royal Commission's recommendations, while the fifth remained neutral on the matter. Nor was the Conservatives' record much better in Surrey, where four of ten Conservative boroughs in metropolitan Surrey bolted the Party to support the plan outright.

Indeed, London County represented the only place in the entire Greater London area where the second-tier reaction to the Royal Commission's report did closely parallel the existing Party patterns.

Outside London County, the use of any direct pressure techniques by the parties simply was not sufficient to hold the second-tier units in line. It was obvious that the county councils would need something else, beyond the considerations of allegiance and party politics, if they were to hope to consolidate their second-tier strength.

Counterattack

This "something else" appeared in the form of an alternative proposal to the Royal Commission's which was formulated by the Surrey County Council's General Purposes Committee under the leadership of Sir Cyril Black. Although this proposal was quite modest in its basic outlines, it is notable for the fact that it represented the only serious attempt any of the county councils made to formulate a positive and constructive response to the Royal Commission plan.

The essence of the Surrey scheme was, first, two sharp thrusts at the proposals advanced by the Royal Commission, and second, two concrete suggestions as to what type of action should be taken to reorganize Greater London's government.

The initial thrust was a stinging criticism of the "tremendous and unnecessary upheaval" in well-established arrangements that would be caused by the Commission's proposals. Here the Surrey Council argued that such "drastic steps could only be justified if . . . an overwhelmingly strong case for change was established."[12] Yet, the Council contended, no such case had been advanced. "Surrey's second thrust was the argument that the proposed Greater London Council would be exercising powers, particularly planning powers, within too circumscribed an area: that it would be a mistake to create this 'monstrosity' simply to do for the built-up area of the metropolis what ought to be done for the south-east region as a whole."[13] In short, the Surrey Council argued that the Royal Commission's plan went too far in terms of its disruptive influences, but not far enough to result in strong regional planning.

The two alternative suggestions advanced by Surrey were, first, to create a Joint Planning Board in place of the proposed Greater London Council. This Board would have executive and financial powers and would cover a geographical area roughly equivalent to that of the Abercrombie Plan (i.e., a thirty-mile instead of a fifteen-mile radius from central London). It would be administered by an independent chairman, would be representative of all the County Councils and the three County Borough Planning Authorities in the area, and would include representatives appointed by associations of the second-tier borough and district authorities, as well as representatives of particular interest

---

[12] *Statement of Views by the Surrey County Council on the Report of the Royal Commission on Local Government in Greater London*, February 1961, p. 17.

[13] "Counter-Attack" (editorial), *The Times*, November 21, 1960, p. 13.

organizations (e.g., transport, power, industry, commerce, organized labour, the Port of London Authority, the police, etc.):

> The Board would have as its primary task the preparation, in consultation with County and County Borough Councils and other interests, of a Master Development Plan for the Greater London Region dealing with all the strategic regional questions such as the main road framework, the rail network, the broad pattern of land uses, the level and main disposition of employment, target population, Green Belt, airports, etc. This Master Plan would have to be approved by the Minister [and] the Development Plans of the individual County and County Borough Councils would thereafter be prepared to fit in with the Master Plan.[14]

The second Surrey suggestion was a scarcely veiled bribe to the second-tier authorities. Here the Surrey scheme called for increased delegation of powers to these authorities, specifically citing the desirability of delegating the local administration of education, health, and welfare and the control of development. The proposal stated further, "it would probably be possible also to delegate elements of the Childrens' Service. To enable this delegation to take place it would be necessary to ensure that District Authorities in the Review Area were at least of a population of 60,000, or not far short of it. . . . It is estimated that throughout the Review Area only a very few District Authorities would need to consider amalgamation with their neighbours."[15] In short, the Surrey Council attempted to offer the increased powers which the second-tier authorities so obviously desired, without any of the pains of amalgamation suggested by the Royal Commission, although the Council was considerably less precise in specifying what these powers would be than the Commission had been.

The London, Middlesex, Essex, and Kent County Councils immediately jumped on the Surrey bandwagon, and all of them, in replying to the Ministry of Housing and Local Government's November 28 letter, indicated that they would now like to see a Greater London reorganization along similar lines. Hence, the Surrey Council did achieve the positive result of persuading the other county councils to admit that

[14] Surrey County Council: *Statement of Views*, p. 19.
[15] *Ibid.*, p. 21.

all might not be perfect in the Greater London area. The counties had finally abandoned the inflexible defense of the status quo that they had presented to the Royal Commission. Yet, this was about all in the way of positive action that did result from the Surrey plan. Most of the second-tier authorities that favored reform were already too well committed to their positions to shift now from the Royal Commission plan to the Surrey scheme. In addition to the fact that they preferred the precision of the Commission's proposals (which clearly spelled out the precise delegation of powers to take place), many of the second-tier authorities simply did not trust the county councils' offer of delegation at this time. They tended to view the Surrey offer as a "death-bed repentance." As a result, they remained suspiciously aloof from supporting the Surrey proposals.

The end result was that the counties had now pulled out all the stops in their efforts to solidify their second-tier support; yet, with the exceptions of London and Surrey counties, the response to the efforts had been minimal. It was a story of too little, too late, with many of the second-tier units still desiring what the Royal Commission had offered and, hence, declining to join with the counties in opposing the Commission's reform plan.

In addition, a number of other units indicated support of the Royal Commission's proposals. The General Purposes Committee of the Association of Municipal Corporations expressed agreement with the plan. Shortly thereafter, in April 1961, Lord Morrison resigned as President of the Association, charging that the Committee wanted to destroy the London County Council. He went on to assert that the Association itself was "so bitterly anti-county council that it is irrational," and held that the Royal Commission's plan represented no more than "local governmental gerrymandering."[16]

The Urban District Councils Association also agreed to go along with the Greater London Council concept, although with considerable misgivings because it feared the disappearance of all its small local government units under the new Greater London Borough amalgamations that the Commission had proposed. In this respect it argued that

16 Letter, Lord Morrison of Lambeth to Sir Harold Banwell, Secretary, Association of Municipal Corporations, quoted in *The Times*, April 12, 1961.

the minimum borough population figure of 100,000 proposed by the Commission was too big. However, the Association's willingness to support the general concept of reorganization, despite these misgivings, represented an attitude of considerable statesmanship. In effect, the Association recognized the need for local governmental reform throughout England and Wales, and it did not want to adopt a position of totally negative opposition to such an effort. Instead, it hoped that many of the existing urban district councils outside the Greater London area could be preserved during the course of this review and felt that the best way to assure this end was to cooperate with, rather than obstruct, the forces of reform. At a later date the Association was to express considerable doubt as to the wisdom of this initial attitude, since it felt it had actually been betrayed during the course of subsequent local government reviews.[17]

Even the County Councils Association indicated considerable sympathy with the Royal Commission, stating that it believed "all the evidence put to the Commission has been carefully considered, and [that it] admired the courage shown in their propounding of a revolutionary plan." The Association did disagree with the proposed Greater London Council idea, however, arguing that this was a "monolithic approach" to local government and should more properly be considered "Regional Government."[18] Yet, this disagreement was not so adamant as to result in an activist position of total opposition to the Commission's plan. Instead, the County Councils Association expressed this initial disagreement, and then retired, rather quietly, from the scene.

Only in the first-tier county boroughs were the county councils able to pick up any active local governmental support at all. The County Borough of Croydon came out flatly against the proposed Greater London Council as "colossal and unwieldy," and it recommended that "all necessary steps should be taken to resist the Commission's proposals."[19] The County Borough of East Ham also went on record

[17] Report of Executive Council, Urban District Councils Association, 29 November 1962, pp. 12-14.

[18] Executive Council Minutes, County Councils Association, 22 March 1961, pp. 6-7.

[19] Report of Finance Committee, County Borough of Croydon, February 20, 1961.

as opposing the proposed reorganization on the grounds that "the county borough has proved itself to be an effective unit in the area, [and] it should be perpetuated."[20] Only West Ham County Borough indicated any basic interest in the proposed plan. It referred to the Royal Commission's report as a "masterly analysis of local government in Greater London viewed historically and functionally" and indicated general agreement with the Greater London Council concept, although it did want a council whose members would be appointed by the constituency borough units rather than directly elected on the basis of Parliamentary constituencies as the Commission had recommended.[21] This, again, was an interesting deviation from the Party line, since West Ham was a Labour-controlled council.

In summary, then, at the first-tier level there was virtually unanimous opposition to the Royal Commission's plan. All five of the county councils (plus, to a lesser extent, Hertfordshire) and two of the three county boroughs disagreed flatly with the Commission's proposals and indicated that they would fight these proposals to the bitter end.

On the second-tier level, however, a majority of the eighty-four local authorities within the proposed Greater London Council area (as finally defined in the London Government Bill) advised the Ministry of Housing and Local Government that they supported the Royal Commission's plan. An analysis of the replies that these eighty-four local authorities sent to the Ministry during the winter of 1961, in response to the request for their general comments on the Royal Commission's proposals, indicates that forty-two of these second-tier authorities expressed basic support for the major components of the plan, while only thirty-six were opposed, and six were undecided.[22]

[20] Letter, Town Clerk, County Borough of East Ham, to Ministry of Housing and Local Government, February 16, 1961.

[21] Report of Local Government Committee, County Borough of West Ham, February 14, 1961.

[22] It is difficult to make a precise classification of the second-tier responses, since virtually all the local councils were favorable to certain parts of the Royal Commission plan, especially the statement that they should be the primary units of local government. In making this analysis, key emphasis has been placed on the local councils' reaction to the proposed new Greater London Council. Those units which were opposed to this Council have been classified as being against the reorganization plan, and those which were for the Council have been classified as being favorable to the plan.

In many cases, these second-tier positions cut across Party lines.

The thirty-nine Labour local councils split on an even two-thirds–one-third basis (with twenty-six opposing the plan and thirteen supporting the Commission's major recommendations, or indicating general sympathy with the basic concept of reform). The Conservative alignment was somewhat more tidy (much to the consternation of the opposition Conservative councils of Surrey and Kent) in that most local Conservative authorities supported the plan. Of the thirty-nine Conservative local authorities, thirty indicated outright support of the Royal Commission, while nine were opposed or undecided. (This local Conservative opposition was to grow in strength, however, when a new borough amalgamation scheme was announced at a later date.) The five remaining Independent second-tier councils split almost evenly, three being for the plan and two opposed; and the one remaining local council, which was divided evenly between Labour and the Conservatives, also opposed the plan.

Despite this majority support for the plan among the second-tier units, the second-tier opposition forces were concentrated in two particular counties, London and Surrey. A tabular analysis of the county distribution of second-tier opposition reveals this concentration of opposition very clearly:

SECOND-TIER COUNCILS:
Reaction to the Royal Commission Plan
Winter 1961

	For plan	*Against plan*	*Undecided*
London County	10*	17	2
Surrey County	5	7	0
Essex County	5	3	1
Middlesex County	14	7	2
Kent County	7	0	1
Hertfordshire County	1	2	0
Total	42	36	6

* This figure includes the City of London Corporation, although this unit is not technically part of London County. The area covered by the tabulation is, once again, the Greater London Council area as finally delineated in the London Government Bill.

The crucially important finding in the above tabulation is that the majority of local councils went along with their county councils' opposition stance in both London and Surrey counties. The fact that the London and Surrey County Councils were able to hold a majority of their local units in line is of crucial importance because it enabled each of these Councils to continue an effective program of opposition to the reorganization proposals. The key reason they were able to do this was psychological. Because the London and Surrey Councils had been able to consolidate their second-tier units to oppose the plan, both Councils could pose as defenders of their local districts' prevailing interests. However, no such guise of altruism was possible in Kent, Middlesex, or Essex counties. Indeed, the Kent position was virtually hopeless. Instead of posing as the protector of its local authorities, the Kent County Council appeared to be bent on grinding these authorities under the heel of its own selfish desires. Under the circumstances, it is hardly surprising that the Kent opposition position eroded rapidly, until this Council finally abandoned its opposition stance completely one year later.

The Middlesex and Essex positions were also highly vulnerable, and in both cases the effectiveness of their opposition was destined to disintegrate even further when Labour lost control of these two County Councils in the April 1961 elections.

Hence, only the London and Surrey Councils passed through their second-tier ordeal as effective opposition forces. Yet, the question remained as to what additional support these two Councils could now obtain in an effort to bolster their positions. Surrey had already advanced an alternative scheme that showed little promise of lighting any great sparks. Where should the opposition forces go from here?

It was at this point that the opposition leaders began to formulate the elements of a new strategy—a strategy that was to differ markedly in both tone and intensity from that which had appeared to date.

Whereas the preliminary opposition efforts had placed considerable emphasis upon positive appeals to loyalty and allegiance, and upon a constructive attempt to formulate an alternative reform plan, the next phase of the reform struggle was destined to become considerably more

Map X

Reaction to
Royal Commission Plan:
Second-Tier Authorities
(Winter 1961)

KEY

Favorable (42)

Opposed (36)

Neutral, or
Favorable to
Alternative
Reform
Concept (6)

0   5 Miles

1 City of London
2 Holborn
3 Finsbury
4 Shoreditch
5 Bethnal Green
6 Bermondsey
7 Southwark
8 Deptford
9 Chelsea
10 City of Westminster
11 Kensington
12 Paddington
13 St. Marylebone
14 Hampstead
15 Stoke Newington
16 Southwark
17 Wood Green
18 Friern Barnet
19 Wanstead and Woodford
20 Penge
21 Beddington and Wallington
22 Merton and Morden
23 Malden and Coombe
24 Kingston-upon-Thames
25 Brentford and Chiswick
26 Hammersmith

negative, and more hostile, in its basic emphasis. Now confusion, obstruction, exaggeration, and fear were to be utilized as symbols of political manipulation, as the opposition forces attempted to expand the scope of their support from among the more passive spectators who had not as yet shown any great interest in the question of reform.

In short, the Greater London contest was about to pass from the phase of initial disagreement to that of increasingly more bitter antagonism.

11. The Strategy of Scale

The Government's initial reaction to the constant drumbeat of criticism that the London Teachers' Association had been directing against the Royal Commission's plan provided the key to the new opposition strategy.

This strategy was quite simply designed to activate as many groups as possible to attack specific aspects of the reorganization plan in an effort to gain further concessions from the Government. If these concessions were forthcoming, they could be used to activate new participants, in addition to eroding the original unity of the Royal Commission's program. Obviously, if this process of activation, attack, and erosion could be kept up indefinitely, the entire organization effort would become so emasculated as to warrant complete abandonment.

For purposes of basic identification, this opposition strategy can be somewhat oversimplified as a five-part process of

1. *Enlarging* the scope of the critical audience to
2. *Attack* specific aspects of the reform plan to realize
3. *Concessions* from the Government to result in
4. *Erosion* of the basic unity of the plan to justify
5. *All-Out Attack* on the entire reform effort.

Although so many groups were destined to become caught up in this process that the reform contest eventually began to resemble a game of musical chairs, it is necessary to analyze only a limited number of these groups in order to catch the full outlines of this opposition strategy at work. For illustrative purposes, three such groups—the teachers, the child welfare workers, and once again, the second-tier authorities—have been selected for such analysis. Finally, the activities of a fourth group—The Committee for London Government—are described to illustrate the nature of the concluding all-out broadside that the opposition forces launched against the entire reform program, once they felt the initial groundwork for justifying such an effort had been laid.

The Teachers

The initial attack launched by the London Teacher's Association against the Royal Commission's plan was crucially important because it led to the initial breakthrough in concessions by the central Government that activated the entire strategic process noted above.

It will be recalled that the Royal Commission had decided that the new Greater London Boroughs should be limited to a minimum population of 100,000, rather than a minimum of 250,000 as had been recommended by the London School of Economics Scheme "A." The Commission realized, when it cut down the population size of these boroughs, that they would not be large enough to take full responsibility for primary and secondary education as had originally been recommended in the LSE scheme. As a result, it had proposed that responsibility for education should be split between the two new tiers of London government, with the Greater London Council being responsible for over-all educational policy and the boroughs handling day-to-day administration.

This proposed split of responsibilities between the two tiers provided the immediate focus of concern for the London Teachers' Association, and this group moved with almost lightning speed to make its criticisms known. The Royal Commission issued its report in October 1960, and in the November 1960 issue of *The London Teacher*, the Association's President commented:

> The handing over of the 'day-to-day running of the schools' to fifty-two newly constituted Boroughs I personally view with alarm and despondency. . . . I regard it as a retrograde step. . . . Since the 1944

Education Act the trend has been for Education to be administered by larger authorities. . . . Considerable friction has arisen where authority has been divided especially between the Counties and Excepted Districts.[1]

Within the short space of one month, this initial concern had branched out into a comprehensive attack on the entire Royal Commission report. Writing in the December 1960 issue of *London Town*, the LCC staff gazette, the London Teachers' Association President asserted:

> Teachers are worried. . . . The educational changes proposed by the Royal Commission are so revolutionary that the full impact of what is intended is only now beginning to dawn on those who will undoubtedly find their whole conditions of service changed. . . . Our advice to all concerned, therefore, is to reject the Report.[2]

During this same month, the General Committee of the Association decided to ask all member teachers to sign a petition calling for rejection of the findings of the Royal Commission as far as they applied to education, and by January 1961 these petitions were already being circulated among the 14,000 LTA teachers.

In February 1961, the Association held its annual conference, and on this occasion, a motion opposing the Commission's proposals was passed unanimously. Although the London Teachers' Association was concentrating its concern upon the educational aspects of the plan, there is little doubt that its members opposed the entire Royal Commission report insofar as this report called for the abolition of the London County Council. In effect, this group felt so strongly about the possible adverse impact of the reorganization plan upon the education services that it was quite willing to throw out the baby with the bath water. Indeed, as the Association's President commented at the annual

---

[1] "The President's Notes," *The London Teacher*, LXXIX, No. 1,279 (November 1960), 69. (The Association's President at this time was Mr. W. H. George.)

[2] W. H. George, "Leave Education Alone!" *London Town*, The L.C.C. Staff Gazette, LXI, No. 732 (December 1960), 390-391.

meeting, "Nobody with any knowledge of education at all loves this particular baby."[3]

As the London teachers kept up this constant patter of criticism throughout the spring, summer, and fall of 1961, the crucial question related to what reaction the Government would make to this outpouring of opposition. The Royal Commission had completed its work in October 1960, when it presented its report to the Minister of Housing and Local Government, and was no longer operative. It was now the responsibility of the Ministry to analyze the Commission's report and to deal with the future disposition of this report. The alternatives open to the Government were threefold: (1) It could ignore the opposition entirely by supporting the report in all its basic essentials; (2) it could place great weight on the opposition arguments by rejecting the report completely; or (3) it could attempt to mollify the opposition by making revisions in the report to meet specific criticisms.

The Government gave its answer in November 1961, when it issued its White Paper on *London Government.* The essence of this answer was alternative three, revision of the report. Although this Government White Paper made only two basic modifications in the original Royal Commission recommendations, both were of such crucial magnitude as to indicate that the London teachers had scored the first direct bull's-eye in the reorganization contest.

The two revisions involved the administrative arrangements for education and an upward shift in the population criterion for the proposed new Greater London Boroughs. In the words of the White Paper:

> The boroughs ought to be larger, and therefore fewer, than the Commission recommended. . . . The structure recommended by the Commission for education is not considered to be satisfactory. On education the Government do not agree that the two-tier system proposed would be likely to work well. They think that, given larger boroughs, education could and should, over the greater part of the area, become a borough service.[4]

[3] W. H. George, quoted in *The Times,* February 13, 1961.
[4] Rpt., Cmnd. 1562, p. 3.

Hence, the two revisions recommended by the Government were intimately bound up in each other, though the Government stated them in reverse order. As its primary concern, the Government felt the proposed functional split of educational responsibilities would not work, and it suggested instead that education should become a borough service. In order to make education a borough service, however, the Government felt it necessary to increase the size of the boroughs above the 100,000 minimum population range recommended by the Royal Commission, and in this regard it proposed that the new boroughs contain a minimum population of not less than 200,000 each.

In addition, the Government made one further concession in the field of education that indicated even more directly how forceful the attack of the London teachers had been in its impact. This additional concession took the form of a recommendation that an entirely separate educational authority should be set up for London's "central area," and that education in this particular area should not be the responsibility of the new boroughs at all. Although the White Paper was quite vague with regard to the precise form that this proposed new central area educational authority should take, it did suggest that it could cover a population on the order of two million, which represented about two-thirds of the population of the existing London County Council area.

Far from satisfying the London teachers, these concessions opened the way for a whole new flood of protest. The opposition forces had now had their first taste of blood, and they prepared to move even more sharply in their attack against the Government's White Paper than they had on the original Royal Commission plan. The key new opening for the London Teachers' Association's attack related to the Government's proposal for the new central area educational authority. The essence of this attack was an exceedingly effective question: Why stop at two million population for such an authority? Why not make it three million, thus leaving the existing LCC educational system completely intact?

The Government was hard put to answer such an inquiry, for the simple reason that no logical answer was immediately available. At this point some of the news media also began to express doubts about this new central educational authority. *The Times*, while still favoring the over-all reform program, questioned: "What sort of a creature would this ad hoc authority be, and how would the central boroughs be reconciled to its existence?"[5] *The Economist* expressed a similar confusion over the implications of "this hybrid central authority."[6] *The Guardian*'s "London Letter" was outright in its criticism of the fact that the new central authority would not be large enough to encompass the existing LCC area.[7] This same criticism was leveled even more forcefully at a later date in *The New Statesman* with the inquiry, "if two million is right in the middle of London, why not let the L.C.C. carry on with its three million?"[8]

By now both the tempo and the scope of the contest were beginning to pick up in earnest as all sorts of individuals and groups began to take firm positions on the Government's White Paper.

In early January 1962, Mr. George Brown, the Deputy Labour Leader in Parliament, described the reorganization as a "crackpot plan."[9] In February the County Councils held a joint consultation session at the LCC County Hall in an attempt to consolidate their strategy. Shortly thereafter, the London County Council issued its own alternative plan which, in major content, resembled little more than a pale shadow of the earlier Surrey scheme.

The Government, alarmed over the growing discontent, attempted to get the reform program back on the track by flexing its muscles in Parliament. On February 19-20, it called for a two-day general debate on the major outlines of the White Paper, and then, in a tricky Parliamentary maneuver, it forced a vote in which the Parliament was asked to decide whether it would "take note of" this Paper. It is difficult, of course, to vote against taking note of anything, and the Government carried this vote handily, 302 to 198. In March it utilized this same strategy in the House of Lords.

[5] "A Plan For London" (editorial), *The Times*, November 30, 1961.
[6] "Baronial Rule?" *The Economist*, December 12, 1961, p. 883.
[7] "London Letter," *The Guardian*, November 30, 1961.
[8] Jeger, *New Statesman*, p. 586.
[9] Quoted in *Daily Herald*, January 13, 1962.

While this Government maneuver was successful, it hardly reduced the disquiet over the way in which the reform program was proceeding. As *The Times* editorialized:

> . . . the opponents of reform have in recent weeks been getting the better of the argument. This was true in the debate in Parliament. . . . The report of the Royal Commission, out of which all of this arose, was cogent, authoritative, and persuasively presented. Since adopting its main recommendations, the Government have allowed the case for reform to look after itself.[10]

It was only shortly after the Parliamentary debate, however, that the first real crack appeared in the ranks of the opposition. On March 1, 1962, the Kent County Council voted to withdraw any further active opposition to the plan, thus becoming the first major county to abandon the fight. The loss of the County Council's second-tier support in metropolitan Kent had, indeed, proved fatal.

One week later, the second crack appeared when the Essex County Council also voted to make a significant alteration in its opposition stance. Instead of adopting a position of all-out criticism of the Government's White Paper, as was recommended by its General Purposes Committee, the Essex Council now recognized the very real potentialities for concession that were in the air. It decided that it would continue to try to persuade its second-tier authorities to oppose the plan, but if such action was unsuccessful, it would compromise by asking the Government to exclude more portions of the Essex Green Belt from the proposed new Greater London Council area. In addition, the Essex Council voted to negotiate for further "fair and equitable compensation" to be paid to it if, by any chance, the reorganization plan was finally approved.[11]

Although Kent and Essex were falling by the wayside, both the LCC and the Surrey County Council were stepping up the pace of their attack. In March, the LCC held a marathon, eighteen-hour, all-night session before voting to send a deputation from the Council to see the

---

[10] "All The Disadvantages" (editorial), *The Times*, March 9, 1962.
[11] County Council of Essex, The General Purposes Committee Report, 6 March 1962, p. 232, and Appendix "A."

Prime Minister and Dr. Charles Hill (the Minister of Housing and Local Government who had succeeded Mr. Henry Brooke). This deputation was received by Prime Minister Macmillan and Dr. Hill in early April, with the only immediately apparent result being a considerable display of coolness on both sides.

The Surrey County Council, in the meantime, was distributing two pamphlets to its residents in an effort to awaken them to the dangers of the Greater London plan. The first of these featured a gigantic S.O.S. ("Save Our Surrey") and depicted an avaricious black octopus (i.e., "London") stretching its greedy tentacles in the direction of Surrey and Middlesex Counties. The second pamphlet showed a mounted knight in shining armor (appropriately wearing an "S.C.C.") charging fearlessly at a snorting dragon complete with, of all things, a bowler hat, horn-rimmed glasses, spats, a black tie, and a wing collar (i.e., the "Ministry of Housing and Local Government").

At the same time this sort of thing was going on, the London Teachers' Association was preparing to open up its second major salvo against the reorganization program. The essential aim of this new attack was to throw the scope of the reform contest wide open by organizing a massive series of parent protest meetings against the plan. The response to this effort was extremely impressive, with more than 1,400 parents' protest meetings taking place in three months. Understandably, the supporters of the reorganization program looked on this latest development with considerable dismay. In mid-April Mrs. John Townsend, the Conservative minority leader on the LCC Education Committee, publicly challenged the London Teachers' Association's "bias" against the plan and protested the use of schoolchildren for political purposes.[12] The following day, the President of

---

[12] *The Londoner*, No. 262 (April 1962), p. 8. The Conservatives charged that the London Teachers' Association was using a campaign of "distortion" and "bias" to scare parents into opposing the Greater London plan. Specifically, they argued this campaign was stressing the following "falsehoods": (1) that the boroughs would "economise" on education; (2) that children would not be able to go to schools across borough boundaries; (3) that the boroughs would have no experienced educational officers or councillors; (4) that present LCC playing fields would be lost to the new authorities; (5) that the changeover would cause chaos and disruption; and (6) that special schools and further educational establishments would be unevenly distributed.

the London Head Teachers' Association defended the protest program in a letter to *The Times* and asserted, "we cannot advance any reasons for the proposed fragmentation."[13] The London Group of the Parent-Teachers' Association, which also backed the protest campaign, likewise denied the charge of bias.

By now other educational groups were joining the battle. The Guild of Teachers of Backward Children and the London Branch of the Special Schools Association wrote to the Minister of Education to express "great concern" over the reform plan and to request a meeting to discuss the entire situation.[14] In early May, an entirely new group called the London Education Protest Committee announced its formation with the intent of coordinating all opposition groups into one massive assault on the Government's proposal "to dismantle the LCC education service."[15]

It would take a fairly rugged civil servant, indeed, to stand up against this battering, and the Minister of Housing and Local Government, Dr. Hill, soon indicated that he had had enough. On May 4, after what was described as "a major Cabinet clash and a flood of protest from parents and teachers,"[16] Dr. Hill announced the Government's second major concession in the administration of the educational services.

The major plank of this concession was to enlarge the population of the proposed central London education authority from two million to three million and thus keep the entire LCC area intact as the new central education authority. The existent London County Council educational system was to remain operative, however, only for a period of five years, after which time the entire situation would be reviewed, with appropriate further modifications being made accordingly.

Thus, the London teachers had drawn blood for the second time. This did not, however, signify the end of their opposition to the reform program. They now decided to press on to see if they could convince the Government to leave the entire LCC organization intact, not only with regard to education but with regard to other key services as well. In this,

13 John Brown, "Letter to the Editor," *The Times*, April 16, 1962.
14 Letter quoted in *The Times*, April 11, 1962.
15 *The Guardian*, May 3, 1962.
16 *Daily Herald*, May 4, 1962.

they were joined by other professional groups who harbored deep concerns over the impact of the proposed reorganization plan upon their particular fields of professional specialization.

The Children's Services

The battle over the administration of the Children's Services was fought mainly in the "Letters to the Editor" column of *The Times*. On May 17, shortly after Dr. Hill had announced the Government's latest concessions in the field of education, a letter appeared in *The Times* which deplored "the breakup of the London County Council's Children's Department into fourteen arbitrary pieces" and strongly urged that the same arrangement that had just been announced for the central education area "is imperative for the Children's Service." The letter was signed by thirteen chairmen of the Metropolitan Juvenile Courts.

A week later three additional letters appeared, all of which supported the above request, and all of which pointed out the dangers of a fragmented Children's Service. The first of these was signed by four members of the London School of Economics staff, one of whom had supported the original LSE Scheme "B." The second was sent by the Chairman of the Association of LCC Child Welfare Officers, and the third by the Secretary of the Association of Child Care Officers.

Shortly thereafter, two more letters appeared, this time from individuals who argued against the appeal of the thirteen Metropolitan Juvenile Court Chairmen. The first of these letters was from the Chairman of the General Purposes Committee of the Association of Municipal Corporations, who supported the proposed reorganization as a step in the direction of getting away from "institutionalized care governed by a remote and distant authority"—a reference obviously intended to apply to the London County Council. The second letter was from Professor William Robson of the London School of Economics, who questioned the alleged superiority of the present LCC Child Care Service and objected to the Juvenile Court Chairmen's appeal as a "good example of opposition to broadly conceived reforms directed by persons interested in one specialized service." One further letter appeared a week later, when the Chairman of the London County Council's Children's Committee challenged the validity of Professor Robson's analysis.[17]

This flurry of letters signaled both the beginning and the end of the relatively brief outburst over the Children's Service, at least for the present. Here there were no great potentialities for parent protest movements, as had been the case in the field of education, since the number of London children in care is, fortunately, relatively small. What is of most interest, however, is not the size of this effort, but rather its ultimate implications. *The Times* attempted to analyze the meaning of this latest outburst of letters to its editor in an editorial which it quite aptly entitled "Battle for Survival":

> Whatever the merits of the demand, its tactical significance is obvious. Each particular concession to the London County Council's indivisibility strengthens its general claim to preservation . . . [and] . . . blunts the point of reorganization. Enough concessions and exceptions and the whole edifice collapses.[18]

Thus, *The Times* indicated an acute awareness of just how serious the situation was becoming: Too many concessions, and the entire reform program would be finished. This is not to imply that the particular participants in the Children's Service controversy were politically motivated to destroy the proposed reorganization plan. On the contrary, the chairmen of the Metropolitan Juvenile Courts acted quite logically, and indeed even altruistically, on this issue. They had seen major concessions being granted in education and, quite understand-

---

[17] "Letters to the Editor," *The Times*: Chairman, Metropolitan Juvenile Courts, May 17, 1962; LSE Group, May 22, 1962; M. O. Hawker, Chairman, The Association of LCC Child Welfare Officers, May 23, 1962; Ethel A. Steel, Secretary, Association of Child Care Officers, May 24, 1962; J. W. F. Hill, Chairman, General Purposes Committee, Association of Municipal Corporations, May 25, 1962; Prof. W. A. Robson, London School of Economics, May 29, 1962; and Mrs. Beatrice Serota, Chairman of the LCC Children's Committee, June 4, 1962.

[18] "Battle For Survival" (editorial), *The Times*, May 31, 1962.

ably, they pressed their own claims for similar concessions. Yet, as *The Times'* editorial had emphasized, this was precisely the danger. If too many concessions were granted to too many groups, the entire reform effort would be reduced to a shambles.

Although no such threat was implicit in the actions of the Children's Service groups alone, if still other groups continued to press for additional exceptions in their particular fields of concern, there was no doubt that the reform program would be in very serious trouble.

The Second-Tier Authorities

The next group to reappear, the second-tier authorities, packed considerably more political punch than the Children's Services' spokesmen. Indeed, these authorities possessed the type of knockout wallop that could well lead to *rigor mortis* for the entire reorganization effort.

In order to understand the new display of restlessness that was now appearing among the second-tier authorities, it is necessary to recall briefly the two basic concessions the Government had made in its White Paper of November 1961. Since this White Paper had suggested that the new boroughs should take over primary responsibility for education, it had concurrently proposed that the minimum population criterion for these boroughs should be upgraded to at least 200,000, in lieu of the 100,000 figure originally suggested by the Royal Commission. In making this proposal, the Government had indicated rather vaguely that it would be necessary to reduce the boroughs to "fewer in number" through such an upgrading, but it was not until one month later, when the Government actually issued a second memorandum on these proposed new borough groupings, that the second-tier units began to grasp the full impact of what this "fewer in number" would actually mean.

Whereas the Royal Commission had originally called for the creation of some fifty-four Greater London Boroughs, which would have left most of the large units virtually unscathed (see Map I, page 27), the Government now proposed to reduce this number to thirty-four boroughs. Under the Government's new proposals, only three second-tier units—Harrow (208,000) in Middlesex County; Lewisham (221,000) in London County; and of all places, the City of London Corporation (4,771)—would remain completely intact within the confines of their existing boundaries.[19]

Once the second-tier authorities started to reflect upon this particular situation, the ardor which many of them had previously expressed for the reorganization plan began to cool quite noticeably.

In Middlesex County, for example, the Government now proposed that the wealthy Conservative Borough of Wembley, a qualified member of the "Big Ten" and a former potential Greater London Borough in its own right under the Royal Commission's original suggestions, should be merged with its considerably less wealthy Labour neighbor, Willesden. The most appalling part of this prospect, as far as Wembley was concerned, was the fact that Willesden, with a 50,000 population advantage, would probably dominate this new borough grouping.

Similarly, the county boroughs of East Ham and West Ham would lose their former independent existence through a joint merger; in London County, the very proper Conservative stronghold of Hampstead was about to be joined with the Borough of St. Pancras, which had created considerable controversy on at least one past occasion by flying a Socialist Red Flag from its Town Hall on May Day; and so it went.

Many of these second-tier authorities viewed all this not so much with a sense of disillusionment as with a reaction that bordered on outright shock. There was now going to be a very real price to pay for all those wonderful new powers the boroughs had previously expected to receive virtually gratis.

As the very audible rumblings of many of these second-tier authorities increased in intensity, the Government once again decided that something would have to be done to quiet the situation. Yet, on this occasion, rather than making another outright concession, it hit upon a highly unorthodox, if nonetheless nimble tactical scheme, which was formulated in the Ministry of Housing and Local Government. It de-

[19] Circular No. 56/61, Ministry of Housing and Local Government, 16 December 1961.

cided to play for time by appointing an "independent" panel of four town clerks to review the proposed new borough amalgamations and recommend any changes they felt to be necessary. These four clerks were from Plymouth, Cheltenham, Oxford, and South Shields, all communities located well outside the confines of the Greater London area. For the time being at least, the Government had quieted the protests of the inner boroughs, which immediately began to divert their major energies to advancing their cause before this new review tribunal.

However, the situation regarding the second-tier fringe authorities, located on the outer edges of the proposed new Greater London Council area, was something else again. From the very beginning, the strategy of these groups had been a consistent one. They felt that reorganization was a fine idea, as long as they were not included within its purview, and with this aim in mind they had been employing might and main to demonstrate that they were really rural extensions of their individual home counties and were in no sense a homogeneous part of the metropolitan London complex.

The situation was most difficult for the Government in Surrey County, for the simple reason that the outlying Surrey authorities were extremely affluent Conservative strongholds which had always sent their full share of contributions to the Party's campaign war chests. Thus, just as had been the case when the teachers had first started their opposition campaign, the big question now became one of what action, if any, a Conservative Government would take to quiet the growing Conservative commotion that was becoming all too vocal on the outlying borders of Surrey County.

The answer this time appeared on May 19, 1962, when Dr. Hill, in a written reply to a Commons question, announced that the Government had suddenly decided to exclude no less than nine of these second-tier fringe authorities (seven in whole, and two in very great part) from the future fate of a Greater London existence. Five of these authorities were located in Surrey County, two in Middlesex, one in Essex, and one in Hertfordshire (see Map XI).

The reaction to this latest Governmental collapse tended to confirm that the reform effort was now beginning to take on the character of the ludicrous. Commenting on the action as it affected one of the severed Surrey authorities, *The Daily Express* trumpeted, "DR. HILL SPLITS EPSOM DOWN THE MIDDLE—An Invisible Iron Curtain Is To Fall Across the Fair and Fat District of Epsom and Ewell."[20] Noting the total exclusion of another Surrey authority, *The Daily Mail* cracked, "Epsom, the Home of the Derby, is past the post in its gallop to get out."[21] Perhaps the most bitingly disillusioned commentary of all appeared in *The Economist,* which lamented:

> Dr. Hill must not let himself be browbeaten by suburban witenagemots. . . . The Surrey Tories may dance in the streets because they still have sack and soke in Banstead [another excluded Surrey district], and the rest of the country may simply shrug its shoulders at London's enduring parish-pumpery. But this is a decision that needs to be questioned—if only because the fate of another dozen peripheral districts wanting to wangle their way out . . . is now in the balance.[22]

This last comment, of course, represented the heart of the matter. To those who had felt that the Royal Commission's study area had been too small in the first place, this latest Government concession was nothing short of a disaster. Yet, the real question now became not whether the fast shrinking Greater London Council was large enough, but rather whether this Council would even survive at all. Under this latest Governmental concession, for example, the Surrey Borough of Epsom and Ewell had been split almost down the middle—with approximately three-quarters of its residents moved out, and one-quarter still left under the jurisdiction of the Greater London Council. The ominous immediate reaction of the local residents of this now eviscerated borough, who still remained inside the new Council's jurisdiction, was to "queue up" and sign petitions telling why they wanted out.

The simple facts of the matter were that the entire reorganization effort was now floundering in some very deep waters. On the one hand, the Government was, quite obviously, running out of concessions to make, because there was precious little left to concede without destroy-

---

[20] *Daily Express,* May 19, 1962.
[21] *Daily Mail,* May 19, 1962.
[22] "The New London," *The Economist,* May 25, 1962.

Map XI

Local Authority Deletions
Greater London Council Area
(May 1962)

KEY

Original Deletions
by Royal Commission

New Deletions by
the Government

0   5 Miles

1 City of London
2 Holborn
3 Finsbury
4 Shoreditch
5 Bethnal Green
6 Bermondsey
7 Southwark
8 Deptford

9 Chelsea
10 City of Westminster
11 Kensington
12 Paddington
13 St. Marylebone
14 Hampstead
15 Stoke Newington
16 Tottenham
17 Wood Green

18 Friern Barnet
19 Wanstead and Woodford
20 Penge
21 Beddington and Wallington
22 Merton and Morden
23 Malden and Coombe
24 Kingston-upon-Thames
25 Brentford and Chiswick
26 Hammersmith

ing the total unity of the original Royal Commission plan. In addition, there were some telltale signs to indicate that the Cabinet leaders in the Government, if not the permanent civil servants in Whitehall, were fast losing their perspective on the entire issue. In early April, for example, Dr. Hill had announced a "provision decision" that the old Metropolitan Water Board, originally established in 1904, was to be abolished and its functions transferred to the new Greater London Council. Yet, this authority had been specifically excluded from the Royal Commission's review, and in its final report the Commission had made no reference at all to the administration of water resources in the metropolitan area. The only apparent reason for this unexpected move was that earlier in the year the Labour-controlled Water Board had disagreed with the Government's national "pay pause" policy and had granted 7½-per-cent salary increases to its employees—an action that hardly related to the organizational structure of the Board itself or to the future operations of the Greater London Council.

Thus, by June 1, 1962, those who were intent upon defeating the reorganization plan might well have taken satisfaction in the progress they had achieved to date. The opposition forces were realizing major concessions in an ever more rapid fashion, and it seemed that the basic strategy they were pursuing promised very real potentialities for total success.

Yet, it was precisely at this point that these opposition forces made a dramatic shift in emphasis with respect to their future strategy. Instead of continuing to pursue a policy of tactical flexibility, jabbing at the most vulnerable aspects of the Government's position, the opponents of reorganization now began to solidify into a massively inflexible position of bitter all-out criticism that defies easy description.

This new hardening of the opposition forces first became fully apparent in the London County Council. It quickly led to the formation of a totally new group, the Committee for London Government, and then spread to the Metropolitan Boroughs' Standing Joint Committee.

The final stage of all-out attack upon the entire reorganization concept had arrived, and in retrospect it soon became obvious that it had arrived so far ahead of schedule as to hurt, rather than help, the forces of opposition.

The Committee for London Government

Following the meeting that had taken place between the Prime Minister and the London County Council deputation in April, Mr. Macmillan and the LCC leader, Sir Isaac Hayward, had exchanged correspondence in which Sir Isaac had concluded:

> I have been asked to assure you that the Council is fully aware of its responsibilities for co-operating with the Government in the preparation and implementation of legislation. The officers have in fact been authorized to provide the Government departments with factual information which may be asked for, and the Council will be prepared to express its views about any other matters arising during the course of any preparatory work.[23]

An indication that the London County Council leadership almost immediately began to develop very serious misgivings about this policy of sweet cooperation appeared in the form of 5,000 copies of a pamphlet which the Council issued in May. This pamphlet characterized the proposed reorganization as "A LEAP INTO THE DARK AND A MONSTROUS UPHEAVAL" (see next page). In mid-May, the Council leadership proposed a second meeting with the Prime Minister, this time with the intention of recommending that a further public inquiry into the entire reorganization program be made. On May 30 Prime Minister Macmillan rejected this request outright, advising the LCC leaders that "the worst thing we could do would be to create further delay and uncertainty by setting up some further committee of inquiry into matters which have already been exhaustively examined by a Royal Commission."[24]

This latter exchange of correspondence marked the end of any potential cordiality between the London County Council and the Government. As one of the Council leaders later stated, "we felt we should no longer go around the corner to supply the rope for our own hang-

---

[23] Letter quoted in *The Londoner*, No. 265 (July-August 1962), p. 3.
[24] Letter quoted in *The Guardian*, December 5, 1962, p. 16.

THE
LONDON
COUNTY
COUNCIL - WHY DESTROY IT?

ing." The LCC leadership now flatly decided that it would not cooperate with the Government in its efforts to implement the proposed reform program. In effect, this decision meant that the Council was to stand completely aloof from cooperating with any working parties dealing with such problems as the transfer of staff, housing, parks, properties, or other matters. The Council did originally indicate that it would provide purely factual information on such transfers in response to specific Governmental inquiries, but as time went on even this degree of cooperation became suspect. By mid-November, Sir Percy Rugg, the Conservative leader on the LCC, was able to charge that the Council had refused even to consider eighteen separate ministerial communications that it had received from the Government on the reorganization plan during the preceding four months.[25]

Coupled with this complete stiffening of LCC attitude was the announcement, in late June, of the establishment of a totally new spearhead of opposition, under the title of "The Committee for London Government."

The Chairman of this new group was The Right Honourable The Earl of Longford, P.C., and his designation to this post represented an obvious attempt by the opposition forces to impart an air of respectability to a controversy that was becoming increasingly more ungentlemanly in both its undertones and its overtones. Although Lord Longford had long been associated with the Labour Party (he previously served as Minister of Civil Aviation and as First Lord of the Admiralty in the postwar Labour Government), like the Royal Commission members, he was not in any way directly connected with the London political scene. His only previous local governmental experience had been in the form of service on the Oxford City Council.

The Vice-Chairman of the new Committee was Sir William Holford, the distinguished London architect and town planner, who had previously presented evidence to the Royal Commission on behalf of London University's Centre for Urban Studies.

[25] Statement by Sir Percy Rugg at 14th Annual Local Government Conference of the National Union of Conservative and Unionist Associations, London, November 17, 1962.

A quick review of the Committee's Council of Patrons indicates that this new organizational effort represented a direct attempt to add a glitter of prestige to the opposition cause. In addition to the Chairman and Vice-Chairman, the Council of Patrons was drawn from such diverse professional fields as economics (Baroness Wootton of Abinger; Mrs. Mary Stocks, LL.D., Litt.D.), theater (Dame Peggy Ashcroft, D.B.E.; Miss Margaret Rawlings; Sir Michael Redgrave, C.B.E.), poetry (John Betjeman, C.B.E.), journalism (Sir Gerald Barry; John Freeman, M.B.E.), and even athletics (Sir Stanley Rous, C.B.E., J.P.).

There was no doubt, however, that the Committee was extremely overbalanced in its Labour sympathies, and it was not until August that it was able to add Sir John Wenham, the former Chairman of the Surrey County Council, to its Council of Patrons, thus numbering at least one prominent local Conservative among its ranks.

In commenting on the initial aims of the new Committee, Lord Longford asserted, "We go into battle under the title 'Let London Speak.' We shall strive by every constitutional means to make it morally impossible for the Government to proceed."[26]

Early hopes that the group might bring a fresh air of enlightenment to the increasingly more bitter controversy were voiced by such newspapers as *The Guardian,* which in its "London Letter" commented:

> The Committee brings a lively impetus and co-ordination to the varied opposition to the Government's plan for London. Its influence will be the more considerable because it shifts the arguments away from the entrenched devotions of County Hall and puts anxieties on a professional, rather than a party, basis.[27]

This *Guardian* comment was prophetic to the extent that the Committee very definitely did bring a strong professional orientation to the reform controversy. This orientation, however, was almost totally negative in its emphasis on the "anxieties" inherent in any reform effort. Actually, the handwriting was on the wall in this respect as soon

[26] Quoted in *The Evening Standard*, June 25, 1962.
[27] "London Letter," *The Guardian*, June 26, 1962.

CHAOS OR PROGRESS
LET
LONDON
SPEAK
on
homes
rates
education
child welfare
town planning
entertainment
sport
THE COMMITTEE FOR LONDON GOVERNMENT

Please do not throw this away but pass it to a friend when you have read it.

ISSUED ON BEHALF OF THE COMMITTEE FOR LONDON GOVERNMENT

The Government's Greater London Plan

NO MANDATE
NO ELECTORAL VOTE
NO PUBLIC INQUIRY

THE PLAN is to **DESTROY** the **L.C.C.** and **MIDDLESEX C.C.** to partition the **HOME COUNTIES** and fragment the **VITAL SERVICES.**

THERE IS NO MANDATE from the people for this scheme.

NO PUBLIC INQUIRY is being allowed such as those held in other parts of the country to let the citizens state their views and objections to new boundaries and municipal amalgamations.

THE GOVERNMENT WANTS TO PLAY DICTATOR and flout the expressed wishes of the citizens.

WHAT IS THE COST? The Government say they don't know, but it is known that in the outer Home Counties **RATES MUST RISE STEEPLY.**

EDUCATION PLANS ARE IN CHAOS because the Government makes a plan which everyone condemns, then delays it without withdrawing it. Forward scheming and proper staff recruitment are impossible.

NO CONTRIBUTION is offered to the growing problems of traffic and transport and overall planning of housing, or to the ending of the miseries of homelessness.

CHILD CARE and the **WELFARE** of the handicapped: Existing organisations are to be disrupted.

HUGE UNWIELDY BOROUGHS will replace the truly local authorities. Fewer councillors means **LESS REPRESENTATION OF THE RATEPAYERS.**

ARTS, ENTERTAINMENT and **SPORT:** The L.C.C.'s imaginative sponsorship, help and control will disappear. They will be **NOBODY'S BUSINESS** in the capital of the country. London will be a capital without the status of Manchester or Liverpool. **(IN EFFECT THERE WILL BE NO LONDON** as a coherent entity.)

TO L.C.C. TENANTS: Your future rents are now an unknown quantity.

HELP US PROTEST against this **MONSTROUS PLAN** by signing our **MONSTER PETITION.**

The All-party Committee for London Government, Chairman Lord Longford, Secretary L. French, 89 St. Stephen's House, Victoria Embankment, S.W.1. WHITEHALL 9627.

VAIL & CO. LTD. LEEKE STREET LONDON. W.C.1

as the Committee issued its very first announcement, at the time of its initial formation.

In this original announcement, the Committee stated that it was "not at this stage committed to any [specific] alternative plan." Instead, its most basic ambition was to circulate a huge petition protesting the Government's plan. Here the Committee made a very serious tactical blunder by stating a target goal of 500,000 signatures for this petition.[28] This initial objective of arousing half a million Londoners to oppose reform virtually assured that the basic emphasis of the Committee's message would have to be directed toward anxiety, exaggeration, and fear. Certainly, it would be difficult to stir up 500,000 apathetic citizens to commit themselves against the reorganization of London's governmental structure through the use of any genteel program of enlightened education.

As a result, from the very beginning, the literature issued by the Committee featured such concepts as "chaos," "destruction," "paralysis," "monster plan," and "Government dictatorship." As the Committee proceeded in its operations, its tone became increasingly more strident, until finally its Chairman made the charge that "the Government is acting with all the despotism of a Fascist State."[29] Comments such as this were hardly of a nature to engender any outpouring of public sympathy for the opposition cause.

Moreover, the Committee made a second serious tactical blunder by placing almost entire emphasis upon a defense of the London County Council. As a result, many tended to view the Committee as little more than an LCC pressure group, and some authorities that were publicly committed in their opposition to the reorganization plan (such as the Independent County Borough of Croydon) refused to support the Committee's work actively at all because they felt it did not relate to their own legitimate interests.

This is not to state that the Committee was lacking in the sincerity of its convictions. Many of its adherents demonstrated a total dedica-

---

28 *The Guardian*, June 26, 1962.
29 Remarks before the Institute of Public Relations, quoted in *The Daily Telegraph*, November 28, 1962, p. 26.

tion to its cause, above all others Mr. L. French, the Committee's Secretary, who put in long and difficult hours in an attempt to coordinate the Committee's efforts with only very minimal staff help. Yet, despite such Herculean endeavors, the very frame of reference of this group made it extremely difficult for the Committee to be much more than a negative "holding operation." The Committee for London Government was debatable, not so much in terms of its dedication, but rather in terms of its very conception, with regard to the amount of long-range good that it might have accomplished for the opposition cause. In the end, it was able to collect only 172,000 signatures for its petition—certainly not an insignificant total, but one which was badly blunted in impact through comparison with the 500,000 the Committee had originally announced as its objective.

Shortly after The Committee for London Government had begun its campaign, still another group—The Metropolitan Boroughs' Standing Joint Committee—voted to join the London County Council in its new attitude of intransigent opposition to the reorganization proposals. The latest series of metropolitan borough council elections, which had been held in May 1962, represented the key lever that triggered off this latest development. These elections were significant for two reasons.

First, in terms of the simple mathematics of power politics, the Constitution of the Standing Joint Committee provides that any "decision of the Committee shall be communicated to the said [member] Councils, but shall not otherwise be communicated unless it has received the support of not less than two-thirds of the Councils present and voting."[30] Since the Committee consisted of twenty-nine members (i.e., the twenty-eight metropolitan boroughs, plus the City of London Corporation), it was necessary for at least twenty of these members to agree on any policy issue before it could become binding upon all Committee members under this two-thirds rule.

Prior to the May elections, Labour controlled nineteen boroughs on the Committee, eighteen of which were opposed to the reorganization

---

[30] Constitution of the Metropolitan Boroughs' Standing Joint Committee, 4 February 1957, Section 12, Voting.

plan, with Fulham representing the only Labour deviant. Hence, the opposition forces fell two votes short of the twenty votes needed to meet the two-thirds requirement, and as a result the Committee was paralyzed in terms of its ability to take any definitive opposition stand. In the May elections, however, two former Conservative boroughs— St. Pancras and Wandsworth—swung over to Labour council majorities, and both these boroughs now shifted to the opposition side. Thus, since the opposition forces now had control of twenty votes on the Committee, they could adopt an outright opposition position on the reorganization plan without Fulham's concurrence. This position automatically became binding on all twenty-nine member boroughs under the two-thirds rule in the Committee's constitution.

The second significant factor that grew out of the May borough elections was the interpretation the opposition leaders placed upon the St. Pancras and Wandsworth victories. In effect, these leaders argued that these two elections had been fought over the issue of metropolitan reform and that the fact that the majority in both boroughs had shifted from the Conservative to the Labour camp represented a public mandate against the reorganization plan, which, in turn, justified a stand of all-out opposition on the part of the Committee.

The Conservatives hotly denied this interpretation. They argued that the elections had not been fought on the issue of reorganization but, rather, had been influenced by local factors. Specifically, they felt that the fact the Conservative Council had raised housing rents in St. Pancras was the key to the loss of this borough and that the fact that the Liberals had intervened heavily in Wandsworth to take away votes from the Conservatives was the key to this election.

It is difficult to weigh such counterclaims, but the only significant research on London local elections that has been done in recent years would tend to support the Conservative claims. L. J. Sharpe of the London School of Economics, in a masterful analysis of the 1961 LCC election, attempted to determine whether the reorganization issue had played any major role in this campaign. His conclusion was that "it is doubtful whether the public viewed the [Royal Commission] Report as a major issue. The nearest thing to a major issue about which there was strong public interest concerned the best method of solving the perennial housing shortage." In support of this observation, Mr. Sharpe made a detailed survey of the extent of local "political knowledge" in one of the voting divisions within the Metropolitan Borough of Wandsworth, and this survey indicated that these local Wandsworth voters knew less about their Party's basic position on the reorganization plan than they knew about any of five other public issues on which they were questioned.[31] Although Mr. Sharpe's analysis covered the 1961 County Council election rather than the 1962 metropolitan borough election, nothing indicated that any great change that would have modified these earlier findings had taken place in the Wandsworth electorate during the intervening year.

The simple practicalities of the matter were, however, that the opposition Labour forces now controlled a two-thirds vote on the Metropolitan Boroughs' Standing Joint Committee, and that they were determined to use this vote to adopt a stance of all-out opposition to the reform program. In July the Committee voted that none of its constituent members could cooperate in any way with the Government in the implementation of this program.

Subsequent events were to indicate that this action was highly debatable in terms of its impact on the opposition cause. For one thing, as was the case with the London County Council, this stand was hardly designed to encourage general public sympathy for the opposition cause, since it simply was not cricket to play the political game in this way. Numerous angry letters denouncing the Committee's stand began to appear in the local press, and some of the more influential newspapers indicated extreme editorial displeasure with this latest development. Even the *Sunday Telegraph,* which considers itself to be a national rather than a London paper, was worked up enough over this move to characterize it as "a gross act of defiance of constituted authority, ill becoming a party supposedly devoted to democratic principles."[32]

Labour's action was debatable not only because it alienated public

[31] Sharpe, *A Metropolis Votes,* pp. 6, 7, 74.
[32] *The Sunday Telegraph,* "Defiance" (editorial), October 14, 1962.

opinion, but also because it placed on the Committee's individual member borough councils a tremendous strain that was both unnecessary and undesirable. Many of these local councils were understandably concerned about the adverse impact that any such lack of coordination and cooperation between themselves and the Government could have on their permanent staff employees. These boroughs could hardly offer any assurances that they were doing their best to protect their own staffs' interests if they refused even to discuss the proposed reorganization plan with responsible Government officials who were working on the implementation of this plan. Hence arose a case of sharply divided loyalties that placed many of the local councils in an extremely difficult position. This concern cut across both the supporters and the opponents of the plan.

Conservative Westminster, for example, which supported the plan, decided almost immediately that it would ignore the Joint Committee's vote and cooperate with the Government, and later in the year the Westminster Council voted to join the Association of Municipal Corporations, to give its views even more weight in this respect. In a similar vein, the Labour Borough of Woolwich voted that it also would cooperate with the Government in exchanging information on the plan, although the Woolwich Council remained opposed to reorganization. As soon as the Woolwich Council made this decision, Lord Morrison of Lambeth refused to speak at a meeting in the Woolwich Town Hall with the comment, "we must not help the executioner to sharpen his axe."[33]

Lord Morrison's remark provides a clear indication of just how hard the opposition line in central London had become since the London County Council had originally announced its position of noncooperation in June. For a number of reasons, however, this hard line was confined to the LCC area. The Surrey County Council refused to go along with this position, despite its continued opposition to the plan, because it felt such action was not in the best interests of any of the parties concerned. The Middlesex County Council also refused to support the LCC–Metropolitan Boroughs' Standing Joint Committee position, al-

[33] Quoted in *The Guardian*, November 3, 1962, p. 12.

though the precise outlines of exactly what transpired in Middlesex on this occasion were somewhat obscured by another in the virtually endless series of misfortunes that had by now come to characterize the operations of this county. In the spring, the Middlesex Council had installed a fancy new voting machine, which automatically computed the councillors' votes by command of a simple press of the button from each of the councillors' seats. At a meeting held on July 26, the Conservative leadership on Middlesex Council proposed a motion pledging the Council's help in transferring various services under the proposed Greater London plan, and after a series of procedural maneuvers, the motion was put to vote and passed, by an apparent margin of 36 to 20. The voting machine was challenged, however, and on a recount, it belched out a different vote of 43 to 33, still, however, in favor of the motion. In turn, this second vote was challenged, but by now the machine, if not the Council, was in a state of total confusion, and the matter was left in abeyance. The end result was that the Middlesex Council had voted to cooperate with the Government, although by an indeterminate margin.

Since both Kent and Essex counties had virtually withdrawn from the battle, neither of these two bodies was interested in participating in the noncooperation movement, and they joined with Surrey and Middlesex in providing information to the Government. Hence, the London County Council, the Metropolitan Boroughs' Standing Joint Committee, and the Committee for London Government took over as the opposition extremists and constituted the hard core of outright intransigence on the issue of cooperation.

Two further events occurred during the summer of 1962 that completed the setting for the Parliamentary battle that lay just ahead. In July 1962, after the Conservative Party had suffered a rather devastating series of defeats in Parliamentary by-elections, Prime Minister Macmillan decided his Cabinet needed a dramatic new look, and in the ensuing Cabinet reshuffle Sir Keith Joseph replaced Dr. Charles Hill as Minister of Housing and Local Government.

Although this new appointment marked the third change in the leadership of this Ministry since the Royal Commission had issued its report some twenty months earlier, Sir Keith promised to bring a new display of dynamism and vitality to this position that was sorely needed. Only forty-four years old, he had experienced a meteoric rise to top Cabinet office within six years after initially entering Parliament. His assets with respect to the reorganization controversy were particularly impressive. In the first place, his knowledge of the London area was lifelong. His father, founder of the London building firm of Bovis, had served as a former Lord Mayor of London (hence the baronetcy), and Sir Keith himself had served as the youngest alderman in the city's history before retiring at age thirty-one to devote his full energies to a Bovis directorship. Secondly, he was fully knowledgeable on the details of the Royal Commission report, having served as Parliamentary Secretary to the former Minister of Housing and Local Government, Mr. Henry Brooke, during the period 1959–1961, when the Commission had presented this report. Hence, Sir Keith's appointment indicated that the advocates of reform were finally to have the type of vigorous political leadership that they would so obviously need in the tough months that lay ahead.

The second major development was the issuance of the final report on borough amalgamations, in August 1962, by the Committee of the Four Town Clerks. Although the town clerks approved the essence of the earlier amalgamation groupings that had been suggested by the Ministry of Housing and Local Government in December 1961, they made just enough minor modifications in the Ministry groupings to reduce the proposed number of new Greater London Boroughs from thirty-four to thirty-two (See Map VII, page 90).[34]

In so doing, they retained all the old areas of basic disagreement (i.e., Conservative Wembley would still be merged with Labour Willesden) and added a number of new ones (i.e., the Conservative Borough of Hornsey, another faithful dues-paying member of the Middlesex "Big Ten," was now about to be submerged by the Labour hordes of adjacent Tottenham).

---

[34] *London Government: The London Boroughs, Town Clerks' Report*, presented to the Ministry of Housing and Local Government (London: HMSO, August 1962).

Thus, the second-tier controversy flared up all over again, this time on an even more chaotic basis. The Borough of Wembley didn't want to be joined with the Borough of Willesden, and the Borough of Willesden didn't want to be joined with the Borough of Wembley; Conservative Hornsey objected to amalgamation with Labour Tottenham; Labour Romford objected to amalgamation with Independent Hornchurch; West Ham opposed merger with East Ham; Barking objected to merger with Dagenham; Wandsworth didn't want to be split down the middle, nor did the Kent Urban District of Chislehurst and Sidcup; and the Surrey District of Coulsdon and Purley was still trying to get out of the reorganization completely, as were the Hertfordshire District of Barnet and the remaining fragment of the Surrey Borough of Epsom and Ewell.

Thus, at the second-tier level, the proposed reorganization was fast approaching utter chaos. The situation was hardly less contentious with regard to the first-tier authorities, or with regard to a variety of other interest associations. Both the London and the Surrey County Councils were still banging away at the plan (although with varying degrees of obstinacy); the majority of the Metropolitan Boroughs' Standing Joint Committee, spurred on by the London Labour Party, had solidified into a mass of adamant opposition; the Committee for London Government had launched its protest campaign, quite literally, by hiring a boat to sail down the Thames so that its leading members could distribute leaflets to the various borough ports-of-call along the way; and all the while, the London Teachers' Association (accompanied from time to time by local doctors, social workers, and others) was attacking the reorganization with the same display of zeal that had led to the first concessions activating this whole process. Only the Middlesex, Essex, and Kent County Councils had been reduced to a state of rather enfeebled confusion, but the intensity of the other opposition forces more than made up for their loss.

By October 1962, an American observer could feel very much at home in the anarchy of political confusion that greeted the statement in the Queen's Speech from the Throne: "My Government will . . . propose . . . legislation . . . for the reorganization of local government

Map XII

Final Borough Groupings
Town Clerks' Report
(August 1962)

KEY

Proposed
Boundaries
of the 32 New
Greater
London
Boroughs

0   5 Miles

1 City of London
2 Holborn
3 Finsbury
4 Shoreditch
5 Bethnal Green
6 Bermondsey
7 Southwark
8 Deptford

9 Chelsea
10 City of Westminster
11 Kensington
12 Paddington
13 St. Marylebone
14 Hampstead
15 Stoke Newington
16 Tottenham
17 Wood Green

18 Friern Barnet
19 Wanstead and Woodford
20 Penge
21 Beddington and Wallington
22 Merton and Morden
23 Malden and Coombe
24 Kingston-upon-Thames
25 Brentford and Chiswick
26 Hammersmith

in Greater London."[35] This statement highlighted the fact that the opposition strategy of "attack-concession-erosion" had not, in fact, succeeded in discouraging the Government from pushing ahead with reform in the new session of Parliament. Yet it did not mean that this opposition strategy had failed to score very heavily. Perhaps the unkindest cut of all in this regard was the comment that a London Labour Party spokesman made in an attempt to chide the Government on the new London Government Bill when it finally did appear in Parliament:

> The first point to note about the . . . Bill is the way in which the Government, whilst professing support for the conclusions of the Royal Commission on Local Government, have moved further and further away from the recommendations of the Herbert Commission.
> The Chairman of the Royal Commission will hardly recognize this Bill as one of his offspring.[36]

In essence, the opposition had done as much as it could do to modify the reorganization plan before it entered the Parliamentary arena. It was now up to the Parliamentary Labour Party to carry the banner for the opposition cause.

[35] Text of the Queen's Speech to Parliament, *Daily Telegraph*, October 31, 1962, p. 21.
[36] Peter Robshaw, "Notes on the London Government Bill" (London Labour Party, mimeographed statement, December 5, 1962).

12. The Parliamentary Struggle

In commenting on the opening of the new session of Parliament, *The Times* editorialized, "except for the reorganization of London government, which the Opposition will presumably fight clause by clause, there are no highly contentious measures in The Queen's Speech."[1] *The Times* underestimated the vitality of the Parliamentary Labour Party. As Mr. Gaitskell, the Opposition Leader, had advised earlier, Labour was prepared to fight the London Government Bill not only "clause by clause," but "line by line" as well.[2]

The extent of the Labour Party's Parliamentary opposition to the reform program, and the types of Parliamentary weapons which the Conservative Government could bring into play in order to overcome this opposition, were the key ingredients in this fight.

When the Royal Commission had first issued its final report in October 1960, it immediately became obvious that the London Labour Party and the London County Council were prepared to pull out all the stops in an effort to block the reorganization program. Considerable time passed, however, before the national Labour Party spokesmen began to swing behind this central London opposition stance. During the early part of the reform contest, many of the Parliamentary Labour spokesmen had remained relatively noncommittal on the issue. It was not until January 1962, when George Brown, the Deputy Labour

[1] *The Times*, "The Programme" (editorial), October 31, 1962.
[2] Quoted in *The Times*, July 2, 1962.

Leader, had denounced the reorganization program as a "crackpot plan," that Labour's Parliamentary opposition began to jell. The following month, during the preliminary debate to "take note of" the Government's White Paper, the Parliamentary Labour Party officially announced its opposition to the reorganization by sponsoring an amendment (defeated 302-198) calling on the Government to revise its policy. Mr. Brown and the other Parliamentary leaders expressed essentially the same concern as a justification for their opposition to the Royal Commission's plan; namely, that the plan would have a destructive impact on the discharge of various professional services in the greater London area.

This Labour Party position was confirmed officially once again in April 1962, when the National Executive Committee issued a statement calling on the Government "not to proceed with these proposals for which they have no mandate."[3] In July, Mr. Gaitskell made his "clause by clause" and "line by line" comment, arguing that "it would not be unfair to describe this as a squalid attempt on the part of the Tory Party to snatch the banner of London for itself by altering the boundaries because they cannot get the votes." In addition, Mr. Gaitskell advised that if the Labour Party won the next General Election it would reserve the right to scrap the Greater London plan and to make what changes it thought necessary in the interests of Londoners as a whole.[4] The Party put the final stamp on its opposition position at its Annual Conference in Brighton in October 1962, when the National Executive Committee accepted a motion that condemned the reorganization as politically biased and ill-conceived.[5]

Thus, by October 1962, all the various wings of the Party—the London Labour Party, the London County Council Labour Party, the national Labour Party (at both the NEC and Annual Conference levels), and the Parliamentary Labour Party—had gone on record as being opposed to the reform program. A strong functional ideological heritage

[3] Statement issued by Labour Party Press and Relations Department, Transport House, London, April 18, 1962.

[4] *The Times*, July 2, 1962.

[5] *The Guardian*, "Pledge to Retain LCC," October 4, 1962.

(see Chapter 7) had welded these separate major Party segments into a cohesive opposition force, the only deviants being a few Labour boroughs, such as Fulham, that still supported the reform program.

In organizing their Parliamentary team, the Labourites could look to a number of astute tacticians in both the House of Commons and the House of Lords. The leading Labour spokesman on this issue in the Commons was Michael Stewart, who could dissect the reform plan with icy brilliance by singling out the potentially adverse impact of reorganization on individual services, especially education and welfare.[6] In the House of Lords, the Party could look to both Lord Longford and Lord Morrison, especially the latter, to lead its attack. Lord Morrison was obsessed with the evils of reform, characterizing the entire plan as "A Tory Plot to Destroy London."[7] After his long climb up the London Labour Party-London County Council ladder, he could not help viewing the reorganization as an attempt to destroy his lifetime's work.

Despite the fact that the Labour Opposition was well entrenched and highly articulate, the Conservative Government—as is true of any British Government—held the key levers of Parliamentary power. First and foremost it could count upon its sheer weight of numbers. Since it controlled the House of Commons, it monopolized the entire machinery of national power. The Conservatives, with their highly disciplined Commons majority of more than one hundred votes, were capable of pushing the reform through over any opposition, no matter how well entrenched or articulate, and this, of course, had been their ace in the hole from the very beginning.

In addition to commanding its disciplined Parliamentary majority, the Government could utilize a number of procedural weapons if the

[6] In addition to his very precise intellectual ability, Stewart had a thorough familiarity with the key issues that Labour would use to attack the Bill. He had formerly served as an LCC teacher, and his wife was one of the thirteen Chairmen of the Metropolitan Juvenile Courts who had signed the letter in *The Times* in May 1962.

[7] Rt. Hon. Lord Morrison of Lambeth, "A Tory Plot to Destroy London," *Reynolds News & Sunday Citizen*, September 2, 1962.

going got rough. Two of these were of primary importance. The first was its control of the scheduling of Parliamentary business, and the second was its control over Parliamentary debate.

Under British procedure, most (although not all) bills originate in the House of Commons, where they are subjected to three readings. The First Reading serves as nothing more than an opportunity to introduce the measure. It is "read" to the House and printed. The very important Second Reading, which generally follows in two to three weeks, is devoted to a debate (usually two days) on the general principles and merits of the bill. After the bill has passed Second Reading, it enters the Committee Stage, which is quite different from any American congressional counterpart. The Parliamentary Standing Committees, which number approximately forty members drawn proportionately from the parties in the House, are not specialized bodies, nor is there any way in which they can suppress bills or hold them up indefinitely. The function of a Committee is not to pass upon the general merits of a bill (this has already been done in Second Reading), but rather to work through the bill in detail. Amendments to the bill can be considered either in Standing Committee, or in the Committee of the Whole House (the Commons, itself, sitting under another name in an effort to speed the consideration of bills). After the bill has been worked over in detail during its Committee Stage, it is subjected to a Third Reading debate (usually one day), when it is given final approval by the Commons.

The bill then moves on to the House of Lords, where it goes through a similar reading and debate process. Conceivably, the Lords can delay the bill for one year (one month for money bills) if they wish to, but this is rarely the case. The Lords can, and do, amend bills, however, and after a bill has received approval from the House of Lords, it is referred back to the Commons for final consideration. The bill then passes out of Parliament, becoming law once it receives Royal Assent.

In addition to controlling the scheduling of a bill through each of these procedural phases, the Government can hasten the progress of a bill by limiting debate. One of the most brutal means of doing so is passage of an "Allocation of Time Order," more commonly known as "the guillotine." The guillotine amounts to closure by compartments. Before debate even begins, the "Time Order" is passed to specify the period during which each clause (or compartment) of the bill will be discussed. Once this period has expired, the guillotine drops, and the debate is chopped off. Thus, the Government has in the guillotine a weapon of considerable potency with which it can expedite Parliamentary business.

The House of Commons

Following the Queen's Speech, which announced the reorganization measure as part of the Government's pending Parliamentary program, the London Government Bill received its First Reading in the Commons on November 20, 1962. In general format, the Bill followed the outlines of the Government's White Paper (as amended by concessions) quite closely. Clause I dealt with the establishment of the Greater London Council and the London Borough councils. Clauses II through VII specified the various functions that were to be exercised by these new authorities. Clause VIII dealt with rating, evaluation, grants, and related financial matters; and Clause IX, with miscellaneous provisions.

The Bill moved on to Second Reading on December 11–12, 1962. Since this was a major debate on the general merits of the proposed legislation, both sides brought up their heavy artillery. Sir Keith Joseph led off the debate for the Government, and Michael Stewart replied for the Opposition. The debate continued into the following day when, at nine o'clock in the evening, it was concluded by George Brown for the Opposition and by Enoch Powell, the Minister of Health, for the Government. The House then divided on the Bill, which was carried by 314 votes to 236, a Government majority of 78. Five Liberals, including the Party leader, Mr. Grimmond, voted for the Bill. However, in addition to Conservative abstentions, four Conservatives (two from

Surrey, including Sir Cyril Black) voted against the Bill despite the fact that the Government had applied a three-line whip.[8] Following its Second Reading approval, Clause I of the Bill was committed to the Committee of the Whole House, while the remainder of the Bill was referred to a Standing Committee.

Following Christmas recess, on January 23, 1963, the Committee of the Whole House began its consideration of Clause I, Schedule 1, dealing with the establishment of the new London Boroughs. The Labor Opposition and the chief Liberal spokesman on the Bill (Mr. Lubbock) immediately moved amendments that would eliminate restrictions on the maximum number of borough councillors. The Bill specified that the boroughs should be limited to no more than sixty councillors, a restriction that was unpopular with many of the Conservative backbenchers who objected that the larger boroughs would be too "impersonal" and "remote" unless more councillors could be added to increase the degree of council liaison with local constituents. As a result, when the amendments came to a vote, there were additional Conservative abstentions. The Labour amendment was only defeated by 222 to 194, a Government majority of 28, while the Liberal amendment was defeated by 218 to 192, a Government majority of 26. The Opposition was delighted with the outcome of this first test of strength, and "both [votes] were greeted with . . . cheers and shouts of 'resign'."[9]

The next day Labour resumed its attack on Clause I, Schedules 1 and 2 (dealing with the new London Boroughs and the Greater London Council) by quickly calling for an amendment that would delay by three years the election of new councillors. The Bill scheduled the first Greater London Council election for April 1964 and the first London Borough council elections for May 1964. Labour attacked both dates on the grounds that no new local elections should be held until after the next General Election, which would offer the people an opportunity to express their mandate on the reform program. This

---

[8] A three-line whip means that the question to be voted on is underlined three times in the daily schedule. In short, it is the Government's way of telling its supporters to be on hand to support the measure.

[9] *The Times*, "London Bill Conflicts Bring Majorities Under 30," January 24, 1963.

was a crucial issue because the Labour Party had indicated it would reserve the right to recast, or rescind, the entire reform effort if it won the next General Election. The Conservative Government, on the other hand, wanted to implement the reform as quickly as possible to prevent just such an eventuality. The Conservatives felt that if the local council elections could be held before the next General Election (which could be no later than October 1964), it would be too late for the Labourites to unscramble the reform omelet even if they did win control of the Government. The Labour argument was that the Conservative Government was proceeding with "indecent haste," in an effort to secure political control over central London prior to the next General Election.

When viewed in this light, the amendment on the local election schedule offered Labour the opportunity to debate again and to attack the entire reform effort. Thus, in concluding the debate on the date of elections amendment, Michael Stewart asserted:

> What we have to lose by this bill are a finely constructed education service, a humane and efficient child care service, an architects department of world fame, and many other services.[10]

A division was taken on the amendment, which was defeated 215-166, a Government majority of 49. The Government then moved closure to cut off further debate on Schedules 1 and 2 of the First Clause, and this was carried 191-124 (majority 67).

Despite the fact that these second-day majorities were larger than those of the preceding day, the Government was deeply disturbed over the effectiveness of the Opposition's Parliamentary strategy. The Opposition, of course, was only doing what came naturally. In the phraseology of one of its members, Clause I represented "the coffin in which the body is to be placed."[11] When viewed in this light, the Opposition had no scruples in attempting to make this coffin as irritating as possible. In so doing, it was concentrating on specific amendments that were designed to pick up maximum support from dissident Conservative backbenchers. The Government, worried about its thin majorities and

[10] *The Guardian,* "Closure Forced on London Bill," January 25, 1963.
[11] *The Times,* "Legislation By Pianola" (editorial), January 29, 1963.

fearful that the Bill would become bogged down in an endless morass of amendments, decided to take drastic action. On January 28 it announced that it would place the London Government Bill under the guillotine.

The Government had no trouble pushing the guillotine through (the "Allocation of Time Order" was passed on January 29 by a vote of 261-188 over bitter Labour protests), but the action was far from popular, even with supporters of the Bill. Sir Percy Rugg, the Conservative leader on the London County Council, indicated that he regretted the application of the guillotine, and *The Times* deplored the action, in an editorial entitled "Legislation by Pianola," as being another in a long line of sufferings endured by the Commons:

> A committee of the whole House has so far spent two days, which is not excessive, on the first clause, a key clause. . . . Some hold that since the guillotine procedure assists the efficient dispatch of business, no government need be shy of invoking it. . . .
>
> The claim is correct up to a point, wholly correct if efficiency is equated with speed. But a price is paid in a diminution of parliamentary control over the content of legislation, similar to its loss of control over public expenditure. . . .
>
> The legislature is already in some danger of becoming more like a pianola than a pianist, mechanically rendering tunes composed jointly by departments of state and whatever organized interests happen to be affected. . . . It cannot do the job if its examination of Bills is habitually truncated.[12]

The guillotine specified the future schedule of debate. Two further days were allotted for the committee stage on the floor of the House for Clause I. The remainder of the Bill would then be taken upstairs, where the Standing Committee was required to report back to the House by March 21. After the Bill was once again reported on the floor, two days were allotted for both report and Third Reading.

In the course of the next two months, the Opposition managed to put down no less than 1,000 amendments to the Bill. Parliamentarians were not sure whether this was an all-time record, but it was certainly

[12] *Ibid.*

close to one. While it is not feasible to trace each of these amendments in detail, it is possible to outline a capsule summary of key issues covered by amendments in order to give some indication of the kind of in-fighting that was taking place:

STAFF: The Government was worried from the beginning about the staff employees' reactions to reform, fearing that such employees might rise up en masse against the plan. As a consequence, it devoted much effort to trying to reassure staff members that their interests would be protected during the reorganization.

On January 9, the Government issued a circular advising that it would create a special impartial committee to deal with staffing problems, and on May 3 Sir Keith Joseph announced that Sir Harold Emmerson (former Permanent Secretary of the Ministry of Labour) would chair the three-man staff Commission to be set up under the provisions of the Bill. In addition, Sir Keith and other Government spokesmen addressed numerous employee associations both before and after the final passage of the Bill. (On September 23, 1963, for example, Sir Keith explained the new Act in considerable detail to a mass meeting of 5,000 NALGO employees in Albert Hall.)

Despite the Government's efforts, the Opposition was able to maneuver very effectively on staff questions, even inflicting occasional defeats on the Government. One such defeat occurred on March 21, when the Standing Committee voted 21 to 17 to support a Labour amendment to the Bill which allowed prevailing LCC conditions of service and scales of pay to apply from April 1, 1965, to officers of the new Greater London Council, despite the fact that the Government argued the amendment was unnecessary.

EDUCATION: Education was another difficult issue for the Government, and one on which the Labour Opposition applied continuous pressure.

On February 26th, the Labour members of the Standing Committee made their major move by proposing a series of amendments to the Bill that would have revised completely the proposed system of educational administration. Under the Government's Bill, the central LCC area was to be administered as a unit by a single education authority (i.e., the Inner London Education Authority), while the twenty new London Borough councils located outside this central area were to have responsibility for administering their own educational programs.

Labour amendments proposed that educational responsibilities in these twenty "outer" boroughs should be taken over by four new education authorities modeled after ILEA. The amendments were defeated, 21-16, after Conservative members of the Standing Committee argued that they were "Typical socialist nostalgia" and a "Trojan horse that would wreck the Bill and cast education as a regional responsibility."[13]

BOROUGH GROUPINGS: The entire Parliamentary proceedings were consumed, indeed obsessed, with debates over the proposed new London Borough council groupings, and (although the question was still premature) over speculation as to the names of these new groupings.

The disappearing boroughs used every means available to preserve their identity (e.g., " 'Doomed' Council will petition The Queen," etc.). Labour spotlighted the issue of borough amalgamations obliquely and ingeniously by proposing that the City of London be absorbed into new Borough Grouping No. 1 (i.e., Westminster, Paddington, and St. Marylebone).

Under the Government's Bill, the City was to retain its identity as a historic enclave, and Labour chided the Government mercilessly for permitting the retention of a historic anachronism of only 5,000 people under a reform program that was designed to modernize London's local government.

However, the Government was able to beat down the proposed Labour amendment in the Committee of the Whole House by a 231 to 186 vote. The issue was raised again later when Lord Morrison proposed in the House of Lords that the City should be amalgamated with four of east London's Labour boroughs (Finsbury, Shoreditch, Stepney, and Southwark). Although this proposal sent the fear of God into the City, it was eventually turned down by the other Lords.

By concentrating on such issues as these, the Opposition was able to keep up a constant pressure on the reorganization program to a point at which the groggy M.P.'s became reduced to a state of total con-

[13] *The Guardian*, "Labour Urges Area Education Plan for Greater London," February 27, 1963.

fusion. The prevailing mood was captured somewhat hilariously, if nonetheless accurately, by a comment in *The Guardian* entitled "London Not In Scotland":

> For ages now it seems the London Government Bill has been with us. . . . So many members are squeezed within its coils—there are at least ninety—that the creature drags itself with prehistoric grunts between the committee and the floor of the House downstairs.
>
> Not surprisingly, some members wander into the committee in error: one did so twice one recent bleak morning and his constituency is at least 250 miles from London. The Bill, now on its 22nd clause, has another 65 to run. The last subsection of the final clause reads thus: 'Except for the amendment to the House of Commons Disqualification Act 1957 effected by paragraph 9 of Schedule 16 to this Act, the Act does not extend to Scotland or to Northern Ireland.'
>
> Perhaps, in view of the increasing home rule awarded to London boroughs, this is just as well.[14]

All the while that Labour was throwing out its massive and unrelenting barrage of amendments inside the Commons, the various professional associations were applying their own brands of pressure outside the Commons.

On January 22, 1963, the Local Medical Committee of the County of London issued a statement calling for the retention of all personal health services under a single central authority comparable to that established in education:

> It will be a tragedy for all concerned, and not the least for the new boroughs, if this fragmentation results in less efficient health services, yet the Government appears blind to this danger.
>
> We doctors, on the other hand, foresee that our patients will suffer.[15]

On January 23, the British Medical Association announced that it had complained about the plan to Health Minister Enoch Powell. "So

---

[14] *The Guardian*, London Letter, "London Not In Scotland," February 20, 1963.

[15] *The Guardian*, "Doctors Fear Split Control In London," January 23, 1963.

far," said a BMA spokesman, "our protests have been brushed aside. Now we shall be approaching M.P.'s to put our case."[16]

On February 13, the Committee for London Government delegation, led by Sir Isaac Hayward and other local mayors wearing chains and official insignia, marched on Commons to present its protest petition containing the 172,000 signatures.[17]

On February 25, "a melancholy procession of 1,000 teachers" took time off from the annual meetings of the London Teachers' Association to protest the reorganization plan.[18]

On February 28, representatives from three child welfare agencies held a press conference protesting the plan, with Lady Wootten warning that, if the reorganization went through, "9,000 children will suffer."[19]

Even the gratuitous dividend of a leap year was not ignored. On February 29, the Conservative members of the Standing Committee on the London Government Bill charged that school-children were being utilized in an opposition propaganda campaign to write letters of protest to their M.P.'s. "The letters bear entirely the same 'proforma' in the expressions they use," complained one Conservative Committee member. The Opposition dismissed the allegations as "rather malicious."[20]

On March 25, at a press conference of the Committee for London Government, Michael Stewart described the Bill as "one of the most confusing and ill-drafted bills ever put before a committee of the House of Commons."[21]

In spite of this assault, both internal and external, the Bill moved forward to final passage. On April 29, it was subjected to its Third (and final) Reading, where it passed by a vote of 285 to 226, a Government majority of 59. Sir Keith Joseph criticized the Opposition's position as being "perverse, parochial and static," while Michael Stewart warned

[16] *Evening Standard,* "Doctors Slam London Plan," January 23, 1963.

[17] *The Guardian,* "17 Mayors Among Petitioners," February 14, 1963.

[18] *The Guardian,* "Lobby By Teachers," February 26, 1963.

[19] *The Guardian,* "9,000 Children Will Suffer," March 1, 1963.

[20] *The Guardian,* "Propaganda Letters From Children," March 1, 1963.

[21] Stewart, quoted in *The Guardian,* "Fight Goes on Against London Bill," March 26, 1963.

that "if a change of Government occurs this year, we shall repeal this Bill. If the change occurs after the new Borough Councils are elected, we shall halt the transfer of functions and break-up of the social services which this Bill seeks to effect."[22]

The Bill had passed through its ordeal in the Commons, bloody but still intact. It now moved over to the House of Lords, where Lord Morrison and company were waiting, with knives sharpened, to give it a lively reception.

The House of Lords

The London Government Bill's journey through the House of Lords paralleled its perilous progress through the Commons. The time span was somewhat shorter (three months versus four months) and the amendments somewhat fewer (500 versus 1,000), but the bitterness of the struggle was every bit as intense and dramatic.

Two major differences between the Lords and the Commons, however, related to membership and procedures. As regards membership, the House of Lords is a venerable body. Theoretically, some 900 members are qualified to sit in Lords, including 840 hereditary peers, sixteen "representative" peers of Scotland, princes of royal blood, the nine Law Lords, and twenty-six Spiritual Lords (i.e., Archbishops and Bishops). Since the passage of new legislation in 1958, this membership has been increased by the creation of new Life Peers and Peeresses, who are recognized for distinguished achievement.

Only about sixty or seventy of the members faithfully participate in debate, however, and what vitality the House of Lords possesses (especially on the Labour side) is usually derived from this latter group of Life Peers (e.g., Lord Morrison), plus some of the more recent hereditary peers. On the whole, if not decrepit, the membership of the House of Lords is characterized by advancing old age. This leads directly to the major procedural differences between the Lords and the Commons.

[22] *The Times*, "Labour Reserves Right to Recast London Plan," April 3, 1963.

Unlike the Commons, the House of Lords does not place reliance upon Standing Committees to work over bills in detail. Instead, the Lords themselves sit as a Committee (comparable to the Committee of the Whole House in Commons) to discuss and debate amendments. In addition, the Lords do not rely upon the guillotine to cut off debate. Instead, the Conservative Government (which enjoys an extremely sympathetic majority because of the historic Conservative leanings of the hereditary peers) can bring about sheer physical exhaustion to wear down the outnumbered Labour peers.

As previously noted, the chief Labour spokesmen on the London Government Bill were Lord Morrison and Lord Longford (the Chairman of the Committee for London Government). They were joined by other peers, including Lord Alexander of Hillsborough (the leader of the Labour Peers) and Lord Silkin (an important former member of the LCC). The Conservative leadership was provided by the Lord President of the Council, Viscount Hailsham (the Leader of the House of Lords and a member of the Conservative Cabinet), Lord Hastings (Parliamentary Secretary, Ministry of Housing and Local Government), and Earl St. Aldwyn (Government Chief Whip).

The fight began in earnest at the opening of the Second Reading, when the Opposition immediately attempted to sidetrack the entire reorganization program by challenging that the London Government Bill was a hybrid bill.[23] After being overruled by the Speaker (and defeated by a vote of 96-29 after the Speaker's ruling had been challenged), the Opposition pressed into a debate on the reorganization which continued through the following day. On April 24, the Second Reading division was carried by a vote of 55 to 27, a Government majority of 28.

[23] A hybrid bill is a public bill that affects private interests. As such, it is referred to a special Select Committee at which objections and counsel can be heard. The delay involved can be fatal. The Labour Opposition had also attacked the measure as a hybrid bill at the beginning of Second Reading in Commons, but they had also been overruled. However, the hybrid bill threat was important. It had originally forced the Government to rewrite the London Government Bill prior to First Reading in Commons, in order to remove any references to the Greater London Council's taking over water services. These services had been administered by private as well as public authorities, and reference to them, if left in the legislation, would probably have made it a hybrid bill.

The Bill entered Committee Stage on May 9. The first Opposition challenges were virtually identical to those that had appeared in the House of Commons. An amendment was proposed that no councillor on a London Borough council could represent more than 3,000 electors (defeated 62 to 27). A second amendment, that the borough elections be shifted from May 1964 to May 1965, was proposed (defeated 37 to 13). So it went while the Bill resumed its "prehistoric grunts" through the Committee Stage in the Lords. On May 13 Viscount Hailsham, discouraged over the slow progress of the Bill, decided to turn on the pressure. He kept the House in session until 2:35 A.M., a sitting of twelve hours and five minutes. This was a new Lords' longevity record for a single sitting, topping the previous high of eleven hours and fifty-five minutes that had been set in November 1934. The session was characterized by angry scenes in which the Labour Peers complained bitterly of "brutality." Lord Alexander lashed out against "physical pressures by a domineering Government" who thought they could play ducks and drakes with a limited Opposition.[24]

The Committee Stage continued into May 21, when Lord Morrison denounced the Bishops and Archbishops for failing to appear after the debate turned to the Government's education proposals:

> I think it is a dreadful thing that not even the Bishop of London is here. I want to say, with such quietness as I can, and with great respect for the Established Church, that if bishops are going to serve in this House we expect them to do their duty, especially on matters in which the Church ought to have a voice.[25]

By May 30, after eleven days and 303 amendments, the Committee Stage of the proceedings was completed. The House of Lords now took a respite before moving to the final Report Stage, and by a curious circumstance, a totally unanticipated external event broke into the open to occupy fully the Lords' attention during this interim period.

The external event revolved around Mr. John Profumo and Miss Christine Keeler. As the implications of this incredible affair splashed across the pages of the press, the Conservative Government staggered

[24] *The Daily Telegraph*, "Brutal Treatment Complaint By Labour Peers," May 14, 1963.
[25] *The Guardian*, "Bishops Criticised for Missing Debate," May 22, 1963.

precariously and very nearly fell from power. There is no doubt whatever that if the Government had not held on at this point the entire reorganization program would have been finished. It was virtually inconceivable that the Conservatives could have survived a General Election, and the heir-apparent Labour Government was firmly on record as opposing the Greater London plan in its present form. In short, the Opposition's strategy of delay very nearly paid dividends.

The Government did survive the crisis, however, and the Bill moved to final report debate in the House of Lords. Another 230 amendments were tabled for Report Stage, which began on June 24. Not all these were brushed aside by any means. On the very first day of Report Stage, two Conservative Peers sponsored an amendment that led directly to a Government defeat. Specifically, they proposed that the fragmented remnant of the severed Borough of Epsom and Ewell should be removed from the jurisdiction of the Greater London Council and returned to its beloved Surrey County. The amendment was carried 35 to 30, a Government defeat by 5. The announcement of the vote was greeted with Opposition cheers and Lord Morrison, grasping for straws, asserted that this was a decisive setback that went to the heart of the Bill. What, he asked, was the Government's intention about the future of the Bill, and of itself? The Lord Chancellor replied, "It is the Government's intention to carry on with the Bill, which is a thoroughly beneficial measure."[26]

The following day the Government proposed another of the many amendments that it had sponsored during the long course of Parliamentary proceedings. This involved increasing the power of the Greater London Council to help the new London boroughs with their slum-clearance schemes. The amendment was accepted. This amendatory process continued into July, with many revisions being defeated, but many being accepted as well. By late July, when the Lords had completed their consideration of Greater London's future, the Bill was returned to the Commons, where the House was confronted with no less than 280 Lords' amendments.

On July 25, Iain MacLeod, the Conservative Leader in the Commons, advised that the Government would utilize a supplementary

[26] *The Daily Telegraph*, "Peers Revolt on London Bill," June 26, 1963.

"Allocation of Time Order" to hasten the final approval of the Bill. Michael Stewart complained that this "merely completed the record of sordid brutality that characterized the Government's handling of the Bill."[27] The supplementary Order was passed 213-158, and the Commons considered the Lords' amendments under a strict time schedule. Many were accepted quickly, including those dealing with an increase in the Greater London Council's control over traffic, the granting of the right to the new boroughs to petition directly for Royal Charters, the exclusion of the severed rump of Epsom and Ewell from the Greater London Council area, and so forth. After the Commons disposed of the Lords' amendments, the Bill received Royal Assent on July 31, 1963.

During the course of the preceding eight months, the Parliamentary struggle over the reform of London's government had been bitter and intense. The Commons spent 20 per cent of the time taken on legislation on the floor of the House considering this one Bill alone, not to mention twenty-one committee sittings. The Lords had broken all-time longevity records. The Bill had been challenged by an endless number of proposed amendments that reached the vicinity of 1,500.

In short, it had been a long, hard Parliamentary pull before the London Government Bill was finally translated into law.

The London Government Act, 1963

While it is beyond the bounds of feasibility to trace all the modifications that took place in the Royal Commission's plan between October 1960 and July 1963, it is possible to highlight the major changes that resulted from the political battle over the Greater London plan. For purposes of summary analysis, four basic revisions were of primary significance:

1. Geographical Jurisdiction. The greatest single concession involved the continuous erosion of the scope of the geographical jurisdiction of the reform program.

[27] *The Times*, "Last Phase of London Bill," June 26, 1963.

When the Government originally created the Royal Commission in July 1957, the review area of this Commission encompassed approximately 845 square miles, extending out from central London in a sixteen-mile radius. The Commission cut down this area in its final report by excluding eleven of the original local authorities (located on the fringes of this review area) from the reorganization program. The Government subsequently continued this process by excluding nine additional fringe authorities from the Greater London Council's jurisdiction.

As a result of the exclusion of these twenty fringe authorities, the total geographical area subjected to reorganization was eroded drastically. Whereas the Royal Commission had begun its study by analyzing an area that encompassed 845 square miles, the Government ended up with legislation that encompassed an area of some 630 square miles.

To those who felt that the review area had been too small in the first place, this subsequent geographical erosion was a tragedy. Many professionals, especially in the planning field, bemoaned the reform program as being too circumscribed. For example, Péter Hall, lecturer in geography, Birkbeck College (University of London), makes the following comments in a study entitled *London 2000*:

> The English have an extraordinary knack for devising pieces of administrative machinery for London that are admirably suited to the conditions of a quarter-century back.
> The important question about the Herbert Commission's report is not: Why did they create the system of government they did?—the logic behind that was almost inescapable—but: Why did they refuse to carry that logic to its 1960 conclusion? Why did they not propose a regional government that would function over a really effective area?[28]

Dr. Hall's question can be answered only by a consideration of the political climate that surrounded reform. It is all well and good to question the Royal Commission, and the Government, for not being bold enough in terms of their geographical thinking, but politics deals with the art of the possible. In light of the battle that ensued over the

[28] Peter Hall, *London 2000* (London: Faber & Faber Ltd., 1963), p. 191.

current Greater London plan, despite its geographical modesty, it is difficult to conceive what would have happened if the area covered by this plan had been doubled or tripled in size.

The geographical erosion that went into the making of the Greater London reform—the 25-per-cent reduction in the size of the original review area—represented the great political concession to the second-tier authorities, especially those that were located on the outer fringes of the metropolitan area.

2 Education. The second great concession occurred in the field of education, and this time it was the professional associations that scored most heavily.

The Government's first educational modification involved a rejection of the Royal Commission's original formula for dividing educational responsibilities between the two tiers, in favor of an allocation of the major educational responsibilities to the new London Boroughs.

The second major modification involved the creation of the new central London education area, which, in turn, led to the establishment of the new Inner London Education Authority and to the preservation of the existing LCC education service.

3. The Borough Groupings. The Government's third key modification grew out of the educational changes noted above.

This was the enlargement of the new London Boroughs from a minimum population of 100,000 to a minimum of 200,000. (In actual fact, the final borough groupings averaged about 250,000.)

4. Other Services. Once the other professional associations became aware of the educational concessions, they began to press for special treatment of their own service specialties. The doctors and the child welfare workers in particular were anxious to see the creation of a special central area for their own services, modeled along the lines of the Inner London Education Authority.

The Government stood firm on this issue, mainly because it felt it could not strip away additional services from the London Borough councils located in the central area. The Government did, however, make numerous adjustments in the allocation of specific responsibilities in order to placate key professional groups.

The fields of traffic, housing, and planning represent good illustrations of this. While the Government did not go as far as the Institute of British Architects would have liked, it did make a number of revisions in each of these services. In the original Bill, the Government had proposed a rather grotesque duplication of traffic powers between the Minister of Transport and the Greater London Council. This was clarified when the Minister was allocated reserve powers only. Although the act retained divided housing responsibilities between the Greater London Council and the boroughs, it strengthened the Council's powers to assist the boroughs in slum clearance. In a like manner, the original Government Bill was modified to require that all local borough planning permissions must conform to the Greater London Development Plan, which is to be formulated by the Greater London Council.

It was fields such as these that represented a halfway house. The Government did not go as far as many of the professional associations might have preferred, but it did permit many shifts in its original position.

In short, the Government, by making concessions such as these, set the stage for the final approval of the London Government Act of 1963. Once this Act became law, Sir Keith Joseph (and the public) got down to the intriguing business of rechristening the new London Boroughs, drawing upon such considerations as:

> *History*—"TOWER HAMLETS" (A resurrected ancient east London name for Stepney, Poplar, and Bethnal Green, which the local Cockneys quickly dubbed Tower 'Amlets);
> *Tradition*—"WESTMINSTER" (for Paddington, St. Marylebone, and Westminster);
> *Logic*—"NEWHAM" (i.e., East Ham and West Ham);
> *Deadlock*—"KENSINGTON AND CHELSEA" (for Kensington and Chelsea); and
> *Fresh new starts in life*—"BRENT" (an attempt to blanket the warring camps of Conservative Wembley and Labourite Willesden).

By the autumn of 1963, the struggle over the Greater London plan was drawing to a close. One final chapter remained, however, before this story was fully complete.

The Conservatives had scheduled the first Greater London Council elections for the spring of 1964. The rationale behind this strategy was clear-cut. The Labourites had threatened to recast the entire reform effort in the event of their anticipated victory in the next national General Election, and the Conservatives were attempting to give their new London government at least an initial lease on life before any such General Election took place. Hence, for better or for worse, the Labourites were going to be forced to face up to the impact of the Conservatives' supposed "political gerrymander" of London's government before they could possibly have an opportunity to make any further forays into the reform arena.

Once these first Greater London Council elections actually took place, the entire picture tended to shift so dramatically that both the Labourites and the Conservatives must have harbored some very deep second thoughts, indeed, about the wisdom of any further forays at all into the mysterious realm of metropolitan governmental reform.

TABLE V[29]

Summary of the Greater London Act of 1963

I. ORGANIZATION

  1. The government of the Greater London area (see Map XII)[30] shall consist of:

     a. a Greater London Council, to be composed of 100 councillors and 16 aldermen. The first Council elections shall be held in April, 1964. Thereafter, all councillors shall retire together every three years, with triennial elections being held on the basis of single-member electoral districts within the London Boroughs;

     b. 32 London Boroughs (see Map XII and attached Appendix), to be composed of a maximum of 60 councillors, and appropriate aldermen to number one-sixth of the councillors. The first London Borough elections shall be held in May, 1964. Thereafter,

[29] *London Government Act 1963*, Chapter 33 (London: MMSO, 1963); also *Metropolitan Boroughs' Standing Joint Committee, London Government Act, 1963*, summary prepared by A. G. Dawtry, Honorary Clerk (October 1963).

[30] Map XII (p. 258) gives an accurate picture of the final Greater London Council area with the exception that the fringe remnants of the Surrey Borough of Epsom and Ewell were dropped from the GLC's jurisdiction by amendment adopted in the House of Lords and later approved by the Commons.

the borough councillors will all retire together every third year, with triennial elections being held within each borough.

II. DIVISION OF MAJOR FUNCTIONS (effective 1 April 1965)

1. The Greater London Council will:
   a. serve as the main traffic authority for Greater London, and as the highway authority for all roads designated as "metropolitan roads" (in addition, the Council may make orders with respect to major trunk roads with the consent of the Minister of Transport);
   b. serve as the local planning authority for Greater London as a whole, and prepare a Greater London Development Plan for submission to the Minister of Housing and Local Government;
   c. provide all "overspill" housing outside the Greater London area; exercise certain comprehensive development powers within the Greater London area (including the provision of certain local housing with the consent of the boroughs involved, or of the Minister of Housing and Local Government); and maintain records showing the over-all housing needs in Greater London;
   d. be responsible for the ambulance services; the fire service; major licensing services; main sewers, sewage disposal works, and main drainage systems; and any Green Belt land falling under its jurisdiction;
   e. provide general intelligence services on the Greater London area by undertaking research and collecting information relating to matters concerning this area;
   f. exercise concurrent powers to provide and maintain parks and open spaces.

2. The London Boroughs will:
   a. serve as the highway authorities for all borough highways except "metropolitan roads" (and trunk roads);
   b. serve as local planning authorities for all borough purposes, including the approval of applications for planning permissions (with limited exceptions), and the preparation of a borough development plan in conformance with the Greater London Development Plan;
   c. exercise full local housing powers (with the exception that "overspill" housing can only be provided with the consent of the Minister of Housing and Local Government);
   d. be responsible for personal health, welfare, and children's services; for public sewers other than main sewers; and for library services;

    e. exercise educational powers as follows:
1. the 20 "outer London" boroughs will be full local education authorities;
2. the education services for the 12 "inner London" boroughs in the central London area will be under the jurisdiction of the Inner London Education Authority (to consist of the Greater London councillors elected from these boroughs and the City of London, plus one additional representative appointed by each of the boroughs and the City). The operations of this Authority will be reviewed by the Minister of Education, who will report to Parliament no later than 31 March 1970 on the feasibility of transferring the education services to the 12 "inner London" boroughs.

    f. exercise concurrent powers to provide and maintain parks and open spaces.

III. FINANCES AND MISCELLANEOUS

1. The London Borough councils will be the rating authorities in Greater London, and the Greater London Council will precept on these rating authorities.
2. The Minister of Housing and Local Government may make a rate equalization scheme for the whole or any parts of Greater London, after consultation with the Greater London Council, the City of London, and any body representing the London Borough councils.
3. For a transitional period of eight years, the Greater London Council is required to pay to the adjacent county councils contributions toward additional rate burdens falling upon these councils as a consequence of the Act.
4. The City of London shall retain its present identity but shall be associated with Borough Grouping No. 1 for administrative purposes. All other London boroughs (with the exception of Borough No. 29, i.e., Harrow) shall be formed from the merger of existing local authorities as set forth in the Act. (The 32 boroughs average approximately 250,000 in population, and the Greater London Council's jurisdiction extends over an approximate 640-square-mile area).

THE 32 NEW LONDON BOROUGHS

(Constituent areas and population of new boroughs are indicated
in parentheses.)

Barking   (Barking, Dagenham—179,000)
Barnet   (Barnet, East Barnet, Finchley, Friern Barnet, Hendon—318,000)
Bexley   (Bexley, Chislehurst and Sidcup [part], Crayford, Erith—210,000)
Brent   (Wembley, Willesden—296,000)
Bromley   (Beckenham, Bromley, Chislehurst and Sidcup [part], Penge,
    Orpington—294,000)
Camden   (Hampstead, Holborn, St. Pancras—246,000)
Croydon   (Croydon, Coulsdon and Purley—327,000)
Ealing   (Acton, Ealing, Southall—300,000)
Enfield   (Edmonton, Enfield, Southgate—274,000)
Greenwich   (Greenwich, Woolwich—230,000)
Hackney   (Hackney, Shoreditch, Stoke Newington—257,000)
Hammersmith   (Fulham, Hammersmith—222,000)
Haringey   (Hornsey, Tottenham, Wood Green—259,000)
Harrow   (Harrow—209,000)
Havering   (Hornchurch, Romford—243,000)
Hillingdon   (Hayes and Harlington, Ruislip and Northwood, Uxbridge,
    Yiewsley and West Drayton—228,000)
Hounslow   (Brentford and Chiswick, Feltham, Heston and Isleworth—
    209,000)
Islington   (Finsbury, Islington—262,000)
Kensington and Chelsea   (Kensington, Chelsea—218,000)
Kingston-on-Thames   (Kingston, Malden and Coombs, Surbiton—
    166,000)
Lambeth   (Lambeth, Wandsworth [part]—341,000)
Lewisham   (Deptford, Lewisham—290,000)
Merton   (Merton and Morden, Mitcham, Wimbledon—189,000)
Newham   (East Ham, West Ham—265,000)
Redbridge   (Ilford, Wanstead and Woodford—249,000)
Richmond-on-Thames   (Barnes, Richmond, Twickenham—182,000)
Southwark   (Bermondsey, Camberwell, Southwark—313,000)
Sutton   (Beddington and Wallington, Carshalton, Sutton and Cheam—
    169,000)
Tower Hamlets   (Bethnal Green, Poplar, Stepney—205,000)
Wandsworth   (Battersea, Wandsworth [part]—335,000)
Waltham Forest   (Chingford, Leyton, Walthamstow—248,000)
Westminster   (Paddington, St. Marylebone, Westminster—269,000)

Part V

PROBLEMS
AND
PROSPECTS

"A city that is at unity in itself"
—Psalm 122:3
The Book of Common Prayer

13. Greater London: The Politics of Metropolitan Reform

The vagaries of metropolitics are wondrous to behold.

With the adoption of the London Government Act of 1963, two central "facts" had emerged with reasonable clarity. First, after seventy-five years, the death knell had finally sounded for the historic London County Council. Second, its successor—the new Greater London Council—faced a precarious future at best. After fighting the creation of this new council tooth and nail, the Labour Party had advanced the very ominous threat of recasting the entire London reform program if it captured control of the House of Commons in the next General Election.

In April of 1964, the Labourites swept the first Greater London Council elections, gaining sixty-four seats to thirty-six for the Conservatives. In May, Labour again captured clear majorities, on twenty of the thirty-two new London Borough councils. Far from destroying the London County Council, the Government's reform program had the practical effect of producing a new "L.C.C. Writ Large."[1] And,

[1] The phrase "L.C.C. Writ Large," from *The Times* [London] (April 11, 1964), refers to the fact that half the newly elected GLC Labour councillors formerly served as members of the LCC, including all key committee chairmen and leaders with the exception of Sir Isaac Hayward and Mrs. Freda Corbett, both of whom retired from the political arena. Hence, the elections had the practical effect of expanding substantially the geographical jurisdiction of the former LCC while leaving its former leadership patterns virtually intact. For a more detailed analysis of the surprising 1964 London election results, see F. Smallwood, "Labourites Sweep London Elections," *National Civic Review* (July 1964).

far from facing a precarious future, this new "L.C.C." appeared to rest on secure political ground indeed, no matter which party won the next General Election.

No more fitting conclusion could be found for the story of London's governmental reform, for, if this story indicates little else, it most certainly highlights our present lack of understanding of the intricacies of metropolitan politics in particular and of the local governmental process in general.

The existing gaps in our knowledge are numerous. A major one involves the realm of theory. Despite centuries of reliance upon local governmental institutions, neither England nor the United States has ever really developed a coherent theoretical framework in which to evaluate the effectiveness of such institutions, especially in terms of their future relevance to the newer challenges of urbanization that have come to characterize modern society. This does not mean that local governmental mythologies do not exist, both overtly and subconsciously; yet these can hardly be classified as providing a meaningful theoretical framework upon which to build a viable local governmental system. Rather, such prevailing mythologies are more usually dusted off to champion a wild variety of divergent causes that bear little, if any, relationship to each other.

What has been lacking is an organized attempt to identify the central theoretical criteria that might help to expose past shibboleths and provide comprehensive conceptual guidelines that could clarify our future local governmental ideologies and development. With the exception of such occasional forays as Roscoe Martin's *Grass Roots,* Arthur Maass's *Area and Power,* Robert C. Wood's *Suburbia,* and Luther Gulick's *The Metropolitan Problem and American Ideas,*[2] the American political scientist has avoided meaningful study of the more theoretical aspects of the local governmental process. The English response to this particular challenge has been equally sparse, especially during recent years, in which little of relevance has appeared beyond occasional papers by W. J. M. Mackenzie and Bryan Keith-Lucas.

[2] Roscoe Martin, *Grass Roots* (University, Alabama: University of Alabama Press, 1957); Maass, *Area and Power*; Robert C. Wood, *Suburbia* (Boston: Houghton Mifflin, 1959); Gulick, *The Metropolitan Problem.*

In turn, America's failure to clarify its own local governmental theory has been compounded by a parochial avoidance of divergent theoretical approaches that fall outside the restricted confines of our native experience. A study such as L. G. Cowan's *Local Government in West Africa* represents a gold mine not only for what it tells about emerging developments in one of the world's most crucially important areas, but also because of its description of the theoretical dichotomy between a French "assimilation" approach and a British Native Authority System.[3] Cowan's analysis represents a relatively rare excursion into unfamiliar climes, however, at least for an American. In the field of comparative local government, the English most definitely can show us something of significance. Here the base for a future effort is to be found in the outlines of such studies as Ursula Hicks's *Development From Below* and W. A. Robson's *Great Cities of the World*.[4]

A second aspect of the local governmental process that calls for the development of a more systematic body of knowledge involves the variety of stubborn practical problems that go into the making of any such project as the Greater London plan. Perhaps, as is indicated in Chapter 6, Professor Duncan is right in asserting that questions involving such considerations as the "optimum" size of cities must inevitably originate in the "realm of values," but certainly we can attempt to restrict somewhat the virtually limitless range of value choices that presently stymies our approach to these very questions. Once again, the subject has not been totally ignored. James Fesler's *Area and Administration,* and more recently Paul Ylvisaker's attempt to suggest "Criteria for the 'Proper' Areal Division of Powers," or the Advisory Commission on Intergovernmental Relations' efforts to analyse the *Performance of Urban Functions: Local and Areawide*,[5] represent the types of studies that can provide both the insights and the hard data

---

[3] L. G. Cowan, *Local Government in West Africa* (New York: Columbia University Press, 1958).

[4] U. K. Hicks, *Development From Below* (Oxford at the Clarendon Press, 1961); W. A. Robson, *Great Cities of the World* (London: Allen & Unwin Ltd., 1957).

[5] James Fesler, *Area and Administration* (University, Alabama: University of Alabama Press, 1949); Paul Ylvisaker, in Maass, *Area and Power*; Advisory Commission on Intergovernmental Relations, *Performance of Urban Functions: Local and Areawide* (Washington: September 1963).

for a more sophisticated approach to these difficult problems in years ahead. Yet, our understanding of many of the most rudimentary functional aspects of the local governmental process is incredibly thin, a phenomenon that is all the more paradoxical in light of the tremendous amount of energy we have, in fact, poured into attempts to classify the more mundane organizational aspects of local governmental structure and procedure.

A third major knowledge gap has grown out of our past failure to develop a more systematic understanding of our metropolitan political systems. Here, however, more recent efforts provide a definite indication of very real progress. In addition to the expanding volume of metropolitan studies of such localities as Miami, St. Louis, New York, Syracuse, Cleveland, Nashville, Toronto, and a host of other cities,[6] we are finally beginning to see the subject of local politics take on the guise of a legitimate classroom concern. As Professors Banfield and Wilson note in one of the more recent texts, "politics arises out of conflicts," and conflicts exist not solely or even primarily because of lack of information or lack of adequate organizational techniques, but "rather because people have differing opinions and interests, and therefore opposing ideas about what should be done."[7]

The Greater London reform contest represents a classic example of

---

[6] See, for example, E. Sofen, *The Miami Metropolitan Experiment* (Bloomington: Indiana University Press, 1963); Schmandt, Steinbicker, and Wendel, *Metropolitan Reform in St. Louis*; Robert H. Salisbury, "The Dynamics of Reform: Charter Politics in St. Louis," *Midwest Journal of Political Science*, V, No. 3 (August 1961); Sayre and Kaufman, *Governing New York City* (New York: Russell Sage Foundation, 1960); R. C. Martin and F. J. Munger (eds.), *Decisions in Syracuse* (Bloomington: Indiana University Press, 1961); J. A. Norton, *The Metro Experience* (Cleveland: The Press of Western Reserve University, 1963); R. A. Watson and J. Romani, "Metropolitan Government for Metropolitan Cleveland: An Analysis of the Voting Record," *Midwest Journal of Political Science*, V, No. 4 (November 1961); D. A. Booth, *Metropolitics: The Nashville Consolidation* (East Lansing: Michigan State University, 1963); F. Smallwood, *Metro Toronto: A Decade Later* (Toronto: Bureau of Municipal Research, 1963); S. Greer, *Metropolitics* (New York: John Wiley & Sons, Inc., 1963); R. Martin, *Metropolis in Transition* (Washington: HHFA, 1963); Advisory Commission on Intergovernmental Relations, *Factors Affecting Voter Reactions to Government Reorganization in Metropolitan Areas* (Washington, 1962).

[7] Edward C. Banfield and James Q. Wilson, *City Politics* (Cambridge: Harvard University Press, 1963), p. 2.

such a collision between differing opinions and interests, and opposing ideas about what should be done. As such, its relevance stems in very large part from its political, rather than its organizational, connotations. Certainly the various administrative components of the Greater London plan do not constitute any elusive Rosetta stone that can be utilized to unravel automatically all America's metropolitan mysteries. Rather, the plan is of particular interest because it can tell us something about the divergent motivations, participants, and strategies that went into the making of a bitter political clash over the specific issue of metropolitan reform—a clash which, when evaluated in light of our own growing body of literature on this same subject, may provide some fresh insights into our appreciation of the metropolitan reform process.

Motivations

Participants in the Greater London contest were activated by four basic motives:
1. Power drives
2. Professional concerns
3. Fears: real and imaginary
4. Ideological rationalizations.

Although there was a high degree of interplay and overlap between these four influences, each is worthy of individual summary analysis.

POWER DRIVES

The Greater London plan represented a predominantly self-contained, and highly reciprocal, exchange of powers, in that certain local "actors" (i.e., the large borough councils, the London Conservatives, etc.) were originally designated to gain increased authority at the direct expense of other local "actors" (i.e., the county councils, the London Labourites, etc.). As a result, power drives induced participants both to support and to oppose the reorganization program. The supporters were motivated by expectant power drives; the opponents, by defensive power drives.

The most apt example of expectant power drives was to be found in the attitudes of the frustrated second-tier councils, especially those of the larger Middlesex boroughs, which favored some system of reform from the outset. It is important to note that the primary thrust that originally led to the entire reorganization program was to be found among these local borough councils. Although surface appearances tended to indicate that the central Government took the lead in advocating reform, this was not actually the case. The underlying pressures first originated at the local level. The true nature of the origins of reform was later obscured by the fact that other local groups, motivated by defensive power drives, later decided to fight the reform program. As the objections of these defensive groups increased in intensity, the entire reorganization effort tended to take on the misleading guise of a dictatorial process, in which it appeared that an adamant higher governmental authority was grinding its heel upon its protesting local underlings. Actually, however, this higher authority did not provide the initial impetus for the reform program, nor did it really know how to handle the subsequent degeneration of this program.

This is not to imply that this higher authority failed to possess expectant power drives of its own. While the Conservative central Government authorities may not have provided the initial impetus for reform, they pressed ahead rapidly once the political implications of the Royal Commission's proposals became fully apparent. When the Labourite opposition accused these central Government authorities of "indecent haste" in their attempts to use the reorganization program as a means of securing political control over London's government, the Conservatives flatly denied this charge. Yet, it is an obvious fact that the central Government did move extremely rapidly on this particular Royal Commission report, much more rapidly than is usually the case. It is difficult to assume that this same aggressive pace would have been forthcoming if the Royal Commission had somehow managed to recommend that a key Conservative local authority should have been abolished in favor of a potentially Labour-dominated council. The intensity of the central Government's expectations may have been somewhat less pronounced than was the case with the frustrated second-tier

Middlesex boroughs, but it would be foolhardy to argue that expectant power drives played no part in shaping the Government's position on reform.

The London Labour Party represented a key illustration of a group that was motivated by defensive power drives. Since this Party was interested in protecting its existing power position, it tended to concentrate on an extremely short-range defense of the status quo. By and large, this same short-range approach toward reform was characteristic of all the defensive groupings. It was particularly obvious in the case of the London Labour Party because, as the reform program unfolded, it became increasingly more apparent that this program's potentially adverse impact on the LLP was not destined to be anywhere near as severe as the Party leaders professed. Each time the Government dropped additional Conservative authorities from the review area as part of its suburban fringe concessions, Labour's prospects of gaining control over the new Greater London Council increased significantly. Yet the local Labour leaders fought the plan bitterly to the very end. They were considerably more interested in protecting an immediate sure thing (i.e., their existing iron grip on the London County Council) than in gambling on potential long-range success with a larger, and more powerful, first-tier authority.[8]

In addition to the London Labour Party, other defensive power groupings were to be found in the first-tier county councils and county

[8] In fairness to the Labourite opponents of reform, it must be admitted that no one originally anticipated the massive Labour sweep that actually materialized during the first G.L.C. elections in April-May, 1964. In part, Labour was able to do so well because of the deletion of Conservative suburban fringe authorities noted above. However, the real key to the Labour success was to be found in the close relationship between the G.L.C. voting and national electoral projections. By the spring of 1964, all the major electoral polls indicated a substantial national swing to the Labour Party, and in the G.L.C. elections this swing was translated into a 7-per-cent Labour gain in those marginal boroughs where direct comparisons could be made with the 1959 General Election voting. Thus, the Labour Party was able to capture every marginal borough in electing its 64 G.L.C. councillors, before returning again in May to capture 1,116 of the 1,855 council seats at stake in the borough elections. While these results were obviously disheartening to the Conservatives, the Liberals actually made the most disastrous showing, being completely shut out in the April G.L.C. election and capturing only 16 of the 1,855 borough seats in the May elections.

boroughs, and in the smaller second-tier authorities that were destined to lose status as a result of reform. Throughout the entire course of the reform contest, it was obvious that power drives, both expectant and defensive, played a crucial role in molding attitudes, pro and con, toward the reorganization plan. It is important to note, however, that these power drives did not constitute the whole story. In many cases they were supplemented, and at times even supplanted, by other, more subtle, motivational influences.

PROFESSIONAL CONCERNS

The major thrust of the professional concerns involved in the reform controversy was overwhelmingly negative in terms of its impact in activating opposition groups.

While, broadly conceived, professionally oriented arguments did provide some grist for the proponents of reform, such arguments were largely confined to abstractions. Supporters of reform, for example, attempted to justify the program in terms of vague claims regarding the increased efficiency to be realized through a rationalization of organizational structure, but these arguments were quite diffuse and carried little weight. The major impact of professional considerations was to be found in the influence that they exercised on a variety of important interest associations—the teachers, doctors, social workers, and the like.

These groups were adamantly opposed to reform on the grounds that it would have an adverse effect on the discharge of their particular service specialties. Their protestations carried considerably more weight than the more nebulous "efficiency" arguments advanced by the proponents of reform. Although the majority of these professional associations tended to take a narrow view of the situation (i.e., they were primarily concerned with potentially adverse impacts on their own particular service specialties), the combined weight of their pro-tests eventually produced a very broad assault on the entire reform effort. The concerns of many of the groups ran very deep. The London Teachers' Association's interest in the comprehensive schools, for example, played a major role in shaping the position of this group, even though the reform proposals failed to take any direct stand, either pro or con, on the comprehensive school question.

While a variety of professional associations strongly opposed the projected reform program, there was little consensus on any alternative schemes. The alternatives that were advanced varied widely, and they were primarily dependent on preconceived value objectives. As a result of their inability to formulate viable alternatives, the professional dissidents preferred to remain with the status quo.

In their defense of this status quo, many of these associations relied upon the use of emotional symbols. Since these symbols grew out of the associations' own deep-seated anxieties, they tended to center upon the manipulation of one of the most powerful of all emotional weapons. With the passage of time, the manipulation of fear, both imaginary and real, played an increasingly more significant role in the proceedings.

EMOTIONAL FEARS

The Greater London contest was dominated by two basic fears—the fear of future uncertainty and the fear of loss of identity. Each of these fears tended to strengthen the opposition side tremendously while providing nothing in the way of support for the proponents of reform.

Fear of future uncertainty was a logical outgrowth of the professional associations' anxieties. In essence, these associations translated their own anxieties into increasingly more generalized fear symbols, by contrasting existing certitudes with future unknowns. Over time, these future unknowns took on ever more ominous overtones, until they finally hardened into sweeping prophecies of dire portent:

"Chaos or Progress?"

"A Leap Into The Dark."

"The Education of the Children of London Will Suffer."

"The Children of London Will Suffer."

"The Patients of London Will Suffer."

"The People of London Must Suffer."[9]

[9] Quotations taken from "The London County Council—Why Destroy It?" (pamphlet published by LCC, September 1962); press statement of child welfare agencies, February 28, 1963; press statement of local medical committee for County of London, January 22, 1963.

These fears regarding future uncertainties were compounded by a second set of more immediately realistic anxieties—fears over the loss of identity. It was this second set of fears that dominated the attitudes of the inner county councils (i.e., London and Middlesex) and the smaller second-tier councils whose jurisdictions were scheduled to be amalgamated with those of their larger neighbors. This development was hardly surprising in light of the fact that both these groupings were, quite literally, fighting for their very lives.

The London experience indicates that the instinct for institutional self-preservation can run every bit as deep as the human instinct for personal survival. Perhaps because the two are so deep-seated and intertwined, the struggle for institutional self-preservation often contains basic elements of dramatic heroics that can engender widespread public sympathy and support. This is especially true if the struggle centers upon smaller groups which are able to convey the impression that they are battling against superior odds.

The impact of this phenomenon was not confined to the London area alone. During the course of the Greater London reform, a series of complementary local government reviews was taking place throughout other portions of the country. One of these reviews centered upon the tiny county of Rutland in east-central England—a county which had "prized its independence for more than 700 years" and was not about to give it up without a fight.[10] Rutland contains some 25,000 loyal inhabitants, and when the Local Government Boundary Commission proposed that it should be abolished through a merger with its neighboring county, Leicestershire (having more than 400,000 population), the reaction of the local Rutlanders was violent in its intensity and Churchillian in its overtones. "We'll fight on the beaches and in the ditches if necessary to keep Rutland free," asserted the housemaster of one of the local Rutland schools. In time, the entire controversy began to take on a compelling David-versus-Goliath appeal. *The Sunday Times,* under the heading "RUTLAND'S LAST STAND," advised its readers:

10 See p. 186, Chapter 9, for a note on Rutland's educational expenditures.

England's smallest county refuses to bow to the knee of the White-hall legions who want to make it a mere rural district of its neighbor, Leicestershire.[11]

Eventually, these Whitehall legions recanted, and Rutland was spared when the recommendations of the Boundary Commission were overruled. It was impossible for any such process of clemency to take place throughout the entire Greater London area, because the reform program would have collapsed if such a policy had been pursued. Yet, it is significant to note some of the major concessions that were made in London. The tiny City of London Corporation, for example, that unique local entity of 5,000 resident souls, was allowed to retain its separate identity from the very beginning, and numerous suburban fringe authorities were permitted to escape from the rigors of reorganization with their skins intact. The instinct for institutional self-preservation was very much a part of the Greater London reform contest.

IDEOLOGICAL RATIONALIZATIONS

All three of the above basic motivations (i.e., power drives, professional concerns, real and imaginary fears) were reinforced by a variety of ideological abstractions that were designed to lend credence to the various participants' preconceived positions. Both the proponents and the opponents of reform employed ideological abstractions for such reinforcement purposes. Once again, however, the opposition side was able to make the most effective use of ideological symbols to strengthen its position.

This use of ideological rationalizations does not imply that either side failed to take such abstractions seriously. Many opponents of reform were quite honest in their ideological attacks on the reorganization program, while many supporters felt that the plan would restore the vitality of local government and halt the trend toward centralization of power. Thus, the Labour Party was able to justify its basic opposition to reform in terms of a functional approach to the local governmental

[11] M. Parkinson, "Rutland's Last Stand," *The* [London] *Sunday Times Magazine*, October 9, 1962, pp. 14-15.

process, while Conservative spokesmen were able to justify both support and opposition stances by drawing upon divergent streams of party ideology.

In very large part, however, this use of ideologies did represent a displacement process. Since many of the participants found it difficult to defend their stands on the basis of purely parochial power drives, they attempted to displace these drives with more attractive ideological rationalizations. There is, of course, nothing new or unique about this. Lasswell has described the political type as one who "displaces private motives with public objects in the name of collective advantage."[12] What is significant to note is that these ideological rationalizations played an important twofold role in the Greater London contest.

On the one hand, they produced a sense of comfort, and even of ethical well-being, for the various participants, with the result that the contest became continually more aggressive with the passage of time. Once the participants had converted their personal interests into ideological causes, they tended to defend their positions with increasing hostility.

In addition, ideologies were utilized to translate individual grievances into broad-based generalities. This permitted the formation of various coalitions that violated the prevailing norms of London politics. Ideological rationalizations, for example, justified the alignment of Surrey County's staid Conservative hierarchy with the Labour forces of central London County. They also led to a natural grouping between the dissident professional associations and these same London County Labour forces.

In short, although their motive power was predominantly rationalizing rather than innovating, ideological abstractions played a very important role in the reform contest. Their major utility stemmed from their very vagueness, which permitted them to be used with a high degree of flexibility. In light of the fact that the nebulous nature of conflicting ideologies contributed to, rather than detracted from, their increased effectiveness throughout the reform contest, it is perhaps easier

12 Harold Lasswell, *Politics: Who Gets What, When, How* (New York: Meridian Books, Inc., 1958), p. 21.

to understand our reluctance to develop any truly coherent and consistent theories of local government.

Other motives beyond those already identified also played a role in activating participants. Some groups, such as the Fulham Borough Council, appeared to indicate a genuine interest in the abstraction of "good government." Most participants, however, were stimulated by concerns that were considerably more practical than this. Financial considerations and status symbols, for example, were a factor in inducing both the outlying county councils and many second-tier fringe authorities to oppose the reform program. On the whole, however, these supplementary motives were not of crucial importance. The primary influences that shaped the Greater London conflict were the four identified above—power drives, professional concerns, real and imaginary fears, and ideological abstractions. These four constituted the quartet that called—if not, in fact, played—the tune in Greater London.

Participants

Participation in the Greater London contest was characterized by two highly distinctive attributes. The first involved the scope of participation; the second, the underlying nature of the participant groupings themselves.

SCOPE OF PARTICIPATION

Despite all its sound and fury, the Greater London contest was, by and large, a private and restricted affair. At times this central fact tended to be obscured by the intensity and the bitterness of the struggle, yet the evidence that is available tends to indicate that the conflict was fought out against a backdrop of widespread public apathy. In their approach toward local government, the great mass of Londoners appeared to reflect the same apathetic attitudes that were to be found among their fellow countrymen throughout the British Isles.

An ambitious nationwide attempt to uncover information regarding the general public's attitudes toward England's local government was launched by the National and Local Government Officers Association in 1957. In all, some 10,000 NALGO members interviewed more than 180,000 people in an attempt to ascertain their concerns about, and their knowledge of, the local governmental process. This NALGO survey indicated that "17 out of 20 householders in England and Wales consider local government to be important in their daily lives, but 1 in 4 has only the haziest idea of what it does." When the 180,000 individuals were asked if they ever attended local council meetings, 6 per cent answered yes, and 94 per cent answered no. When they were asked if they belonged to local interest, or electoral, associations, 17 per cent said yes, and 83 per cent said no.[13]

The NALGO findings of widespread apathy are supported by occasional articles that appear in British scholarly journals. One recent study in the *British Journal of Sociology* involved an evaluation of public knowledge regarding the 1958 local elections in Newcastle-Under-Lyme—an industrial community of some 75,000 people located about midway between Birmingham and Manchester. Based on a sample of 800 electors, the researchers found that "there was widespread ignorance about the election and only limited interest in it." The survey covered two rural wards and four urban wards, and, perhaps surprisingly, the lack of knowledge was most acute in the latter:

> The ignorance of the urban voters about their candidates was astonishing. In all four borough wards, only 33 voters named both candidates correctly, and 419 could name neither. Out of 101 respondents in Ward 5, only 1 knew the names of both candidates, and 98 knew neither.[14]

A good part of such widespread public apathy outside the central London area can undoubtedly be explained by the fact that there are so many uncontested local elections in England. According to the most recent statistics, the national average of uncontested seats in county

13 *Public Service* (official journal of NALGO), XXXI, No. 5 (May 1957), 146-148.
14 F. Bealey and D. J. Bartholomew, "The Local Elections in Newcastle-Under-Lyme," *British Journal of Sociology*, XIII, No. 3 (September 1962), 273-283.

elections is 65.6 per cent, while for rural district council elections this figure soars to 76.1 per cent.[15] In other words, two-thirds of all the county councillors and three-quarters of all the rural district councillors seeking office in England are automatically assured of election because they are running unopposed.

In London County, on the other hand, every seat on the LCC was contested in every election between 1949 and 1961. Thus, the London County Council established the unique distinction of presenting the voters in each of its electoral divisions that key element of the democratic process—the opportunity of choice. When the Registrar General's official statistics are adjusted to reflect this fact, it can be seen that the LCC electorate exceeded the national average turnout by some 10 per cent to 20 per cent during the postwar era.[16]

Percentage of Total Qualified Electorate Voting:
All Council Seats

Year	LCC vote	England: average of all counties
1946	24.9%	23.3%
1949	40.7	28.9
1952	43.4	23.5
1955	32.4	21.6
1958	31.5	20.0
1961	36.4	(Not yet available)

As the above table indicates, however, the LCC turnouts actually were not overly impressive. The highest total in the postwar period (43.4 per cent) saw a little more than two of every five voters exercising their franchise, and the more typical turnout saw only one of every three voters exercising the franchise. Because of the fact that even the contested LCC elections did not light any great sparks, it should hardly be surprising that the general public failed to show any great interest

15 R. C., *Written Evidence*, V, p. 646.
16 *The Registrar General's Statistical Review of England and Wales for the Years: 1946, 1949, 1952, 1955, 1958* (adjusted), Part II, Tables: Civil (London: Her Majesty's Stationery Office); London County Council, Election Statistics, April 1961 election of County Councillors.

in a rather complex reorganization plan that dealt with the structural reform of Greater London's government.

Indication that the general public did not, in fact, show such interest is to be found in the limited number of studies that have been made on the subject of electoral attitudes in the London area itself. In a 1962 survey of the Clapham electoral division of the Metropolitan Borough of Wandsworth, L. J. Sharpe of the London School of Economics discovered a widespread lack of knowledge regarding the proposed Greater London plan. Only 37.2 per cent of his sample who had actually voted in the 1961 LCC elections were able to identify their Party's stand on this issue, while 30.6 per cent of the voting sample misinterpreted their Party's stand, and 42.2 per cent indicated that they did not know what the issue was all about. The corresponding figures for the nonvoters indicated an even more general lack of knowledge.[17]

A similar lack of knowledge was uncovered in a study conducted by Ian Budge, a Yale University graduate student who has also engaged in opinion research in the London area. In 1962 Mr. Budge interviewed a sample of Party leaders drawn from throughout the Greater London area and a sample of local voters in the Middlesex Borough of Brentford and Chiswick. He then attempted to compare the reaction of these two groups on a number of local issues, one of which was the proposed London reform program. Whereas 97 per cent of the Party leaders expressed a definite commitment, either pro or con, on this issue, only 47.6 per cent of the local Brentford and Chiswick voters expressed any definite preference. Of the 52.4 per cent of the local voters who had no preference, 31 per cent indicated they knew nothing about the issue.[18]

Further indications of the prevailing public disinterest which Messrs. Sharpe and Budge discovered could be found throughout the Greater London area. Perhaps the most telling commentary of all was made by a local suburban newspaper in the northern portion of the review area. After making a survey of local reactions to the plan in the summer of 1962, this paper, *The Walthamstow Independent,* concluded, "So Many

---

17 Sharpe, *A Metropolis Votes,* pp. 84-86.
18 Letters from Ian Budge to F. Smallwood dated November 15, 1962, and December 1, 1962.

People Just Couldn't Care Less."[19] There is no doubt that all available evidence, as sketchy as it may be, points to a widespread lack of public concern over the reorganization of Greater London's government.[20]

As a result, the only time the issue did spill over into the public arena was when specific attempts were made to activate public opinion on a short-range basis. The London Teachers' Association's mass protest meetings with the parents of school children served as an apt illustration of this technique. On the whole, however, the Greater London contest was dominated by intensive infighting between a limited number of groups, which varied widely in terms of both their internal cohesiveness and their external commitments.

THE NATURE OF THE PARTICIPANTS

The Yale studies of community power structure have indicated the high degree of relevance that "scope," or issue-area, has to the activation of different political actors.[21] In London, certain groups who reacted vigorously to the specific issue of metropolitan reform followed the Yale pattern very closely. These groups—the teachers, the doctors, the social workers, and so forth—could not be classified as part of any

---

[19] *The Walthamstow Independent*, "The Truth About The Merger," August 10, 1962.

[20] One close observer of the London scene explains this widespread public apathy as follows:

> Part of the London problem is the rootlessness, the insecurity, especially in the central areas where almost nobody owns his own home and mobility is normal. . . . Many Londoners are not aware of their boroughs. They will tell you that they live in Kentish Town or Chalk Farm, rather than St. Pancras; in Limehouse or Mile End, rather than Stepney; in St. John's Wood, rather than Marylebone . . . (L. M. Jeger, "The Human Awful Wonder of God," *New Statesman, op. cit.,* p. 586).

Yet, while this sense of borough anonymity may have characterized the general public's approach toward reform, it did not hold true with respect to the various borough council leaders, many of whom were vitally concerned with the problem of institutional self-preservation noted earlier.

[21] See, for example, Robert Dahl, *Who Governs?* (New Haven: Yale University Press, 1961); R. Wolfinger, "Reputation and Reality in the Study of Community Power," *American Sociological Review* (October 1960), pp. 636-644; Nelson Polsby, *Community Power and Political Theory* (New Haven: Yale University Press, 1963).

stable London political hierarchy or elite. Instead, they became involved in this particular reform controversy only because they felt that certain of their legitimate value objectives were being threatened in a very direct manner by the Government's reorganization proposals. In short, some of the key participants in the Greater London contest represented spontaneous pluralistic groupings of persons who responded aggressively to the specific issue of metropolitan reform but who presumably would have remained silent on other significant community conflicts.

In addition, however, there was a second class of participants who very definitely did indicate the traits of highly influential power elites. This second class of participants—the local political party leaders, the county council leaders, and the like—constituted the hard-core political hierarchy of Greater London. Presumably, they would have been activated by any major political conflict in the London area, regardless of the particular issue-area involved.

The two classes of participants differed quite widely in terms of their internal structural cohesion. Many of the hard-core "power elites" were extremely tightly organized and controlled from the top, whereas the spontaneous groupings tended to be considerably more diffuse. A classic illustration of a tightly-structured elite grouping was the London County Council's Labour majority.

After the London Labour Party captured control of the London County Council in 1934, a series of organizational directives was issued to all Labour councillors. During more than a quarter of a century of unbroken rule, these directives hardened into a system of iron discipline. The kingpin of the LCC Labour hierarchy was the Leader of the Council, and his key lever of power was his authority to appoint all chairmen and vice-chairmen of the LCC committees. In turn, these committee leaders paid due homage to the Council Leader by reelecting him to his leadership post each year. By means of this automatic system of circular reciprocity, the LCC Labour hierarchy eventually took on the characteristics of a completely closed shop.

Over the course of time, the impact of this Labour Party's disciplinary pattern permeated every aspect of the Council's deliberations, primarily because of the major role the committees played in guiding the Council's program. Prior to each committee meeting, the Labour members of the various committees held a private caucus to determine precise lines of policy. Once established, these lines were to be followed by all Party members. As Section III of the LCC Labour Party's Directive on "Organisation" explained:

> ... Normally, of course, the [Committee] agenda will have been discussed in a group meeting held prior to the Committee, and decisions arrived at as to the line to be taken.
> That is why it is most important to attend the group meetings. This is the member's opportunity to raise points of difference, and a member missing this meeting should not come into the Committee and raise difficulties for the Chairman. He or she can easily ascertain from a colleague the line that it has been decided to follow.

Once the Party's policy line had been duly ratified by the full Committee, there was little that individual Party members could do to modify it at a later date, even on the floor of the Council. As Section V of the Party's "Organisation" directive warned:

> Every member is entitled to ask up to two questions at any Council meeting, but he or she should ascertain beforehand from the Chairman of the Committee concerned that the question will not cause the Party any embarrassment.[22]

The effects of this autocratic approach to Council deliberations were widespread. For one thing, it robbed these deliberations of any vitality, to a point where it was hardly surprising that general apathy marked the public's attitude toward Council affairs. Since every conceivable item of policy had been decided long beforehand, the LCC meetings took on all the spontaneity of an automatic computer grinding out myriads of precise statistics.

In addition to deadening the public's interest in Council affairs, the

[22] London County Council Labour Party, "Organisation" (mimeographed), signed by I. J. Hayward, Leader of the Council, and W. G. Fiske, Chief Whip (undated).

Labour Party's tightly structured leadership on the LCC was of considerable importance to the Greater London reform contest. On the surface it might appear that this tight structural hierarchy would help the Council majority to mount an effective opposition program, by permitting it to present a solid phalanx against the reform proposals. In actuality, however, the system hurt the Council. The fact was that this phalanx hardened into a monolithic mass that was unable to offer anything in the way of creative originality as an opposition force. The only significant response to the reform proposals that came from the LCC Labour majority was to be found in the testimony of an individual Party member, Mr. Hugh Jenkins. Mr. Jenkins, however, stood far from the top tier of the LCC leadership, and the fact that he dared to offer testimony at all represented an act of considerable political courage.

With this sole exception, the contributions of the LCC Labour majority toward the reform of London Government were totally negative and lacking in imagination. The significant opposition spokesmen were to be found outside, rather than inside, the ranks of the LCC hierarchy. It was Sir Cyril Black, a Conservative from Surrey County, who demonstrated the initiative to formulate an alternative reform plan. It was Michael Stewart, a Labour member of Parliament, who presented the most articulate case for the opposition. It was a variety of professional associations that attempted to modify the plan in a manner which they felt would make it more effective. In no case did the top leadership of the LCC majority step forward to provide the type of creative guidance that might have helped, rather than hindered, the future development of London's government.

This is not to imply that the London County Council represented an ineffective administrative organization that was racked by corruption or scandal. To the contrary, it was a highly efficient administrative body that had compiled a brilliant list of achievements in housing, education, the health services, and a variety of other fields. The problem was, however, that years of tight party rule had robbed the Council of its political vitality to such a degree that its top leadership was unable to make any effective response during the Council's gravest hour of trial.

Whereas the LCC majority served as a classic example of the highly structured opposition force, the spokesmen for the various children's service groups represented a case of the more spontaneous opposition coalition. In the case of these groups there was no semblance of tight hierarchical organization in any sense comparable to the LCC Labour leadership. Instead, the children's service spokesmen consisted of a mixture of formal and informal groupings—members of the Association of Child Care Officers, chairmen of the Metropolitan Juvenile Courts, interested spokesmen from the academic community, and the like. There is no doubt that such coalitions represented an illustration par excellence of the issue-area participant in action. Most, if not all, of the children's service groups had little sustained contact with the London political scene. They were activated on this particular issue-area by an altruistic belief that the reform plan represented a serious threat to the future administration of the particular service with which they were concerned. In light of this belief, they were willing to assume a political role in an attempt to preserve an existing value system which they found to be highly meaningful.

The same dichotomy between the informal and the highly structured groupings that characterized the opposition forces was also to be found among the proponents of reform. An apt illustration of an informal support grouping was the London School of Economics contingent. The central Government, on the other hand, represented the chief example of the tightly structured proponent group. It is interesting to note, however, that the central Government, like the London County Council hierarchy, also experienced its share of difficulties in responding to the reform program. The major problem here was not one of structural stultification, but rather a discontinuity in political leadership.

Throughout the course of the reform contest, the central Government received extremely able staff leadership, especially from Dame Evelyn Sharp, the Permanent Secretary of the Ministry of Housing and Local Government. The Government's major difficulty related to the fact that the implementation of the Greater London plan demanded a great number of political decisions that could not be made at the staff level. Because of a successive turnover of Ministers during the course of the reform contest, this top political leadership became uncoordinated and inconsistent. It was not until Sir Keith Joseph was named Minister of Housing and Local Government in the summer of 1962 that the required leadership initiative was forthcoming. From this time forward, the Government consolidated its position and moved steadily ahead with the reform program.

Thus, in the final analysis, the structural divergencies between the various opposition and support groups were of somewhat limited significance. Obviously, effective action on either side was forthcoming only when the various groups had access to positions of community power. The key ingredient was not really ease of access, however, but the quality of the leadership itself. Some groups—such as the London Teachers' Association—were able to make highly effective use of relatively limited resources, while other groups—such as the London County Council Labor majority—were frozen into ineffectual positions despite their access to considerably more massive power resources.

The Greater London experience tends to indicate that, if metropolitan governmental reform is to be realized, it will not be totally dominated by any elite revolutions of formal community power leaders. Rather, it will be highly dependent upon a rich degree of political sophistication and sensitivity on the part of a wide variety of less formal groups who may decide to play this particular game. The tactics and strategies that were of most significance in Greater London were primarily a reflection of the innate leadership ability displayed by many informal groups, some of which were able to run circles around those who occupied positions on the topmost tier of the formal community power hierarchy.

Strategies

The opponents of reform were forced to carry the offensive throughout the Greater London contest. The proponents of reform attempted to neutralize these opposition attacks through a continuous series of concessions. The basic objectives of both sides followed closely the Schattschneider strategic concerns (Chapter 8) regarding the scale of the battle. When evaluated in light of American experience, however, the strategic roles adopted by the two sides presented something of a reverse twist. In London, the opponents of reform attempted to enlarge the scale of the battle, while the support forces attempted to restrict this battle.

This twist resulted from a basic procedural variation that distinguishes the English and American approaches toward local governmental reform. In the United States, the issue of metropolitan reorganization is generally decided by a public referendum. Under such circumstances, it is essential for those who favor reorganization to make a vigorous effort to enlist widespread public support for their program. They must take the initiative in selling their proposals to the public, since they can hope to realize their aspirations for success only by enlarging the scope of their support to secure a majority vote in the reform referendum.

In London, the issue of metropolitan reorganization was ultimately decided by a higher governmental authority, rather than by means of any direct public referendum. This higher authority—the central Government—favored the reorganization program from the very beginning. Since this central Government possessed the conclusive strategic advantage throughout the reform contest (i.e., its disciplined Parliamentary majority), it was anxious to limit, rather than enlarge, the size of the interested audience in the hope of restricting potential political conflict. The more controversial the reform plan became, the more difficult it would be to force Parliamentary action on this issue. In keeping with this all-important objective of limiting the size of the audience, the Government attempted to quiet down controversy as soon as it arose. The method it used was to buy off potential opposition through specific concessions to any group (e.g., the London teachers) that became overly vocal in its criticism of the plan.

The opposition forces, on the other hand, were continually trying to open up the scope of the battle. Since they were obviously in continuous danger of losing the contest (i.e., they did not enjoy the Government's ultimate strategic weapon of a disciplined Parliamentary majority), they could hope to reverse this losing trend only by making the plan so controversial that the Government would be forced to drop it. In attempting to pursue this objective, the opposition eventually turned to such direct pressure groups as the Committee for London Government. In turn, these groups employed increasingly more emotional symbols in an effort to induce new opponents to join the battle. In this manner, the Greater London contest followed the Coleman outline (Chapter 8) very closely. It was translated from the specific to the general, and it degenerated from disagreement into antagonism.

This opposition strategy very nearly succeeded. The supreme test for the Government came when it was no longer possible to grant further concessions without destroying the overarching unity of the entire reform effort. At this point, it became necessary for the Government to adopt a new strategy. It was forced to take off its gloves and engage in a direct power struggle with no holds barred. The Government accepted this challenge during the final Parliamentary phase of the battle when it employed the guillotine, and every other weapon at its disposal, to push the reform program through Parliament. It is extremely doubtful that the program would have been adopted if the Government had not been willing to adopt such drastic tactics. It is certainly highly debatable whether the program could ever have had any chance of success at all if it had been forced to undergo the same referendum procedure that is characteristic of the American approach toward the issue of metropolitan reform.

In terms of surface appearances, many of the motives, participants, and strategies in Greater London were quite different from those which are to be found in the typical American city. Underneath this surface, however, there were enough basic similarities to give pause for thought. One of the most significant findings to emerge from the Greater London story is the fact that all those who opposed the reform program were not necessarily misfits or dissatisfied fanatics. On the contrary, many groups found in the prevailing unstructured metropolitan system legitimate values—psychological, professional, and otherwise—that they felt were well worth protecting and preserving.

This again begs the question as to the degree of knowledge which we presently possess on this crucially important issue of metropolitan government. More recent studies are beginning to indicate that there are, perhaps, many more meaningful values in our existing unstructured metropolitan systems than we had at first assumed to be the case.

Thomas R. Dye, for example, has pointed out that Philadelphia's existing "decentralized political structure [is] functional to the metropolitan system" in a number of significant ways, many of which are very directly related to the psychological well-being of its inhabitants, especially minority groups.[23] In a similar manner, Vincent Ostrom, Charles Tiebout, and Robert Warren have indicated that, contrary to surface appearances, Los Angeles' highly unstructured metropolitan area possesses "a very rich and intricate 'framework' for negotiating, adjucating and deciding questions that affect . . . diverse public interests."[24]

This is not to be interpreted as a plea against metropolitan government per se, but rather as a warning that we are dealing here with a highly turbulent issue that cannot be translated into effective action without a thorough knowledge of local conditions and a highly sophisticated expression of local leadership. Above all else, the Greater London experience indicates that metropolitan reform is not solely, or even primarily, an organizational issue; rather, it is a political question that involves the reconciliation of many opposing interests, opinions, and ideas. From start to finish the London reform program was forced to wrestle with Almond's political "input" functions, despite the fact that it was primarily concerned with modifying the administrative "output" components of London's governmental system. In so doing, it most certainly added credence to Professor Hugh Whalen's observation that "a realistic reform program must temper the practicable in an administrative sense, with the practicable in a political sense. . . . In this, as in all other political questions, consensus must be worked for and won; and it is foolish to suppose that agreement is delivered by the stork, or miraculously worked by a hidden hand while men slumber."[25]

As regards the magnitude of this political task, it is extremely significant that, in London's case, the great majority of motivational influences at work were "negative" in that they tended to activate the

[23] Thomas R. Dye, "Metropolitan Integration by Bargaining Among Sub-Areas," *American Behavioral Scientist*, V, No. 9 (May 1962), 11.

[24] V. Ostrom, C. M. Tiebout, and R. Warren, "The Organization of Government in Metropolitan Areas; A Theoretical Inquiry," *American Political Science Review*, LV, No. 4 (December 1961), p. 842.

[25] Hugh Whalen, "Democracy and Local Government," *Canadian Public Administration*, III, No. 1 (March 1960), 13.

opponents, rather than the supporters, of reform. Power drives were instrumental in activating both support and opposition groups, and ideological rationalizations were likewise used by both sides. The major thrust of professional considerations, however, was to stimulate strong opposition to the plan, and the fear and anxiety arguments were almost totally negative in activating opposition groups.

After full recognition of such political difficulties, however, we can hardly bury our heads in the sand and shy away completely from the massive environmental challenge we face today. At the present time, we are participating in an urban upheaval that is producing totally new residential patterns. If we are to believe Doxiadis' predictions, today's metropolis is already coalescing into tomorrow's cosmopolis, and we can hardly afford to sit on our hands indefinitely under such explosive circumstances. Certainly, the basic forces at work here show no signs of abating. As Scott Greer has noted, "the metropolitan community is continuously improvised; its evolution is organic, not rational; change is crescive, not revolutionary; problems are solved by trial and error, rather than by fiat."[26]

It is in making our improvisations, and in subjecting ourselves to such tests of trial and error, that we cannot afford to lose sight of a second basic fact. The city has always been a human institution that has harbored deep human hopes and aspirations:

> Visions of man's ultimate destiny on earth, and indeed, often in heaven, have usually taken shape around the image of the city. To build some kind of New Jerusalem or Celestial City has appeared to demand the most consummate artistry of which men are capable. . . . Prophetic revelation and Utopian gospel have, through the ages, presented visions of this imagined place. Though these visions have been blurred by the mists and disillusionments of history, yet the dream continues to recur in ever new forms.[27]

The unique significance of the Greater London plan was to be found in the Royal Commission's assertion that London's government was

[26] Scott Greer, "The Emerging City: Myth and Reality," in Greer, *Governing the Metropolis* (New York: John Wiley and Sons, 1962), p. 148.

[27] Humphrey Carver, *Cities in the Suburbs* (Toronto: University of Toronto Press, 1962), p. 23.

something more than an administrative mechanism; that it was not just "a machine, or a piece of organisation," but rather "a living thing . . . in which . . . each part is integrally concerned with each other part." As a result of this basic belief, the Commission developed a dualistic approach toward London's governmental needs, which encompassed both the functional requirements of the metropolis and the difficult value judgments that go into the making of a viable and healthy local governmental system.

Many, if they grasped this approach at all, tended to view the Commissioners as mystics at best. Most, however, failed to see such a humanistic, value-oriented approach as being of any relevance to the needs of the modern metropolis. "What was appropriate to the Greek city-state of 500 B.C. is not therefore suitable to 20th century London."

Perhaps in an age which pays lofty tribute to the virtues of functional specialization, such displays of skepticism should not have been surprising. Yet, there still appears to be considerable merit in an observation Graham Wallas made little more than half a century ago:

> Children will not learn to love London while getting figures by heart as to the millions of her inhabitants or the miles of her sewers. . . . Perhaps before we have a poet who loves London as Sophocles loved Athens, it may be necessary to make London itself somewhat more lovely.[28]

The Royal Commission on Local Government in Greater London had its vision of a New Jerusalem which, with all its faults, represented no less than the vision of the old Jerusalem as it was praised in the Psalms—"a city that is at unity in itself."[29]

Whether or not this vision was an accurate one is a matter that will reveal itself in the course of time. It was the very existence of the vision in the first place, however, that made the bitter fight over its realization worth all the effort.

[28] Graham Wallas, *Human Nature in Politics* (London: Constable & Company Ltd., 1962 reprint), p. 209.
[29] Psalm 122:3. The quotation is from *The Book of Common Prayer*. The King James Bible version is "a city that is compact together." I first noted this particularly apt quotation in Professor W. J. M. Mackenzie's 1952 Percival Lecture at Manchester University, entitled "The Government of Great Cities."

Appendix

15. Mrs. Marjorie McIntosh, Chairman, Education Committee, London County Council
16. Mr. Norman G. M. Prichard, M.Sc., J.P., Chairman, Housing Committee, London County Council; Chairman, Metropolitan Boroughs' Standing Joint Committee
17. Mr. Christian Berridge, Clerk of the Council, Essex County Council
18. Mr. Kenneth Goodacre, T.D., D.L., Clerk of the Council, Middlesex County Council
19. Sir William Hart, G.M.C., Clerk of the Council, London County Council
20. Mr. W. W. Ruff, Clerk of the Council, Surrey County Council
21. Mr. G. E. Smith, Town Clerk, County Borough of West Ham
22. Mr. A. C. V. Waite, Deputy Clerk of the County Council, Surrey County Council
23. Mr. W. E. Jackson, Deputy Assistant Clerk to the Council, London County Council
24. Mr. J. S. Mills, M.C., L.I.B., Second Deputy Clerk of the Council, Essex County Council
25. Mr. F. W. Strike, Senior Staff Member, Kent County Council
26. Dr. W. G. Harding, Divisional Medical Officer, London County Council

V. Second-Tier Councils
   (*Metropolitan Boroughs and Corporation of London*)
27. Councillor Charles Slater, J.P., Mayor, Metropolitan Borough of Finsbury
28. Councillor James Olley, Leader of the Council, Metropolitan Borough of Stepney
29. Mr. M. Casey, Town Clerk, Metropolitan Borough of Finsbury
30. Mr. G. T. Lloyd, Town Clerk, Metropolitan Borough of Holborn
31. Mr. C. F. Thatcher, Town Clerk, Metropolitan Borough of Fulham
32. Mr. E. J. Jones, Treasurer, Metropolitan Borough of Holborn
33. Mr. C. C. Taylor, Deputy to the Town Clerk, City Corporation of London
   (*Essex County Districts*)
34. Mr. E. R. Farr, Town Clerk, Corporation of Barking
35. Mr. K. Lauder, Town Clerk, Borough of Dagenham
   (*Kent County Districts*)
36. Alderman H. T. Parkin, J.P., Borough of Beckenham

37. Mr. P. J. Bunting, Clerk, Urban District of Penge
    (*Middlesex County Districts*)
38. Mr. N. Crumpsty, Town Clerk, Borough of Wembley
39. Mr. W. H. Jones, Town Clerk, Borough of Twickenham
    (*Surrey County Districts*)
40. Mr. C. Heyworth, Town Clerk, Borough of Richmond
41. Mr. L. V. Powell, Town Clerk, Royal Borough of Kingston-Upon-Thames

VI. Professional Associations
42. Sir Harold Banwell, Secretary, Association of Municipal Corporations
43. Mr. W. C. Anderson, General Secretary, National and Local Government Officers Association
44. Dr. F. Grey, Secretary, Local Medical Committee for the County of London
45. Mr. Malcolm MacEwen, Chief Information Officer, Royal Institute of British Architects
46. Mr. W. D. Partridge, Deputy Secretary, County Councils Association
47. Mr. V. R. Shaw, J.P., General Secretary, London Teachers' Association
48. Mr. Wyndham Thomas, Director, Town and Country Planning Association
49. Mr. Laurence Welsh, Secretary, London County Council Staff Association

VII. Academic
50. Sir William Holford, Chairman, Centre for Urban Studies, University College, London; Vice-Chairman, Committee for London Government
51. Professor William A. Robson, Chairman, Greater London Group, London School of Economics and Political Science (LSE)
52. Mr. Bryan Keith-Lucas, Nuffield College, Oxford
53. Mr. Peter Self, Greater London Group, LSE
54. Mrs. Ruth Glass, Director of Research, Centre for Urban Studies, University College, London
55. Mr. S. K. Ruck, Research Officer, Greater London Group, LSE
56. Mr. L. J. Sharpe, Research Officer, Greater London Group, LSE
57. Mr. D. Peschek, Research Assistant, Greater London Group, LSE

VIII. Press and Journals
  58. Mr. Gilbert Jenkins, Editor, *The Surrey Comet*
  59. Mr. J. M. Richards, Editor, *The Architectural Review*
  60. Mr. Charles Leatherland, Assistant Editor, *The Daily Herald;* Former Chairman, Essex County Council
  61. Mr. R. M. Taylor, Managing Editor, *The Croydon Advertiser*
  62. Mr. Derek Senior, free-lance writer; former Local Government Reporter, *The Guardian*
  63. Miss S. McCormick, News and LCC Reporter, *The Daily Telegraph*

 IX. Political Parties and Associations
  64. Mr. J. Blake, Research Officer and Secretary, Greater London Committee, The Liberal Party Headquarters
  65. Mr. H. Brabin, O.B.E., Local Government Officer, Conservative and Unionist Central Office
  66. Mr. L. French, Secretary, Committee for London Government
  67. Mr. Patrick McNair-Wilson, Director, London Municipal Society
  68. Mr. C. A. J. Norton, Local Government Office, Conservative and Unionist Central Office
  69. Mr. Peter Robshaw, Secretary, The London Labour Party
  70. Mr. Michael Ward, Local Government Officer, The Labour Party, Transport House

Index